Superhobby Investing

Making money from antiques, coins, stamps, wine, woodland and other alternative assets

by Peter Temple

HARRIMAN HOUSE LTD

43 Chapel Street
Petersfield
Hampshire
GU32 3DY
GREAT BRITAIN

Tel: +44 (0)1730 233870
Fax: +44 (0)1730 233880
email: enquiries@harriman-house.com
web site: www.harriman-house.com

First published in Great Britain in 2004

Copyright Harriman House Ltd

The right of Peter Temple to be identified as the author has been asserted
in accordance with the Copyright, Design and Patents Act 1988.

ISBN 1-897-59733-9

British Library Cataloguing in Publication Data
A CIP catalogue record for this book can be obtained from the British Library.

Printed and bound by Ashford Colour Press Ltd, Gosport Hampshire.

About the author

Peter Temple has been working in and writing about financial markets for the last 34 years. After an 18 year career in fund management and stockbroking, he became a full time writer in 1988.

His articles appear in the Financial Times, Investors Chronicle and a range of other publications. He has written more than a dozen books about investing, mainly aimed at private investors.

He and his wife live in part of a converted bobbin mill in the Lake District National Park.

Superhobby Investing

Acknowledgements

I started out writing this book knowing a little about some of the areas that I planned to cover, but with huge areas of ignorance about many of them. Fortunately I have been able to call on several experts, collectors and superhobby investors. I have picked their brains, gone to them for tips about research angles, and in some cases they have been good enough to check through the chapter that covered their particular area of interest and alert me to any nuances I had failed to pick up, or to the more obvious howlers I had made.

In no particular order of precedence, therefore I would like to thank the following for their unstinting help, patience and forbearance: Gail McGuffie at LAPADA; Sue and Ian Dalzell; Barry Townsley; Val Porter-Godman; Philip Athill at Abbott & Houlder; Peter Blaskett of the Signature Gallery in Kendal; Martin and Pat Masters of Thomond Antiques in Kendal; Daniella Donghur; staff at Sotheby's; Bruce and Kim Stanfield, who auction art for P&O Cruises; Barnaby Faull at Spink; Peter Duppa-Miller at the International Bond & Share Society; Keith Hollender; Colin Steele; Julian Roberts; Christopher Proudlove, Simon Roberts and Tim Schofield at Bonhams; Dave Selby; staff at Spink's coin department; staff at Coincraft; Ian Goldbart of Noble Investments (UK); Tom Hulme and colleagues at Teather & Greenwood; Leighton James-Giles and colleagues at Close Brothers; Martin Churchill at Tax Efficient Review; Marc Sinden; Tim Kirk and colleagues at Tilhill; Dr Robert Weinberg and Rhona O'Connell at the World Gold Council; Laurence Chard; Richard Purkis and Adrian Roose at Stanley Gibbons; Colin Harding at Scotia Philately; Richard Watkins at Spink; James Thompson; Alan Gray at Sutherlands; Ann Armstrong; Gordon Doctor at Peter J Russell; Kiran Kumar at The Whisky Exchange; Jim Budd; James Sherry at Vineyards of Bordeaux; and Anthony Foster at Foster Bonhote.

Various publications I write for regularly have allowed me to use their columns to explore some of the ideas contained in this book. In this respect I must thank Kevin Brown at the 'Financial Times', Richard Beddard at Ample, Jonathan Savill at Cue Communications, and Frank Hemsley at Fleet Street Publications for their help. I first got interested in the tangible assets scene through writing articles about scripophily and gold for 'Accountancy'.

At Harriman House, thanks go to Philip Jenks, Myles Hunt, Nick Read and Stephen Eckett for embracing the idea of this book so enthusiastically and for editing, designing and producing the finished product at a speed that puts most traditional publishers to shame.

Last but above all not least, my wife Lynn Temple, whose idea this book was, has contributed to the book in many ways. Lynn conducted or sat in on most of the interviews we had with experts in many fields, attended auctions, researched particular topics in depth for me, and compiled and maintained the database on relevant web sites and information sources on which a number of the tables in the book are based, wrote some of the text, and proofread the finished version of the manuscript. Completing the book would have been a much lengthier task without her help and she has, as always, my grateful thanks for her diligence and support.

Peter Temple

May 2004

Contents

<table>
<tr><td>Chapter

1</td><td># Superhobbies - A new investment option</td></tr>
</table>

We called this book 'Superhobby Investing' because it covers the area at the intersection of investing, collecting and other serious hobbies. The idea is to examine how you can ratchet up a hobby or a collecting passion into an investment option.

If you are a stock market investor, this book will show how you can use the tangible assets that are normally part and parcel of collecting as a means of diversifying your portfolio.

Or you may simply own, or have inherited, some 'superhobby' assets - a stamp collection or a set of first editions, say - but never thought of them as potential investments.

Using this book, you can find out how to assess their value and how to convert them into a durable and profitable portfolio.

There is no shortage of examples. The stamp collection you started as a child, or inherited from your grandfather, could provide an impressive return. If you have furnished your home with antiques over a period of many years, the chances are that they have increased in value. One good painting, carefully chosen, can prove a fantastic investment.

What we want to do in this book is to show why developing one or more superhobbies can be a good idea, and to look at the forms this tangible asset investing can take.

There are a number of common themes running through the book, and we'll look at each topic systematically. In each superhobby investment category - whether it's art, antiques, books, forestry, stamps, wine or whisky - we will be focussing on some key aspects.

These are: the background to the market; whether or not a particular superhobby is really right for you; the long-term returns you can reasonably expect, based on past history; whether or not there are tax advantages you can use; how best to buy and sell and through whom; and where to go for more information on your chosen superhobby investing area.

But before we begin let's outline some of the issues that have led us to the conclusion that looking seriously at the alternative, particularly tangible, investments that the superhobby concept represents is a good idea.

Why superhobbies?

A superhobby is simply a collecting area or some other interest taken to a more systematic level. It may be an interest you decide to take up seriously after reading this book. Ultimately, only you can decide which interests are the right ones for you. We hope this book will help you do that.

What you need to recognise, however, is that superhobby investing requires that you make a serious financial commitment to the area you choose. Like any investment, it will repay the attention you devote to research. We think, however, that researching superhobby investment choices can be just as interesting as trying to spot undervalued companies.

So let's start off by looking at the reason why you should be thinking about diverting some of your hard-earned cash away from the stock market and into a superhobby.

Conventional investments are untrustworthy

Running through the whole investment process is the axiom that risk and return are closely linked.

Here are a few ways that axiom manifests itself.

Government bonds are 'safe' (supposedly!) but have low returns; pooled investments like unit trusts are safer than individual ones; blue chip equities are more risky than bonds but usually have higher returns; loss-making enterprises or very young companies are even riskier than blue chips, and investors in them have the potential to make higher returns still.

While statements like this are true, they don't tell the whole story. Government bonds are only safe in the sense that they have a government guarantee that interest will be paid and capital returned at maturity, but in certain circumstances their prices will go down. If inflation rises or interest rates go up, bond prices will fall. Many pooled investments, like technology unit trusts, have proved treacherous.

Investing in a unit trust doesn't absolve you from thinking about your investment. You have to pick the right area to invest in and, however diverse a fund, it will lose money if the area it specialises in moves out of favour or the manager isn't up to the job.

> ## Conventional investing has failed
>
> - Shares, and bonds, have proved riskier than expected
> - Funds can be badly managed
> - With-profit funds have produced low returns
> - The protection offered by some funds has been illusory
> - Securities markets could be trendless for a long time

You also don't need to be financially sophisticated to know that insurance company with-profit funds have not yielded the returns those investors in them once expected. Granted there are generally some guarantees, but recent events have shown that returns, in the form of bonus rates, can change both dramatically and arbitrarily.

Investments that promise equity linked returns and protection of capital often have clauses in them that mean they lose money spectacularly if markets head south. Just ask the investors in so-called 'precipice bonds' for their opinion.

In other words, what the recent bear market in shares should have taught investors is that there are no short cuts to investing success. If you can't discover where the risk in an investment might be, it doesn't mean there is no risk, but simply that you have not looked in the right place for it.

We don't have a crystal ball. We don't know where world stock and bond markets - and the investments that are linked to them - will go from here. There are those who believe that the strong rally in world stock markets that began in March 2003 is the beginning of a new bull market. Others see it as simply a prelude to further long term weakness. The reality could be that it will fizzle out and that markets will move sideways for an extended period, rather as they have in Japan since the pricking of the property based bubble there at the beginning of the 1990s. The prolonged period of low interest rates in the US may usher in an era of more rapid global inflation.

A decade of the drooping Nikkei - is this what's in store for the UK?

In any case the inherent unreliability of stock market returns should prompt any rational investor to look elsewhere. This is why tangible superhobby investments are worth closer investigation.

Diversifying your assets is good

Conventional wisdom in investing is that diversification reduces risk. Learned academic studies have measured how and why this works. It's true, for example, that holding as few as eight individual shares, for example, will reduce your risk significantly, in fact by almost as much as holding 50 or 100 shares would do.

Professional investors and many individuals also reduce risk by investing in other types of securities, notably in fixed income investments like bonds, but also in less conventional (but still essentially stock market related) investments like hedge funds and venture capital.

The aim of all this activity is to produce a smoother pattern of returns, in other words to reduce volatility. Investors do not want the value of their investments to zigzag alarmingly. They would rather see returns that are predictable and for the value of their portfolio to show a smooth upward trajectory.

One of the ways volatility is reduced is by having a mixture of different types of assets that are not strongly correlated with each other. Bonds generate income constantly and may show capital growth when shares are weak, for example.

When shares are strong, bonds may be weak. Hedge funds pride themselves on performing well whatever the market conditions.

Diversification in securities is not true diversification

- Conventional diversification is usually only within securities markets
- True diversification avoids market mood swings
- True diversification extends your time horizon
- Tangible investments are a good counterweight

The flaw in this diversification argument is that all of these investments that are widely used by professional and amateur investors alike are based around the securities markets. Securities markets - the markets for shares and bonds - are highly liquid. It's easy to buy and sell. Investments made through securities markets have a real-time price. At any moment of the day you can tell how much your investment is worth.

But there are times when this may not necessarily be a good thing. Stock and bond market investments, and those like hedge funds and unit trusts that are related to them, are vulnerable to shocks to the financial system. The fact that they are liquid can tempt investors to sell when they should hang on for a better price, and to buy when they should take their profits or steer clear. Markets like this are often feverish places, and however diversified your stock market investments are, they will reflect the market's mood swings.

> **Calculating how much to invest in superhobbies - an example of a strategy**
>
> - Mr. X has equity in a house worth £250,000, a share portfolio worth £500,000 and cash of £50,000. Total assets £800,000.
> - Invest 10% of total assets in 'tangibles' = £80,000.
> - £80,000 equates to 16% of his share portfolio, a good compromise.
> - Dividing it into four lots of £20,000 gives Mr. X diversity and a reasonable investment in each.
> - Mr. X selects four areas that interest him - stamps, wine, art, and classic, cars.
> - He invests gradually in each area, taking advice, using his uninvested cash, and where necessary supplementing it by selling poorly performing shares.

Owning a range of tangible superhobby investments is a good counterweight to all this feverish speculation. Investments of the sort we describe later in this book are less liquid than stock market investments, although not as illiquid as is commonly supposed. At first sight this lack of liquidity might seem a disadvantage. But it can mean that you are less prone to making poor short-term market driven decisions when you own them.

Long-term investment is an underrated technique

So you should diversify the type of asset you own, whether it's a bond, share, hedge fund, unit trust, or other form of investment, and diversify within each of those categories. In the same way, it also makes sense to diversify your investments according to the length of time they may need to come to fruition.

If you buy a speculative share you might hold it for a day, a week, a month or two, and then sell it. It might make sense to switch your assets between stocks and bonds over the course of a few years, depending on the ebbs and flows of the economic cycle and trends in the respective markets.

Many alternative forms of investment - take wine and forestry, for example - can take years to reach their full value but, if you buy wisely, are likely to increase in value. Trees grow; wine improves with age. This means that the patient investor can make substantial percentage returns simply by sitting on the investment and doing nothing.

Long term investing favours tangible assets

- Many dealers use tangible items as their own 'pension fund'
- Values increase because supply is restricted
- Values should at least keep pace with inflation
- Supply of tangibles more restricted than property

It makes good sense to diversify not just the type of investment you own, but also the timescale over which their best returns will be realised.

Many dealers I have spoken to, in the antique trade, in art and photography, in the book trade, and in stamps use this medium as a home for all or part of their long-term savings. Many avid collectors use their chosen field in the same way.

There is a simple but fundamental reason why long-term superhobby assets work as an investment medium. Supply is restricted.

There is only one Van Gogh 'Portrait of Dr Gachet' (one of the most expensive pictures ever sold), only a limited number of Chippendale chairs, only a limited number of bottles of 1990 Chateau Petrus, only a limited number of first edition Dickens novels, a limited number of high quality 1840 'penny blacks', and only a limited amount of gold bullion.

There's only one 'Portrait of Dr Gachet'

This means that at the very least the greater the amount of purchasing power in the world economy, the more the value of objects like this will rise over time. Scarce objects should at least keep place with inflation and should rise in value with greater affluence in markets where collecting and investing is common.

The same argument is sometimes made about residential property, although this is more questionable. While residential property prices tend to rise over time, they are subject to the vagaries of the planning regime and demographic changes.

The house we used to own in the London suburbs appreciated less in value over the 18 years we owned it than if we'd invested the same amount in a loft in Wapping, because of the trend away from the suburbs and towards inner city living. When we bought the house, it would have been hard to foresee this trend. It was in the end dictated by longer working hours and high salaries for City workers.

Investing in houses may not be the answer

On the other hand the house we now own, an 18th century construction in the Lake District National Park, is probably a better bet. This is because genuine 18th century properties cannot be built in the 21st century and because National Park planning restrictions mean that the supply of new property in the area is strictly limited.

The arguments that apply to our current house apply equally to a long-term investment in an 'old master' painting. Because it is old, it has a value all its own that cannot be replicated. It is therefore a desirable object in its own right and its value should increase at least in line with the general price level.

In summary, most superhobby-type investments are likely to increase in value over time because 'they ain't making them any more'.

Absence of investment income less important when rates are low

Few superhobby investments produce income. Or to put it another way, all of their gain comes in the form of capital growth. Of the ones we cover in the book, possibly the only exception to this is forestry. Forestry investment can be structured in such a way that you can receive a regular tax-free income.

Is this lack of income a drawback? It depends on your viewpoint. Some investors need to derive income from their investments. But many long-term investors will go for years without taking dividends. In fact it is often an advantage to let income roll up inside an investment to allow compounding to do its work. And there are many commonly used investments, like zero coupon bonds, that investors use in order to save for specific long terms goals like retirement or school fee provision which have no income paid in the form of dividends.

So rather than think of tangible alternative investments as having no income, think instead of their total return and the hidden income that is rolling up inside them.

Even if you find this hard to grasp, remember that interest rates are pretty low right now. Normal savings accounts return next to nothing. In the UK, long term savings accounts provide an income of little more than 3%, even for quite substantial sums, and less than this when tax is taken off.

Absence of income, and charges, should be ignored

- Most tangibles don't produce income
- No different to, for example, zero coupon bonds
- Absence of income less important when rates are low
- Storage and insurance charges no different to fund administration costs

---

This means that what you forgo by having investments that produce no income is that much less. What you are giving up in interest on a bank deposit is much less significant than it would be if rates were much higher.

Critics may say that holding tangible assets for investment yields a negative income. This is because valuable items held for investment may need to be stored and insured. This imposes a cost that is supposedly not present in investments made through the securities markets.

This is true up to a point, but not really that significant. Some items (such as gold) can be held in such a way that storage and insurance costs are eliminated. In other cases insurance costs are in fact less than for normal household contents, particularly if you have good security measures in place at your home anyway. Some items, like stamps, are easy to hide away, and their true value is not apparent to the untutored eye.

Let's also remember that holding stocks, bonds or unit trusts as an investment is not cost-free either. Most brokers and asset managers impose administration charges, charges for valuations, and the like. Unit trusts frequently have both initial and annual charges. They can be reduced (if you buy through a fund supermarket, for example) but rarely avoided. ISAs and PEPs are also subject to charges.

Liquidity is better than you might think

In the stock and bond markets, even investments that do not distribute income are sufficiently easy to sell for investors seeking an income to be able to sell small amounts periodically to raise funds.

This is less of an option in the case of superhobby investments. For one thing a collection (of books for instance) may have a value as a collection that exceeds the value of the sum of the parts. This means that to sell a small part of it may diminish its value disproportionately. In the case of other forms of tangible investment, selling a small lot may be uneconomic. Alternatively your investment may be concentrated in a few items of high value, and therefore it may be 'lumpy' or difficult to sell if you only want to cash in a small amount.

You need to pick your choice of investment very much with this in mind. The more homogeneous the item, or the lower the individual value of the pieces that comprise your collection, the easier it will be to realise small amounts of income periodically. So for example wine, stamps or limited edition prints, as opposed to fine art or classic cars, might be a better choice if this aspect concerns you.

Selling through auction rooms is usually possible. While commissions are hefty, sellers do have some control over the minimum value realised by setting a reserve price. Price data from auctions is also readily available and makes it possible to check the price of many items beforehand and get a good idea of what an item you want to sell might fetch, or how many pieces you might need to sell to raise a specific amount.

Despite the commissions that have to be paid, the saleroom is a good place to sell because of the potential for a bidding frenzy, with competing buyers eager to own your piece. On the minus side, you may not sell at your desired reserve price and, if the category you have invested in is an esoteric one, you may have to wait several months for an auction in which it can be included to come along.

Liquidity issues leave you in control

- Buy through a trusted dealer; sell through a saleroom
- Auction system allows you to establish a minimum sale price
- Procedures for selling mean less chance for impulsive sale
- Intrinsic value provides comfort if sale fails

With tangible investments you can control whom you buy from. This might be a trusted dealer who specialises in your particular superhobby area and with whom you have built a relationship.

Or you can use an intermediary, like a saleroom, that will be able to give you some advice on prices and put you in touch with would-be sellers and buyers through the auction process. You can control the price you sell for by simply not selling if you consider the price likely to be achieved does not meet your expectations. But read the auctioneer's small print first to be sure on this point.

In stock market investments, there is every chance - if you are like me - that an item of company news might prompt you to sell a share because you feel it may have suddenly become a more risky proposition.

Works of art, and other tangible investments, cannot go bust. It follows therefore that you may feel less pressure to hurry a sale simply because you feel the climate has changed for the worse. There is always the option of retaining the item for the time being and selling it later when conditions have improved, secure in the knowledge that the item has an intrinsic value in its own right and in many cases an aesthetic appeal that you can enjoy in the meantime.

Aesthetic appeal

Aesthetic appeal is often the biggest plus point for those attracted to superhobby investing. Many individuals begin collecting by accident before they even entertain the idea of doing so as an investment.

Here's a personal example. In our home we have a collection of contemporary mixed media art from an artist we know well who has been a close personal friend for more than 30 years, a small collection of old bond and share certificates, some original cartoons, some limited edition prints from internationally recognised artists, a small collection of first editions, a number of Victorian watercolours and some modern ceramics that could be classed as collectors' items. We have never really viewed any of these as an investment. They are simply beautiful or appealing things - often with a story attached - that we like to have around us.

We have also indulged in some more systematic superhobby investing by buying a small portfolio of investment grade stamps. Another area that attracts us is wine. Why these particular areas?

The first because of its similarity to stock market portfolio investing; the second because it is comparatively easy - as we'll find out in a later chapter - to invest regular amounts in wine and build up a portfolio over a long period. Both stamps and coins can be stored securely and independently in conditions that best protect their value.

But these are personal preferences. They are topics we already know a little about and, provided you deal through a reputable dealer, investment in them is not bedevilled by fakes and forgeries. They also have well documented price histories, although do check independently that the price you will deal at is competitive before handing over the cash.

Aesthetic dividend is a big compensation

- Tangibles offer aesthetic pleasure instead of a cash dividend
- Tangibles tend at least to hold their value in real terms
- Returns not strongly correlated with the stock market

The aesthetic dividend from these tangible investments we have at home is important to us. And, if you take up superhobby investing it should be to you. They can be a conversation piece, and a source of pleasure. Looking at a painting on your sitting room wall or handling a Graham Greene first edition gives you a reason not to be too worried about the shorter-term ups and downs in the market. If you can't achieve the price you want when you come to sell them, then you can wait and continue to enjoy their beauty in the meantime.

The big argument for investments like this is that with a few exceptions they tend to hold their value in real terms, you have the aesthetic dividend, and a chance of making decent returns that are not strongly correlated with the stock market, but rather with the general level of economic prosperity.

In the course of this round-up of reasons why tangible assets are a good long term investment medium, I have mentioned a few of the areas we will cover in later chapters. I want now to look at why we have chosen some areas and excluded others, and what all of the superhobbies we look at later have in common.

What alternatives?

When we set out to put the ideas for this book into a coherent form, we were faced with a bewildering number of options. There will inevitably be some areas that readers feel should have been included here but are not. So here are the reasons we picked the areas we did.

These are the essential attributes of our superhobby investment categories:

Must have an established network of dealers

This is essential simply from the standpoint of liquidity. There are a number of more modern areas where collectors do exist, often pursuing their hobby in relative isolation. I know, for example, of one individual who collects old petrol pumps and vending machines, and another who collects used railway tickets. They may increase in value, but there may not be a large number of collectors from whom to buy and sell. It's OK for a hobby, but not for superhobby investing.

Must be permanent and lasting assets

While it is true that many tangible investments can be destroyed (rare books can be torn up, antiques broken, forests burnt down), if you look after your investments carefully they can be more or less permanent assets. There are shops in London selling vases from Ancient Greece dating from the third century BC. And there are 18th century long case clocks around that are still in perfect working order, despite being considered wasting assets by the Inland Revenue. We wanted to avoid, however, looking at investments that had a finite life. Racehorses are an example. While you can make money from owning racehorses, the fact remains that they are 'high maintenance' items. They will also keel over sooner or later, at which point your investment ceases to exist.

Must not be securities-based

For reasons that we explored earlier in this chapter we want to avoid looking at investments that reflect the tangible assets we are interested in but which are based around tradable securities. So while it is possible to buy shares in antique salerooms, stamp dealers, gold mines, timber companies and various others, the focus in this book is generally on the physical ownership of the items themselves.

This isn't a hard and fast rule. There are collective investments in forestry and in films, and there are securities you can buy that give you direct exposure to the price of gold. But in all of the areas we have looked at, direct physical ownership of the item in question are both possible and preferable.

Must not be property

Finally, we have avoided property. Though for many people property has been a favoured investment area, it could be the subject of a book in its own right. There is another reason. If one of the prime reasons for superhobby investing is to achieve diversification away from our existing assets, then most of us already have a sizeable stake in the property market ourselves, if only through the house we live in.

If you don't own a house, then of course this remark doesn't apply to you. But most people need to look at the assets in which they have invested or the cash they have available for investment, and include the equity in any property they might own.

Investing further in property might be the correct decision at a particular point in the economic cycle, but we suspect it isn't the case at present. Either way it does not achieve the diversification that is both desirable and necessary.

With all this in mind, what areas do we think fall into the superhobby category as potentially lucrative areas into which you can diversify?

Before we list them, we need to get a couple of things clear.

The first is that most of the markets I'm going to describe are not homogeneous. So what we'll do in each chapter is to include comments on some niche collecting areas and investment media that may be of interest as superhobby investments in their own right. In each case these are by no means an exhaustive list of the options you have, but merely suggestions.

You may not, for example consider yourself to be in the market for 19th century French impressionist painting, but there is affordable art available from around this time period in the form of collectable early photography, watercolours and limited edition prints, areas that we think we are likely to hear more about in the future.

With this proviso in mind, here are the broad themes we have selected to explore further in the chapters that follow:

Main market	Some distinct sub-markets
Antiques	Furniture, silver, china, Victoriana, clocks
Art	Photography, prints, drawings, watercolours
Books	Crime, SF, Children books, modern authors
Banknotes	Scripophily
Classic cars	Supercars, commercial vehicles
Coins	Gold coins, Greek and Roman coins
Film and theatre productions	Sale and leasebacks, film productions; EIS
Forestry	Direct, collective
Gold	Coins, certificates, other 'white' metals
Stamps	Postal history, antique stamp boxes, desk sets
Whisky	Cask, collectable bottles, distillery ownership
Wine	Bordeaux, champagne, fortified wine

As you can see this gives us plenty of scope to examine all aspects of the tangible investment scene, even though we have excluded some pretty big areas. We haven't for example looked at toys, or jewellery, or sports memorabilia, all of which are big areas. We simply don't have space, within the confines of this book, to look at every single one.

Read on to find out the basics of these markets, what sort of returns you might be able to make from each of these areas, how to buy and sell sensibly, and where to get the data and advice you need to make an informed decision.

Each of the remaining chapters will cover the topic in question in a broadly similar way with plenty of tabular material. The last chapter of the book looks specifically at auctions as a medium for buying and selling - its advantages and disadvantages and the intricacies involved. At the end of the book we've included a directory and a glossary to make it easier to understand and find the information you need to be a successful superhobby investor.

Finally, we should stress that our aim has been to look at each particular area as objectively as possible from the standpoint of an individual approaching the subject for the first time and to compare each particular category in the same way, particularly with reference to potential returns, costs of ownership and transaction costs.

We have talked extensively to many collectors and dealers in the course of researching and writing this book and some have been good enough to comment on the draft of the relevant chapter. Nonetheless it is inevitable that established and experienced collectors and dealers in all of these areas may find the approach we have taken as giving possibly too brief a coverage of their pet area.

If so, remember that we do not claim to be experts in each individual area, but we have tried in this book to bring to our comments on them a systematic investment-orientated approach that at the very least might be thought provoking and challenging, even to expert collectors. It might even encourage them to explore new avenues. In short, we hope that there is something in this book for everyone.

Chapter

2 | Antiques

Of all the superhobbies you can take up, collecting antiques is one of the most popular. The proof is the rash of TV programmes devoted to the topic. These range from the perennially popular 'Antiques Roadshow' to others such as 'Flog It!' and 'Bargain Hunt'.

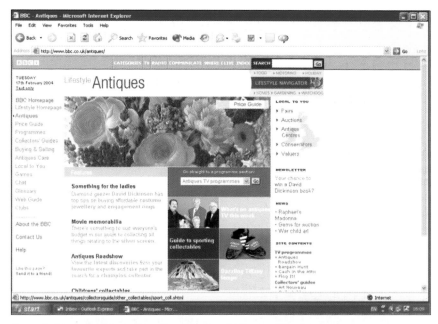

Superhobbys on the telly - the popular Antiques Roadshow

These may make entertaining TV, but their emphasis is the opposite of the purpose of this book. Programmes like this concentrate on the value at auction of items acquired many years ago or family heirlooms that have lain gathering dust in the attic.

Nevertheless programmes like this provide useful lessons for would-be supercollectors.

One is that results achieved at auction are unpredictable. Another is that the most seemingly mundane items can be worth more than you might think. And they show that condition, while not the be-all and end-all, is crucial when it comes to getting a good price.

Finally, think back to the old TV series 'Lovejoy'. It demonstrated, to any who had not suspected it already, that the antique trade can be a minefield.

If you venture into the antique trade, do so with your eyes open. Most dealers are honest and their stock genuine. But you will from time to time come across some disreputable dealers (thankfully a small minority), some fake and reproduction items artfully got up to look like valuable originals, and some stolen goods.

Lessons from the TV

- Auction sales are inherently unpredictable
- Seemingly mundane items can be valuable
- Condition matters
- Provenance matters
- The auction market has its share of villains and forgeries

What this really means is that establishing the provenance of the items you buy is vital. Provenance really means establishing that they are the genuine articles and that the person selling them to you acquired them honestly. In turn this means buying through a dealer you trust, or through a saleroom which has taken steps to establish provenance.

Many big auction houses will refund your money if you can demonstrate that a piece you bought at auction is a forgery. Even with this protection, it will pay you to walk away from a bargain rather than get landed with a fake or stolen item.

You don't necessarily need to be a fully qualified expert to invest in antiques. It helps, however, to have one on call in the shape of a dealer you know and can trust. Don't be afraid to pay for quality. If something appears to be unduly cheap it is probably cheap for a reason. That reason may be poor quality, poor condition, doubtful provenance, or simply lack of aesthetic appeal, or a combination of these factors.

Remember, however, that you are dealing in an unregulated market. So you need to keep your wits about you. It is, however, a market that occasionally has anomalies that can be uncovered by diligent research. Rather like the stock market, in fact.

With that in mind let's have a look at some of the basics of antiques as a 'superhobby'.

Basics

As with most of the superhobbies listed elsewhere in this book, it helps to specialize. It is the only way you can make sense of a market this size. The antique trade is so diverse that it is impossible to become expert on every single area. Nor should you try. After all, not all antiques will either interest you or be to your taste or your budget.

But there are a few easy steps you can take to start things off. The first is to pick an area that interests you. Pick one that is also appropriate to the physical space you have available at home, the type of property you live in, and the depth of your pocket. If you can try to focus on an area where you may have some interest or contacts that can give you an edge.

Once you have picked an area (and we'll cover some of the popular ones later) read up on it first. Reading up is only a start. Even with extensive reading you are unlikely ever to be able to match the depth of experience and expertise of a dealer specialising in that particular area.

Here's an example. There is a dealer in antique clocks about 20 miles from where I live. He has a stock of over 50 antique clocks, the principals in the business span two generations, and they have on call more than 1400 out of print books on horology. They know more about clocks than I ever will.

So the second step, before you buy, is to go and talk to a few dealers. Most antique dealers are people who have a great love of antiques and many years experience of handling, buying and selling them. It makes them the best advisers that superhobby investors have to have to take their first steps in the antiques market.

> ## First steps in antiques
> - Choose a couple of areas to specialize in
> - Read up on it before you start buying
> - Find a couple of dealers you can trust
> - Adopt a portfolio approach to spread risk

The golden rule is 'talk before you buy'. Get the dealer on your side and indicate that you are considering investing a significant sum of money. Tell him you are talking to other dealers. That way a dealer sees you as a potential long term customer and, because others are competing for your business, will not try and sell you a piece that is overpriced or of doubtful authenticity. Generally dealers will want you to return and spend more money. They want a satisfied customer.

When it comes to making your first purchase there are a couple of things to bear in mind. One is to buy the best pieces you can afford from the most reliable sources you can find; the second is that aesthetic appeal and good quality craftsmanship are what ultimately determine value.

Portfolio investment is just as important in antiques as anywhere else. Don't put all your eggs in one basket. Spread your money across a number of items. By doing this, not only do you spread your risk, but you also have a larger and more interesting collection. Think long term, and be prepared for a few knocks along the way. Don't expect all your antiques to make you a fortune.

Don't forget that just as the stock market and individual sectors of it can go up and down, different genres of antique go in and out of fashion. Not all the shares you invest in will do well. The same is true of individual antiques. But if you buy carefully, the star performers should outweigh the also-rans.

Above all, buy things of beauty. An ugly piece does not become a thing of beauty simply because it is 200 years old.

Collecting Areas

Which areas of the antiques market you choose to invest in depends on your circumstances, where you live, and your pocket.

We live in a small but picturesque house in the Lake District, built in 1753. Regardless of the depth or otherwise of our pocket, it would be futile to fill it with large, highly polished items of antique furniture. There isn't the space. And they would never have been seen inside a building like this, originally a miller's cottage.

It's better for us to buy small items that would have been used in the late 18th and 19th century in a country area. Assuming you want your antique investments in your home, then the space you have and the style of the building you live in dictate what you buy.

But here are a few areas where there is a ready market.

Ceramics

This is a generic term that takes in, among others, bone china, pottery and porcelain. It is a very well established area for collectors. But there are a few rules to follow. To value and identify individual items correctly, you need to know the marks of individual makers and their significance. However, this is not the whole story. Potters seldom marked items made before 1870. This is where expert analysis of the general style and the quirks of individual potters come in. Good dealers can help with this.

More important still is that the pieces themselves are attractive and above all flawless, with no chips or cracks. If you buy with care, they should be a consistently good investment.

19th century country crafts

A member of our family is an experienced dealer in items like this, as well as other rustic items like kitchen implements, toys and small items of furniture like stools and chairs.

Dating from the 19th century (and earlier of course) items like this have great charm. They usually show up some facet of the history of that era. And they nearly always hold their value.

What about some examples? Samplers, on which girls and young women practiced their stitching technique by embroidering homilies and letters of the alphabet, are a subset in their own right and eminently collectable. Primitive animals (either in the form of paintings and toys) and portraits of children and especially dogs have shown big increases in price recently. Cast iron doorstops and household tools fashioned in the shape of small animals can fetch surprising amounts.

The attraction of items like this for us personally, quite apart from having a family member to advise on acquisitions, is that they are often small and modestly priced. We recently saw a cast iron nutcracker in the form of a squirrel priced at more than £100, and an attractive pair of carved wooden elephant bookends for not much less.

Silver

This has always been considered a good investment, although prices in the last ten years have been less than dynamic. This may change, if only because precious metal prices have been staging something of a recovery of late.

There is, however, a two-tier market in silver antiques.

Early marked pieces require substantial capital. Further down the price scale, the market is currently subject to the whims of the export trade, notably to Italy. Here, silver is bought for fashion reasons and fashions can change. Remember too that silver and jewellery are also often prime targets for thieves. So, if you own antique silver, good security and insurance is essential.

Furniture

This can be an excellent investment. In particular, items made in Britain from oak, elm, walnut, or various fruit woods have shown very good returns over quite a number of years.

Prices of furniture stalled in 2002 in the aftermath of the September 11th 2001 terrorist attacks. Antique furniture has been very popular with American buyers in the past. So much so that when they are absent, prices dip. There is a silver lining to this particular cloud. Buyers ship furniture abroad, thus diminishing the available supply. When they return, prices should resume their rise. Whether they will return any time soon is, of course an open question.

Let's not forget, though, the particular way that antique furniture scores highly. Irrespective of its investment potential well-made antique furniture has function as well as beauty. It can be sat on, slept on, eaten off, or just admired for its beauty. This is something you cannot do with conventional stock market investments. And it's not easy to steal.

Clocks

Clocks, particularly long case clocks, are perennial favorites of many antique collectors and investors alike. One reason is that the Inland Revenue considers them to be machinery, which of course they are. It means that for tax purposes they are deemed a wasting asset. The importance of this is that gains in their value are not subject to capital gains tax.

In mid 2003 a 300-year old long case clock made by Thomas Tompion, doyen of 18th century clock makers, sold at auction for over £340,000. Some wasting asset!

Clocks of the early Victorian era and earlier are worthwhile investments. In the case of pieces from the later Victorian era, however, it is a different matter. Mass production and rather ugly design conspire to reduce both their aesthetic appeal and collectibility.

Contemporary antiques

'Contemporary' means items, particularly furniture, from the 20th century. These can cost as much as much older items, but it is an open question whether they have true investment potential. The exception here is probably items that reflect well-established artistic and architectural movements like Art Nouveau and Art Deco and the work of established players like Charles Rennie Mackintosh. There can be investment potential in quality contemporary arts and crafts but one must beware of falling for the fad of the moment.

Condition

It is axiomatic that whatever you collect must be in the best possible condition. This is a theme that recurs throughout this book. Condition governs value. In property, it is often said that the three most important aspects are location, location, and location. So also in most superhobby investing, condition, condition and condition are the three things that matter most.

The antiques you invest in should be in the best condition. It sounds simple enough. But let's examine for a moment exactly what we mean by that. A pristine piece can be just as suspect as one with obvious damage. It is very important in an antique that signs of age are present. Indeed the patina that some antiques acquire with age is one of their attractive features. Remember that wear should be consistent with the age of the piece itself.

What you should avoid are obviously damaged items or poorly renovated ones.

There are many heavily restored pieces on the market. But how do you spot them? The evidence of your eyes will often be enough. A good dealer will tell you if an item has been restored. If he or she doesn't and you subsequently find that the piece you bought has been restored, you could return it and ask for your money back.

For this reason, a quality antique shop or antique centre offering receipts is often the best place through which to invest. LAPADA and other trade associations for dealers police issues like this with a fair degree of vigilance. They will arbitrate if you don't feel as though you are getting a fair crack of the whip.

With auctions, by contrast, only if the piece is clearly a fake do you stand a chance of restitution.

Condition, condition, condition

- Only buy from a dealer that gives receipts
- Wear and tear should be consistent with the age of the piece
- Trade bodies offer arbitration if you feel aggrieved
- Read up on caring for your investment

Fakes are by no means a rarity. The number of reproduction items and total fakes existing in the market is on the up. There are also many items from the Continent (especially from Eastern Europe) coming into the UK now that have doubtful provenance and consequently little future value.

Keeping items in good condition after you have bought them is also important. There are many dos and don'ts, some of which are not entirely obvious. LAPADA, one of the major trade associations for antique dealers, has a range of leaflets dealing with the care, handling and upkeep of furniture, ceramics, silver and other items.

Security measures

Antiques are often stolen, especially small portable pieces like jewellery, china, pictures and small items of furniture. There are a number of precautions you must take to protect your investment.

The first is to keep receipts of any items you buy. Have items you have owned for more them five years valued by a specialist valuer. Dealers and LAPADA offices can provide names of suitable ones near where you live.

All valuable items should be photographed individually with colour film, preferably in natural light and against a plain background. Put a ruler or a 50p piece alongside to give an indication of their size. Keep an inventory of all valuable items with details of labels and identifying marks, and dimensions. Put this list in a safe place so that it too cannot be stolen.

Foiling thieves
- Make sure you are fully insured
- Keep an inventory, measurements, photographs and receipts
- Mark items with your postcode

If it can be done without detracting from the value of piece, mark your antiques with your postcode and the first two letters of your house name or number. Marks should be made on parts that are not visible or those that are cleaned.

Make sure that all items are insured for their full market value and that you can verify their value to an insurance company's satisfaction and that you satisfy their stipulated security measures. Having antiques on your policy will not necessarily add significantly to your premium. Antique items typically cost in the region of £2.50 per £1,000 of value to insure.

Is it right for you?

Let's look at the questions you need to answer to determine whether antiques could be a superhobby category with a place in your wider portfolio of investments.

▊ Are you investing for the medium to long term?

There are few quick turns in the antique trade. Even for dealers, big killings are rare. You must recognise that by buying from a dealer, you are funding the dealer's profit margin in the price you pay. If you buy at a saleroom, the auctioneer's profit margin (in the shape of the buyer's premium, and sellers commission) is also hefty. This means you need to keep the piece for a number of years to recoup this cost and make a good return.

Do you have adequate capital?

No deep pockets are needed to invest in antiques. Items can be had for as little as £50 and yet prove a good investment. Furniture, ceramics, pictures, glass, metal, and quality toys can be purchased at prices ranging from £50 to £500 or £5,000 and more. It is relatively easy to assemble a portfolio of antiques with, say an initial £5,000. The more cash you have to invest, the more ambitious you can be about what to buy.

Are you prepared for storage, insurance and maintenance costs?

You need space to display your investment. Since they are things of beauty it makes no sense to lock them away. As we noted earlier, this means that what you collect is dictated by the size of property you have available. If you have items that are small, portable and have obvious value, you will need to invest in secure cabinets for them and have them separately insured.

Right for you?

- Long term investment - no quick turns
- Buy what suits where you live and space available
- Deep pockets not necessarily required
- Factor in insurance, security, restoration costs
- Prices in some categories indirectly dependent on US stockmarket
- Tax concessions only in 'wasting assets' (eg clocks)

Breakable items need to be handled with extreme care and placed somewhere where they will not come to harm. You will need to spend time and money caring for your antiques, whether it is restoration work (all but the most basic is best done by an expert), or simply a coat of polish now and again.

Are antiques a true diversification away from the stock market?

Like many areas covered in this book, the prices of antiques reflect the general level of affluence of the collector base. They are worth only what someone is prepared to pay for them. Americans have been among the most avid buyers of antiques in the past. It follows that the propensity of Americans to travel and the movement in the international value of the dollar can have a significant impact on the price of items they like.

At the time of writing (early 2004) many dealers in the UK report an absence of American buyers. It could mean a buying opportunity for well-capitalised UK purchasers.

Why is this relevant to portfolio diversification? Well, what it means is that the degree to which antiques represent true portfolio diversification is somewhat hedged around. Antiques are to some degree dependent on a prosperous cadre of American buyers. If US stock markets or American property prices take a dive, prices of antiques that are popular with American collectors will probably do the same. You need to bear this in mind.

Do you have an interest in social history?

Many people enjoy antiques for their aesthetic qualities and for what they reveal of the social history of the period. A prerequisite for successful investing in antiques is that you enjoy these aspects of your investment as much as its potential for producing financial returns.

Our own personal collecting interests really lie outside of the antiques category, but we have bought a number of small items appropriate for the house we live in. These include old cotton bobbins, small pieces of pewter, Victorian bookends, an early 19th century wooden jewellery box, and a number of other small items. These are far from being investments, but have some sort of resonance with the building we live in and are a frequent talking point.

Are there tax considerations?

Because antiques are, by definition, old and have increased in value over time, they cannot be regarded as wasting assets. And, needless to say, they are not viewed as such by the Inland Revenue. There is an important exception to this, which is any item with moving parts.

These are regarded as wasting assets and therefore not subject to capital gains tax. Watches, clocks, and old scientific instruments are normally exempt from CGT. And of course gains on sales of other items may be tax free if the profit you make is less than the annual exemption.

What returns can you make?

What returns can you make from a superhobby investment in antiques?

Like almost all other tangible assets, antiques do not produce an income in the conventional sense, so we can forget this as an investment objective. However, if you have invested in a number of antiques, and you need to raise cash, you can always sell some and generate income that way. Don't overdo it, though. Dealing is a way of getting a feel for a particular market, but if you do it too frequently the taxman could view your trading as a business and tax you on your profits.

Some lovers of art and antiques affect a lack of interest in their financial value. In fact this is true across many superhobby areas, both among collectors and even some dealers. And it is usually precisely that - an affectation. Few of those who deal in, buy, or inherit antiques do not want to know their monetary value. And any buyer of an antique will continue to be keenly interested in its resale price. Any investor or dealer who tells you different is not being entirely honest.

This is a different matter from the claim that is often made, probably correctly, that antique collectors may start out as hard headed investors, but then become so attached to their collections that they cannot bear to realize their investment returns when the time comes.

So what sorts of returns are on offer from superhobby investment in antiques? And how long do you have to wait to realise them? One problem with this is that the antique market is so diverse. Generalising about values is impossible. In reality there is no single antique market; rather, there are several different ones. One way of getting around this problem is simply to take a sample of items purchased by an informed buyer.

The table below shows a range of items in the personal collection of a dealer we know. It shows the date the items were purchased and an estimate of what they are worth now.

Table 2.1 - Antiques: Examples of returns

Item	Year bought	Price paid(£)	Est.value (£)	Compound return (%pa)
Oil painting of dog - listed artist	1977	50	900	11.8
Oak gate leg table	1978	300	2,000	7.9
Long case clock	1982	450	3,000	9.5
Oak mule chest	1984	400	900	4.4
Victorian cast iron moneybox	1994	50	120	10.2
Blue and white Davenport jug	1994	65	200	13.3
18th century country stool	1995	60	200	16.2
Tea caddy c. 1860	1995	70	150	10.0
Staffordshire flatback pottery figure	1995	50	150	14.7
Victorian rocking horse	1995	250	650	12.7

The returns demonstrated here are self-evident. There are higher returns in general from porcelain and lower returns from furniture. On average, returns in double figures look capable of being captured through intelligent buying.

More generally, an art market research firm recently provided a national newspaper with details of its estimates of the general trend in prices fetched by a spread of 18th century items in three different categories: furniture, porcelain and silver. The data covered the ten years from 1993 to 2002.

Porcelain appreciated steadily, increasing in all but one of the years in question and rising in total by around 90%, an average annual gain close to 7%.

Silver fell in price between 1993 and 1996 and has since recovered, but its overall gain over 10 years is a modest 8% or so in total.

Furniture dipped in the early part of the period, dropping in 1994 and increasing only fractionally in 1995, but then appreciated quite nicely after that, rising around 54% overall, or an average of 4.2% a year, or 6.7% a year if measured from the trough.

Remember that these gains are simply those seen in the general category in question for that particular age of piece. Individual pieces and those of different eras may have performed better or worse.

It is also worth remembering that these changes reflect only general levels of prices achieved at auction and do not reflect buyers premium, sellers commission and insurance costs over the period in question. These can take a big bite out of returns.

Buying and selling

Antiques are long-term investments. Good profits can sometimes be made quickly if you know your market and are lucky. But as with the stock market you need to beware of selling a good investment too cheaply. Hold on, and your profit might be greater in the long term. Buy intelligently, and only sell if you have a specific reason for doing so, or get an offer you can't refuse.

The basic first step is to go to a shop, antique centre or fair that has reputable and knowledgeable dealers. There you are more likely to buy an honest piece that will be easier to sell at a profit in the future.

Get a detailed receipt, and with reputable dealers you have the law on your side if there is a problem. Fakes are just a disaster. To avoid them, always get a receipt that describes and dates the item. Good, reputable, dealers will have no problem doing this. If a dealer refuses to do so, be on your guard.

When you come to sell, some dealers will buy pieces outright, and some will also sell on commission. That is to say they will display your piece for a period of time, and take a specified percentage of the sale price if they sell it. This can work, but you need to have the terms and conditions, and details like insurance, sorted out to your satisfaction before entering into an agreement like this.

Canny buying and selling

- Only buy from reputable dealers and get a receipt
- Trade in a small way to get a feel for the market
- Avoid buying at large auction rooms
- If you sell at auction, place a realistic reserve
- Bargains can be had in out of the way auctions, fairs and sales

---

Buying antiques (or indeed any collectable item) at auction can be hazardous for all but the most expert. Items not scrupulously examined at the preview may have flaws that will affect their value. After you have bought them is simply too late to find this out. Very few auctions offer real guarantees about the goods sold, other than taking back fakes. The rule is strictly 'caveat emptor'.

At auctions too you will be bidding against knowledgeable specialist buyers and those representing wealthy collectors. Dealers will drop out of contention once the potential margin on an item disappears, but competition between determined and rich private buyers can drive the price up way too high.

In circumstances like this it is all too easy to get carried away and bid too much. This is a condition known as 'auction fever'. It is a source of some amusement for wily trade buyers who know the value of and potential profit on each item. We'll look in more detail at how auctions work in the last chapter of this book.

What works against buyers can be to the advantage of sellers. The saleroom is as good a place as any to sell antiques but do place a reserve on lots you sell in case there is a sluggish day, few willing buyers, or some low bidding. You may incur a charge if the reserve is not met.

A final point to bear in mind is that you can sometimes get real value for money by buying as far down the chain of buyers and sellers as possible. Each time an item changes hands, a dealer will be making a margin on it.

Prominent dealers and auction houses have expensive overheads, but visiting country fairs and small auction rooms can often produce bargains. Follow this route if you know what you are buying and are disciplined to refuse less than perfect pieces. With a big city-centre dealer you may get a certificate of authenticity and a better guide to a piece's provenance, but you will pay extra for it.

Fairs are a good way of meeting a lot of dealers at the same time. This is particularly true of the professionally organised multi-day affairs. The largest of this type, held several times a year at Newark showground, has 4,000 dealers in one place, but is only for the knowledgeable and energetic. Other more modest fairs are organized regularly during the year throughout the UK and widely advertised.

Table 2.2 – Antiques – key web addresses and contact details

Company	Web address	Email	Phone	Type
Antique Collectors Club	www.antique-acc.com	sales@antique-acc.com	01394 389950	Data
Antiques Atlas	www.antiques-atlas.com	Iain@Antiques-atlas.com	n/a	Links
Antiques Magazine	www.antiquesmagazine.com	subscriptions@antiquesmagazine.com	01214 278731	Publication
Antiques Trade Gazette	www.atg-online.com	info@antiquestradegazette.com	020 7420 6600	Publication
Antiques World	www.antiquesworld.co.uk	contact@antiquesworld.co.uk	n/a	Links
The British Association of Paintings Conservators-Restorers	www.bapcr.org.uk	secretary@bapcr.org.uk	02392 465115	Association
BADA	www.bada.org	info@bada.org	020 7589 4128	Association
BBC Antiques	www.bbc.co.uk/antiques	antiques.roadshow@bbc.co.uk	n/a	Information
Bonhams	www.bonhams.com	info@bonhams.com	020 7393 3900	Dealer
British Antique Furniture Restorers	www.bafra.org.uk	headoffice@bafra.co.uk	01305 854822	Association
Christie's	www.christies.com	info@christies.com	020 7839 9060	Dealer
Invaluable	www.invaluable.com	customer.services@invalubable.com	020 7487 3401	Links
LAPADA – The Assn.of Art & Antiques Dealers	www.lapada.co.uk	lapada@lapada.co.uk	020 7823 3511	Association
Phillips	www.phillips-dpl.com	inquiry.desk@phillips-dpl.com	020 7318 4010	Dealer
Sotheby's	www.sothebys.com	On site	020 7293 5050	Dealer
UK Institute for Conservators	www.ukic.org.uk	ukic@ukic.org.uk	020 7721 8721	Association

Where to go for more information

Antiques are a huge subject. There are many thousands of dealers in the UK alone. Rather than list them, this section shows those reference publications and web sites that contain more information and large numbers of links. These are the gateways that would-be antique collectors can go to and explore at their leisure.

Trade Organisations

Formerly known as the London and Provincial Antique Dealers Association, LAPADA (www.lapada.co.uk), which now styles itself The Art and Antiques Dealers Association, offers guidance on buying and selling antiques. Its database can be searched either by dealer or item of interest. The site has information on the care and restoration of pictures, furniture, silver, ceramics and glass with free printed leaflets available in each case.

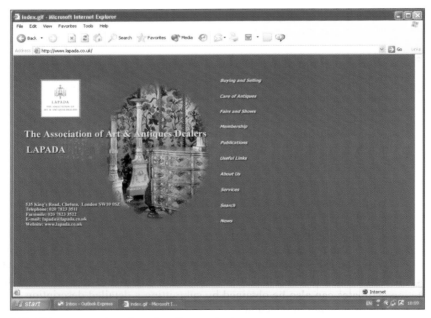

LAPADA represents art and antiques dealers

LAPADA also publishes a useful handbook: 'Buying and Selling Art and Antiques - the Law' by an expert in art and antiques law. You can buy it online. There are numerous other links. They include insurers, police forces, magazines and forthcoming fairs and shows. The LAPADA site also has details of the firm's conciliation service, which mediates disputes between dealers and their customers, and details of gift vouchers and its wedding present service.

The British Association of Antique Dealers (BADA) (www.bada.org) has a list of its members, searchable by category and region. There is information on buying and selling antiques and on choosing a reputable dealer.

BADA organises the Annual Antiques and Fine Art Fair in London. This takes place in March and details of it are on the site. The association also offers an antique assessment service. This is not a valuation, but a way whereby recognised experts can confirm the age and appropriate description of an antique. A free arbitration service is offered in the event of a dispute between a customer and a BADA member.

You can buy BADA gift vouchers on the site. These can be spent in a range of BADA member shops and galleries throughout the country.

The British Association of Paintings Conservator-Restorers (www.bapcr.org.uk) is the professional organisation for picture restorers. Members' meetings, featuring illustrated talks, are open to the public for a small charge.

The British Antique Furniture Restorers Association (www.bafra.org.uk) lists accredited conservator-restorers throughout the UK. The site also has articles, news and useful links.

The United Kingdom Institute for Conservators (www.ukic.org.uk) is the representative body for professional conservators and restorers in private and institutional practice. The site has information on choosing and working with a conservator.

Auctioneers

Bonhams (www.bonhams.com) has an auction calendar with online catalogues, an item search and results of past sales. Contact details for the numerous specialist departments are listed.

Christie's (www.christies.com) has an auction calendar together with online catalogues. You can buy these or view them online. Christie's Lotfinder will search the online catalogues and email the results to you. It is also possible via the site to enter absentee bids in Christie's auctions around the world. Free online auction estimates can also be obtained by submitting a detailed description and photograph of the item in question.

Sotheby's (www.sothebys.com) has an auction calendar, online catalogues for viewing and purchase, and previous auction results. Similar to Christie's it offers free auction estimates. Allow up to six weeks for a reply.

The firm's tax and heritage department assists clients and their advisors in the UK on all tax and legal problems relating to works of art and other objects auctioned by Sotheby's.

Publications

The Antiques Trade Gazette (www.atg-online.com) offers weekly news, comments and analysis from the international art and antiques trade. Also included on the site are comprehensive illustrated price guides, classified advertisements, fair and auction calendars, and directories. Access to the site is free to registered users. You can subscribe online to the print edition of the magazine. At the time of writing this cost £76 for the year.

Antiques Magazine (www.antiquesmagazine.com) is free to use, except for online databases. These are available to magazine subscribers only. The site features a calendar of fairs and auctions, radio and TV programme listings, saleroom reports and a bookshop. The companion site www.antiquescompanion.co.uk has a directory of restorers, services and suppliers.

Antique Collectors Club (www.antique-acc.com) has books on antiques, art, furniture, ceramics and much more. Their publication 'Antique Collectors Magazine', with articles by dealers and collectors, is available online for a modest subscription.

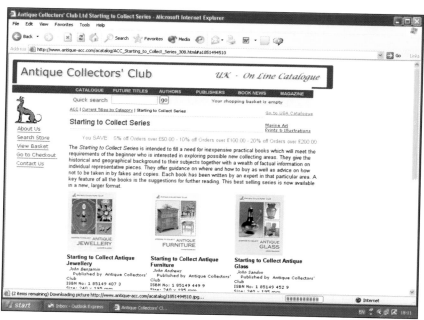

Antique Collectors Club - a good source of reference material

Books on the subject of Antiques are too numerous to mention, but a useful publication is Miller's Antiques Price Guide, which can be purchased from Amazon (www.amazon.co.uk).

Further Information

Antiques Atlas (www.antiques-atlas.com). This lists antiques for sale with dealer contact information. There is also information on UK fairs, an online bookshop and an email alerting service for database updates.

Antiques World (www.antiquesworld.co.uk) is a UK directory of information on antiques and collectables. Included on the site are links to fairs and markets, a list of clubs and societies, links to study courses, book reviews and articles. There are also links to restoration and conservation organisations, and to research and educational organisations.

The BBC Antiques site (www.bbc.co.uk/antiques) is a very useful resource. There are links to fairs, auctions, antique centres, conservators and valuers. The collectors' guides cover all topics with an introduction and relevant information for the subject area. Also covered is information on buying and selling, the care of antiques including restoring and insuring, a glossary of terms, and buyer's guides from the BBC's own experts. There are also links to the BBC's antiques programmes: The Antiques Roadshow, Bargain Hunt, Flog It!, and Cash in the Attic.

Invaluable (www.invaluable.com) lists art and antique dealers, antique centres, auctions and fairs. The auction search facility can search catalogues from up to 1,000 auction houses worldwide.

The company's 'Invaluable Appraiser' is an online database of historical auction prices with four million realised prices sourced from over 2,500 auction houses over the past 10 years. The cost for this service at the time of writing is £212 per year.

The company also operates 'Trace' (www.trace.co.uk) which aims to locate and recover stolen art, antiques and collectables. Over the past ten years they have assisted in the recovery of over 4,000 objects valued at £65m.

3 | Art

If art is your chosen superhobby you are in good company. Many astute City bankers and brokers collect art personally. They use it as an alternative to the stock market and property. Public companies hang art in their offices. Some even have full time curators, although corporate art is often either bland or very abstract, for fear of offending political correctness.

More important perhaps, there is at least one well-known example of a leading pension fund making a substantial long-term investment in art. The facts surrounding this example help to make the case for art as an investment medium.

Railpen (or the British Rail Pension Fund, as it was then called) began investing in art in 1975 because it wanted a hedge against inflation. It put a total of £40m into more than 2,400 works of art. These included sculptures, impressionist paintings, and work in many other genres. Many of the pieces were lent to museums to reduce insurance and storage costs.

Once index linked government bonds made an appearance in the early 1980s, the need for such a hedge disappeared. Eventually it was decided to sell the collection. The programme of sales was interrupted in the early 1990s because of a slump in the art market. The last of the items in the collection was finally sold in late 2003.

Over the period in question the Railpen art collection appreciated from an initial £40m to £172m, a rate of return four percentage points better than inflation. So, though critics scoffed at the idea for many years, the fund had the last laugh.

There is one distinct difference between art and antiques, wine or whisky. Art has no function other than to be decorative. If you own antique furniture you can sit on it or eat off it. Invest in wine, and you can simply enjoy it by drinking it. But art is simply to be viewed and admired. It has no practical use other than to please the eye.

While there is some difference of opinion and personal taste in certain quarters of the antique market over the relative merits of different pieces, there is greater unanimity over the merits of a Queen Anne chair or a Staffordshire pottery figure than there is, say, over the artistic durability of a minor Victorian watercolour painter or the latest 'hot' contemporary artist.

It is a matter of personal taste. Technique can be analysed objectively, but differences of opinion remain. I prefer Turner to Constable, Mondrian to Pollock, Caravaggio to Canaletto, but all are undeniably great artists. Needless to say, for me at least, owning a work by one of these artists has never been an option.

This makes art a more hazardous investment medium, but perhaps a more varied and interesting one.

Basics

Great art is visually appealing. There is no mystery to it. What you see is what you get. But there are a few general guiding principles to cover before we look at some of the main collecting areas.

The first is that the art market has increased substantially in size in the last 25 years. Some estimates suggest that there may be a million people around the world now who consider themselves art collectors, compared to perhaps 10,000 a quarter century ago.

The estimated 30m stamp collectors worldwide dwarf this number, of course. But then the average art collector spends rather more on his passion than the average stamp collector.

The second point is that the art market is not one market but many. Each big-name artist is a market in his or her own right. Particular schools of artist and artistic movements are separate markets, and prices on works of art by individual members of a particular movement may move in and out of favour together. Unlike some other superhobby areas, art is hard to standardize.

Third, there are also permutations on what constitutes art. Not just painting, but also sculpture, prints, photographs, and even video. Each of these constitutes a separate market with its own dynamic and price trends. Within these separate markets there are also different price strata, each with its own patterns of behaviour.

Fourth, the art market is undeniably cyclical in character and appears to move in sympathy with trends in the stock market.

Like the stock market, art prices dropped sharply in the 1930s and did not recover until after the war. They also fell in 1974/75, when stock markets were reeling from the oil crisis and again, more mildly, in 1982, in the early 1990s and again in the last couple of years.

> ## Art market basics
>
> - Art market bigger and more 'democratic' than 20 years ago
> - Each major 'school' of art and major artist is a separate market
> - Not just painting, but sculpture, photography, watercolours, prints
> - All art markets appear to be cyclical

The market is frequently driven by the spending power and taste of American collectors. If Americans are too fearful to travel, telephone and internet bidding can substitute for being present in person. Leading auction houses also hold many sales in America. But the vibrancy or otherwise of the American economy and the international value of the dollar is a potent influence on the health of some parts of the art market.

Here's an example. The dynamic US economy in the 1990s drove up the price of paintings by American impressionists. This was hitherto a respectable, but fairly low profile area. As things stand now with a weaker dollar, it may be that the tastes of collectors with Euros in their pockets dictates prices and trends in the international art market for the time being.

If you are new to art, how do you begin? Do you simply collect paintings or other forms of pictorial art like prints and photographs? Do you collect sculpture as well as painting? What era do you collect?

To some degree this is regulated by the space you have available - hanging paintings normally takes less space than bulky items of sculpture - and on your budget. Impressionist paintings tend to be expensive. Victorian watercolours are relatively modestly priced. Contemporary art can be cheap, but it is harder to discern which contemporary artists have the staying power to make good long-term investments.

There is one iron rule. Only after an artist has died does one know for certain that the supply of his or her work is restricted and that some form of scarcity value can start to apply.

Paradoxically though, it is only through producing consistently good work in some volume through their lifetime that artists can come to the attention of dealers and achieve recognition. Picasso was a prolific artist, yet with a style so distinctive that he remains one of the most collected artists and one of the best performers in the auction market.

We come back to the question of what to collect. One astute private collector we know describes his approach as being to buy 'icons'. They are pictures and artists that are instantly recognizable. They attract buyers like a magnet and ultimately command a premium price. Think of Andy Warhol's screen prints of Marilyn Monroe, for example. In another example, a recent Sotheby's sale had a set of limited edition, abstract photographs of a graffiti-covered Berlin Wall, by Fritz von der Schulenberg. An example of a modern icon, perhaps?

Warhol's 'Marilyn' - the ultimate 'icon'

Most savvy art investors say to buy the best you can afford, buy few pieces rather than many, and buy what you like and hope that your taste coincides with the affluent art buyer of the future.

> ## What to buy
>
> - 'Icons'
> - Something appropriate to where you live
> - The best you can afford
> - An original style rather than a derivation

It is also important to recognize that some art is derivative. That is to say it is imitating another style. The result can be equally appealing in terms of its visual impact, but from an investment standpoint the only course of action is to seek the original rather than the derivation. This means you need to read up on the history of art, even contemporary art, before you begin your investment quest, or take along an expert to evaluate a piece you want to buy.

Collecting Areas

Collecting areas ultimately depend on the depth of your pocket, But you don't necessarily need to spend lavishly to get a good investment.

The record price paid for a painting was for the 1905 masterpiece by Pablo Picasso, 'Garcon a la pipe' sold in May 2004 at Sotheby's in New York for $104m, beating the previous highest at $82.5m paid for Van Gogh's 'Portrait of Dr Gachet' in 1990, by the Japanese businessman Ryoei Saito at the peak of the Japanese property boom. In an auction two days later, he paid $78m for Renoir's 'Au Moulin de la Galette'. Those prices represent the high water mark for impressionist paintings.

In forth place in the all-time record price league is Peter Paul Rubens's 'Massacre of the Innocents'. Lord Thomson of Fleet bought this in 2002 for $70m. There are four Picassos, three Van Goghs, a Cezanne, a Rubens and a Renoir in the top ten highest priced paintings of all time.

At the bottom end of the price scale are limited edition prints, the work of new artists, photographs, some watercolours, and other highly enjoyable artistic work that can sell for less than £1,000 a pop. A recent auction of modern and contemporary art at Bonhams, for example, included ceramics by Picasso with prices in the £2,000-3,000 range, Picasso etchings for £5,000, and Roy Lichtenstein limited edition lithographs priced in the £5,000-7,000 area.

In fact these lower priced alternatives are one of the hottest areas of the market because, as the art market has become more democratic and opened up to a wider section of the public at large, interest in affordable art has increased.

In other words, let your taste determine what you collect and don't be too put off by issues of price. Recent evidence suggests that lower priced art often performs better than the most expensive pieces.

This happens because the art market is one of fashion. Particular movements and artistic media come into and out of fashion and collectors are always hunting for undervalued items. It makes no sense therefore to chase the latest 'hot' fad. Better to find areas that seem to have gone to sleep, buy quietly, and wait for a revival of interest.

Collecting areas are really too numerous to single out more than a handful for individual mention, but here are a few areas where there is a ready market.

Old Masters

The saying in the art world is that new money buys new art. It follows perhaps that many old masters are owned by old money, reluctant to sell paintings that may have stayed in the same family for generations.

Old master paintings arguably come up less frequently at auction than contemporary works but that's not to say there is any shortage of material. The best fetch high prices. But they rarely reach the sort of stratospheric levels reserved for impressionists and more modern works. One trend noted recently in the old master market is that, rather like other areas of the art world, the top quality works remain in strong demand but lesser works often fail to sell at auction if priced too ambitiously.

However, this need not rule out the average investor from the old master market. For example, old master drawings can also be had for relatively low prices and are often things of great beauty. Collecting old master drawings has been a tradition among British art lovers since the 18th century.

Depending on the reputation of the artist in question, drawings can be bought for prices from £1,000 up. In 2003, a drawing by no less an artist as Rembrandt, for example, was auctioned off, with a catalogue estimate of £15,000-£20,000, while Sotheby's offered a Tiepolo caricature with an estimate of £8,000 - £12,000 that sold for £16,800 including the buyers premium. A recently discovered drawing by Rubens was offered at £55,000.

The scale of work on offer varies considerably. Michaelangelo destroyed many drawings made as preparation for his most famous work, and instances of his drawings in private hands are rare and fetch commensurate prices, usually in the hundreds of thousands.

In many old master sales, however, beautiful drawings from lesser names sell for a few thousand rather than tens of thousands. Prices overall have been firm after many years of dormancy as this area has come back into fashion. To take just one example, seventeenth century French drawings saw prices little changed or lower from 1993 through to 2001, but since then they have increased sharply and are currently at more than double the levels of two years ago.

Some affordable collecting areas

- Old master drawings
- Victorian watercolours
- Photography
- Signed limited edition prints (in low numbered editions)
- Contemporary art

There is sometimes an issue involved with identifying the work of old masters. Prominent artists employed pupils who in some instances did as much work on a picture as their master and who in later life faithfully imitated his style. Differentiating between the work of master and pupil can be a tricky business. But if attribution is in doubt, the price paid will reflect this uncertainty.

Impressionists

Works by French impressionist painters are mistakenly regarded as the 'bankers' of the art world, perhaps because impressionism is thought more accessible than either old master or contemporary art.

It is true in that many, if not most, of the highest priced paintings sold at auction fall into the impressionist category. This reflected a vogue for French impressionist art on the part of well-heeled Japanese buyers in the late 1980s. But prices currently stand at about 70% of their peak 1990 level, and as the number of collectors reached by the art market has broadened so tastes have become more cosmopolitan. Other art movements, such as the modernists like Modigliani, Klimt, Leger and others, have come into vogue.

Impressionism was not just confined to France. A parallel boom developed in American impressionist art during the 1990s. This came about as a result of keen interest from new American collectors, particularly those enriched during the internet bubble. Whether or not this price level is any more durable than that seen ten years previously for French impressionists remains to be seen. Prices of US impressionist paintings more than tripled between 1993 and 2002 but fell back in 2003.

Similar, though less extreme trends were seen in impressionist drawings and watercolours. While the market for the best American impressionist paintings has since largely dried up, drawings and watercolours in this category are considered by some experts to have potential for further appreciation. They are often much more modestly priced. British impressionist watercolours have followed a similar trend, doubling in price between 1998 and 2003.

Unless your pockets are deep, however, this is an area for investors to avoid. It has been thoroughly mined over many years and the chances of finding an undervalued gem are strictly limited.

Watercolours

Generally available for modest prices and becoming more fashionable, watercolours represent a good medium for the would-be investor. The market for English and Scottish watercolours and drawings is well documented. A lot of watercolours are in private hands, coming onto the market as a result of deceased estates and as new generations swap traditional art like this for contemporary pieces.

Britain is reckoned to be the spiritual home of watercolours and there are many themes available, not just landscapes. Artprice.com, the art price web site, has information on ten different movements within the British watercolour and drawings market and prices vary considerably.

The post impressionists have the best long term track record, having risen almost six fold since 1993 with Pre-Raphaelites doing next best, notably Dante Gabriel Rosetti and Edward Burne-Jones. Works by minor members of the brotherhood also sell well.

Eighteenth and nineteenth century landscape and portrait painters are perennially popular. Impressionists and modernist artists in this medium have more than doubled over ten years. Classic British watercolours from the 1760 to 1830 period have increased in price by almost as much.

Some pop art is also included in the watercolour category but prices of work like this appear more volatile. Prices here have doubled over ten years, but as little as five years ago were selling at less than their 1993 level. Price levels also dropped back sharply in 2003 from the peak levels reached in the previous year.

This market is one where knowledge can pay off. Watercolours still find their way into provincial antique shops and even charity shops and builders' skips. The knowledgeable buyer can pick up a bargain. On the other hand, condition is very important for watercolours, particularly avoiding any fading or foxing in the picture.

Photographs

Photographs have often been touted as affordable art, and photography shares some artistic movements in common with painting. In the last five years the acceptance of photography as an art form has increased dramatically. So much so that it is now common to see major galleries rightly including photography in their collections and exhibitions.

From a superhobby standpoint there are a few rules to bear in mind. For investment purposes it is best to buy those examples where the print was made close to the time that the original negative was taken. Some dealers will also, in some instances, sell negative and positive together.

One intriguing area is macrophotography. This is close-up photography, particularly of plants, printed to significantly larger than their real-life size. Would-be investors need to be aware that a specialised genre of this sort means that the avenues for liquidating their investment through auctions may be less frequent. They may prove a good investment, but they are a less liquid one than some other categories.

Contemporary photography is also an interesting area. Here, prints are issued in limited editions and the negative subsequently destroyed. Some dealers reckon that buying the work of new photographic talent early is the best policy. The reason is that prices at early showings of new work are generally underpriced, and photography is an artistic medium where differences in quality and talent are perhaps more readily apparent than in other forms of contemporary art.

Having said that, some observers regard the market as exceptionally fickle, and subject to the whims of relatively young collectors.

The big names in photographic art begin at Gustave Le Gray and continue to Man Ray, Ansel Adams, Henri Cartier-Bresson and many others. Photography from the 19th century naturally fetches premium prices. Interest in American photographers like Adams exploded during the 1990s, with many newly rich internet entrepreneurs opting to collect American art, of which this was simply one manifestation. Prices of Man Ray's work also seem to defy gravity, despite occasional examples coming to light of his work being forged.

While recent auction results for photography have been less than spectacular, there is little doubt that photography will come again. In the year to October 2003, according to Artprice.com, prices for photography sold at auction dropped by around 35% overall. This put prices back to levels previously seen in 1998.

The price trends are not uniform. Both vintage and contemporary photography, two areas that had led the earlier boom, dropped back. But prices for modernist photography, such as that of Man Ray, have remained buoyant. Photojournalism of the likes of Henri Cartier Bresson and others has also been a firm market, although there was some evidence of prices dipping towards the end of 2003.

Overall though, despite recent falls, photography stacks up well in terms of long term returns. Research suggests that price rises in the region of 8-10% a year have been seen on average over a 25-year period.

Limited edition prints

Prints, typically produced by a serigraphic (silk screen printing) or lithographic process, are an interesting way for those with modest budgets to gain exposure to the art market. Prints are produced in limited editions, after which the silk screen or printing plate is destroyed. Like photography, there has been an increasing recognition of printmaking as a legitimate and highly skilled art form in itself.

The obvious rule applies that the more limited the edition, the more collectable it is. A print from an edition of 25 is likely to be more collectable than one from an edition of 250, unless the artist in question is particularly well known.

The box over the page gives examples of prices of limited edition prints from some well known artists.

Current prices of limited edition prints		
Artist	Price (£)	Edition size
Beryl Cook	750	495
Sir Terry Frost RA	295	150
Stephen Bartlett	350	75
Donald Hamilton Fraser RA	325	175
Derek Pilotis	75	500
Vassilena Nikiforov	200	225
Ellie Barnes	125	395
Alexander Ivanov	100	385

Note: Based on gallery catalogues and author's own purchases

Other items that add value to prints are an individual signature by the artist on the mount, and any embellishment to the print done by the artist after printing. Some artists make limited edition prints available to be sold in non-gallery market places such as the art auctions held on some cruise ships.

Those buying at auctions like this can rest sure in the knowledge that the artist is making great efforts to promote their work and this can only have a positive effect on subsequent prices of the items.

Prices of prints are said generally to be slower to increase in value, but on the other hand much less volatile than the prices of original works of art. Recent evidence suggests, however, that limited edition prints have done well in a livelier market for affordable art.

Contemporary art

This is a huge area, and the best known names are well publicized: Tracy Emin, Damien Hirst, Andy Warhol, John Piper, John Bratby and many others. Prices range from the affordable to the expensive and the trick here is to spot a 'coming' artist before his or her work attains wide recognition. Those who spotted the potential of early work by John Piper and John Bratby, for example, were rewarded for their perception by five fold increases in price over less than a decade.

The box opposite shows a league table of the richest contemporary artists, based on their cumulative auction sales since 1970.

Top ten richest living artists	
Artists	**Value of auction sales since 1970 ($m)**
1. Jasper Johns	151
2. Gerhard Richter	124
3. Cy Twombly	88
4. Robert Rauschenberg	61
5. Fernando Botero	57
6. Frank Stella	57
7. Karel Appel	56
8. Antoni Tapies	43
9. David Hockney	38
10. Georg Baselitz	34

Source: Art Sales Index; Art Review

Would-be investors need to take care in areas like this, however, because more than most, art it subject to the whims of fashion, and the scale and durability of a living artist's body of work is hard to judge accurately.

Condition

Condition is less of an issue when buying some works of art than it is for other items like books and stamps. Many artistic media are less fragile than paper, for example. But there are still aspects of a work of art that need to be checked for and, if humanly possible, avoided.

Tears and rips in canvas, loose or badly fitting frames, poor or unsuitable quality frames, art that has slipped in its mounting, or discoloration due to acidity in the mounting are all important issues and should be addressed before buying. If the piece is being bought 'as is', a price adjustment should be made to reflect the cost of any remedial measures. A specialist craftsman should always undertake these repairs. If in doubt on these points, walk away.

Condition is a particular issue when buying watercolours. Here it is vital to avoid buying pieces that are faded as a result of having been hung in direct sunlight. You should also avoid any discoloration in the main body of the picture such as the 'foxing' of brown spots like those that commonly occur in old books.

Security measures

Like antiques, art is regularly stolen, especially since it is normally small enough to be easily portable. There are a number of precautions you must take to protect your investment.

First keep receipts of any items you acquire and any other documentation such as certificates of authenticity. Keep track of auction results for the artists whose work you have and if necessary have your collection periodically revalued by a professional valuer.

Keep photographs. All items should be photographed individually with colour film, preferably in natural light and against a plain background and a note made of any identifying marks. You should keep an inventory of all items with details of any identifying marks, and the dimensions of the work, much as you would for antiques.

Mark all pieces on the reverse side with your postcode and the first two letters of your house name or number.

Make sure that all items are insured for their full market value and that you can verify what this is to an insurance company's satisfaction and that you have their stipulated security measures in place. This will not necessarily add significantly to your home contents policy.

Is it right for you?

Let's look at the questions you need to answer to determine whether art might have a place in your wider portfolio of investments.

Are you investing for the medium to long term?

Most individuals buy art to keep it for the long term, but prices can move rapidly in the art market. As the examples earlier in this chapter show, it is perfectly possible, provided one buys well at the right time, to achieve significant price appreciation in as little as two years. What complicates this rosy scenario is dealing costs, particularly if you buy and sell at auction. The buyer's premium and seller's commission paid to auction houses needs to be taken into account when calculating potential profits. It is the scale of these charges that tends to make art investors hold on for the long term. In effect, there is a 40% spread to overcome before you start making money (see chapter fourteen for a concrete example of this).

Do you have adequate capital?

This is a vexed question. At the top end of the market, museum-quality art sells for millions. From an investment standpoint, however, it is not necessary to invest at this level to make useful gains. Rather the reverse in fact. Serious pieces can be had at auction for upwards of £1,500-2,000, and a reasonable portfolio put together for £25,000. If your capital is less than this amount, there are certain sections of the market where art is eminently affordable. These include limited edition prints, watercolours and photography. Lower priced art is by no means the poor relation. It has performed very well in recent years whereas middling pieces produce more pedestrian returns.

Are you prepared for insurance and maintenance costs?

An investment in art will yield no income, although the Japanese owner of one masterpiece did attempt, unsuccessfully, to persuade people to pay to see it. Owning art entails extra costs for insurance, framing and perhaps some gentle restoration much as we described in the previous chapter. Quantify these costs before you commit yourself.

Is portfolio diversification an objective?

Art reflects the whims and affluence of different sections of the collector base. International art market trends tend to reflect the fact that most collectors buy the art produced in their own country. Upsurges in wealth in one country, for whatever reason, may produce a boom in that country's painters and artists.

The demise of the internet bubble, the weakness in the dollar, and the reining-in of executive compensation in the US, seems to suggest that the favourites of US collectors may wane in influence for a time.

Right for you?

- Some price volatility
- High costs if you deal at auction
- Low minimum investment
- Extra costs - insurance, framing, restoration
- Low correlation with stockmarket
- No tax benefits

From the standpoint of diversification, however, you can argue that - timing differences apart - the art market is not that different from the stock market. Artists and artistic movements come into and move out of favour like stocks and sectors.

From this you might assume that art might not be sufficiently different to the stock market to offer meaningful diversification. But American academics who have measured price trends in the art market suggest that most art categories have a very low, and in some cases negative, correlation with the stock market. This would make them an ideal superhobby investment medium.

Are there tax considerations?

The short answer is 'no', although there have been instances where restricting tax concessions on securities-based investment has fostered a boom in art ownership in particular countries that have imposed them.

Returns

The art market is one where it is easy to work out the returns that have been made by investors in particular categories. This is true despite the diverse nature of the market. The reason is that auction houses and statistical services have kept comprehensive records of prices achieved on the same or similar items successively coming up for sale.

The best-known work in this area has been by two American academics. Michael Moses and Jianping Mei work at NYU's Stern Business School. They have tracked art prices at Sotheby's auctions using data as far back as 1925 and other data back to 1875. Some 5300 works had been sold more than once, enabling the price comparisons to be made. Their work suggests that works in the bottom quartile by price showed the highest return, around 11.5% a year. Works in the top quartile rose by only 6.6% a year.

In the post war era, Mei and Moses calculate that annual returns for the art market in total for the period 1952-2002 were in the region of 13%, marginally better than the stock market over the same period. On their calculations, art has outperformed the stock market, as measured by the S&P500 index, by 18% over three years and by 8% over five years to 2002. For the most part, the 2002 data was the latest available as at the time of writing.

The returns seen for different price categories over shorter time periods, however, tend to be more closely packed together and in the 1999-2002 period, mid-priced art did better than either top-priced pieces or the low end of the market.

In terms of collecting themes, impressionists have still to recover to the best prices seen in 1990. Old master and 19th century painting generally has risen consistently, with some cyclical blips.

Prints show an interesting divergence from the main trend. According to Artprice.com, in the 1996-2002 period prints priced at less than €1,000 showed an average annual return of 16%, easily beating the 12% or so seen by paintings in the €100,000 and over price bracket.

Other academic researchers have also conducted projects to examine longer term price trends. The table opposite shows some of those based on repeat sales and the conclusions they came to.

Table 3.1 - Art - Returns calculated by academic studies of repeat sales

Author	Date	Genre	Average real return (%pa)	Period covered by data
Anderson	1974	Paintings in general	3.0	1780-1970
Baumol	1986	Paintings in general	0.6	1652-1961
Frey/ Pommerehne	1989	Paintings in general	1.4	1635-1949
Frey/ Pommerehne	1989	Paintings in general	1.7	1950-1987
Pesando	1993	Modern prints	1.5	1977-1991
Goetzmann	1993	Paintings in general	2.0	1716-1986
Chanel et al	1996	Paintings in general	5.0	1855-1969
Goetzmann	1996	Paintings in general	5.0	1907-1977
Pesando/Shum	1996	Picasso prints	1.4	1977-1993
Mei/Moses	2001	Various	4.9	1875-2000

Note: In some instances real returns were estimated from nominal ones.

This shows consistent positive real returns from art, the scale of the returns depending on the period taken and the category in question. In general data from the more recent era appears to show higher real returns.

A recent article in the Wall Street Journal examined auction records for a number of artists over periods of five and fifteen years and tabulated a number of them giving recommendations based on the views of experts, as to what artists might be regarded as 'buys', 'sells' or 'holds' now. The table below shows some data extracted from this article. The artists in question are generally the pricier ones, and these should not necessarily be construed as my 'buy' recommendations, but they do give an illustration of the types of returns that can be achieved over the medium and long term, and of the variations in returns.

Table 3.2 - Past returns from artists currently viewed as 'buys'

Artist	Average auction price in 2003 ($000s)	Percentage price change over	
		5 years	15 years
Albert Bierstadt	773	126	1871
Gustave Caillebot	2,700	469	461
Paul Cezanne	5,500	59	20
Dan Flavin	135	19	217
Paul Gauguin	2,100	259	110
Keith Haring	58	42	300
Damien Hirst	267	131	n/a
Jeff Koons	519	287	1786
Roy Lichtenstein	1,100	185	181
Rene Magritte	1,100	15	261
Roberto Matta	226	251	493
Claude Monet	4,500	55	-17
Sir Alfred Munnings	247	141	427
Mark Rothko	5,400	1889	451
Ed Ruscha	448	865	356
John Singer Sargent	51	-85	-55
Cindy Sherman	67	121	3292
Wayne Thiebaud	430	129	136

Source: WSJE 29rd January 2004

Buying and selling

Art is synonymous with buying at auction. One reason is that auction houses make a point of having frequent large sales of particular genres of art. They produce lavish catalogues containing price estimates.

Not all items at auction are outrageously expensive. Some auction houses, like Bonhams, for example, make a point of having a number of modestly priced lots, and the same is true of provincial auction houses where, away from the spotlight, there may be bargains to be had. A recent Sotheby's sale of contemporary art contained many pieces with estimated prices of under £2,000 and several at under £1,000.

Elsewhere many cruise lines operate art auctions and this can be a useful source of material, particularly since serious bidders - especially for more offbeat contemporary work - tend to be few and far between. While most material is fairly mundane, there are opportunities to acquire investment-grade art for prices in the low thousands, and also attractive originals from up and coming artists who supply material to cruise lines at attractive prices because of the exposure their work receives. For investment-grade art, some cruise lines operate a buyback policy that effectively limits the buyer's downside risk.

Buying and selling - key points

- Not all auctions are all 'big ticket' items
- Factor in buyers' premium, VAT and shipping before you bid
- Buying through dealers often cheaper for some items
- Buy against the trend, in recession, or from forced sellers
- Provincial dealers fairs and auctions cheaper than London ones

---

Remember, however, when buying at auction you need to factor in the buyers premium (usually 10-20% of the hammer price) and storage costs, shipping costs and the like. This can add up. You also need to guard against overbidding for a particular piece. Research the piece you want to buy beforehand and work out what it is worth to you. Make sure you view the lot before the sale. When it comes to the auction, dealers will not pay over the odds because they need to make a margin, but avoid getting into a bidding war with another private individual. Buying at auction is not an ego trip.

Don't be depressed by this seemingly costly and uncertain buying process. There are several ways to get the market to work with you.

One is to buy against the trend. Avoid fashionable areas but look in detail at those that have fallen out of favour and where prices have been left behind.

Buying during a recessionary period - if you have the capital to do so - is another way of improving the returns you make.

Sales following an auction where a number of lots failed to meet the reserve may be a way of acquiring interesting pieces without going into the competitive arena of the auction. Sales from deceased estates and forced sellers are another way that art can be acquired at good prices.

A final point to bear in mind is that, like antiques, if you know your stuff you can sometimes get real value for money by buying as far down the chain of buyers and sellers as possible.

Each time a piece changes hands, a dealer will be making a margin on it. As noted in chapter two, city centre dealers and auction houses have expensive overheads. You may be able to find bargains by visiting country fairs, provincial galleries, and small auction rooms. If you know what you are looking for and are disciplined enough not to pay too much, you might be surprised at what you can find.

Where to go for more information

There is plenty of information about the art market on the web, and the following is a brief review of some of the key sites and publications.

Dealers/Auction houses

Agnews (www.agnewsgallery.co.uk) is one of the leading international art galleries in the world. A selection of current stock can be viewed online with images and information. Prices are only given on application. Agnews' specialist areas are listed on the site and regular shows are held at its Bond Street premises.

Bonhams (www.bonhams.com) has a sales calendar and the results of past sales. Catalogues can be ordered online.

Christie's (www.christies.com) has an auction calendar and past sales results. For those interested in learning more about art, Christie's education department offers courses varying from short evening courses to master's programmes.

Christie's magazine is published seven times a year and at the time of writing is available on subscription for £35 per year. The numerous articles include special previews of items for sale in Christie's salesrooms throughout the world.

Sotheby's (www.sothebys.com) has details of forthcoming auctions together with auction results. Sotheby's Institute of Art offers short daytime and evening courses for the public in a wide variety of subjects covering fine and decorative arts and contemporary art.

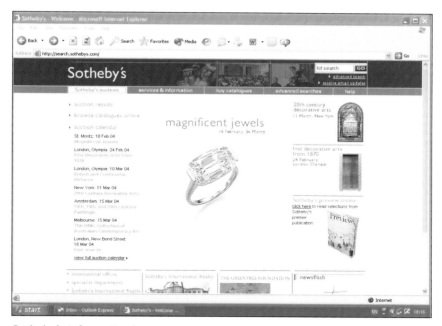

Sotheby's informative homepage

Sotheby's magazine 'Preview' is published seven times a year and is available on subscription at a cost of £48 per year at the time of writing. It has lavish artwork, interviews, commentary, in-depth reporting and a worldwide auction calendar. A free version is available online.

The Contemporary Art Society (www.contempart.org.uk) hosts the annual selling exhibition 'Artfutures', with selections made from the best works from student shows and artists themselves.

Further Information

Artprice (www.artprice.com) collects, processes and analyses data from art auctions covering 2,900 auction houses worldwide. Their reference databanks on the art market list 306,000 artists from the fourth century to the present day.

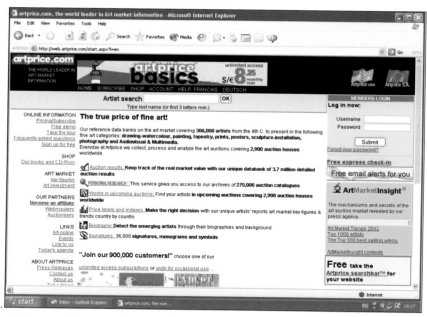

Artprice - data on auction results for art

The extensive free content on the site covers comment and analysis on the art market from ArtMarket Insight, the press agency arm of Artprice, information on artists, auction records, and a searchable database that can be accessed by title, sale or artwork date, and hammer price.

Paying subscribers to Artprice have access to much more detailed information. This includes artist's price levels and indices, biographies and future sales. An 'occasional user' subscription is also available.

For further detailed investment information, the firm's econometrics department offers subscribers quantitative information and analysis plus customised tools.

Art Sales Index (www.art-sales-index.com) was founded in 1968 and has more than 2.6m auction entries by 250,000 artists on its database. This is available on subscription only. The site does however offer much free content including numerous graphs and charts tracking prices worldwide. The online bookshop has numerous reference books to help research artists and prices.

The Art Sales Index enquiry service is available for a fee if you do not have access to the database. One use of this service relates to paintings coming up for auction. If you want to bid, and are unsure how high to go, Artprice will scan their database and provide you with some relevant parameters to help you come to a decision.

The Art Loss Register (www.artloss.com) is a permanent computerised database of stolen and missing works of art, antiques and valuables, operating on an international basis.

Art Review (www.art-review.com) is a leading art magazine for 20th and 21st century art and style. It offers interviews and analysis, and critics' views.

The Art Newspaper (www.theartnewspaper.com) has news, comments on the art market, book reviews, and exhibition listings. The print version can be subscribed to online.

British Arts (www.britisharts.co.uk) is a useful web resource for all art related matters. The site includes an A-Z list of well-known British artists, some with biographies, and a list of galleries where their work can be found.

Galleries (www.artefact.co.uk) is a UK monthly arts listings magazine and is available from galleries, hotels, and the like, and also by online subscription. The magazine includes information on current exhibitions and stock on display at 500 commercial and public art galleries.

Kara Art (www.karaart.com) has a comprehensive list of art fairs and festivals worldwide, plus some information on contemporary art. A free email newsletter is available.

Devised and run by two American academics, the Mei/Moses Art Index site (www.miemosesfineartindex.org) offers indices, graphs, numerical values, and research and press reports. Users must register.

24-Hour Museum (www.24hourmuseum.org.uk) is an independent charity funded by the Department of Culture, Media and Sport. It aims to promote UK museums, galleries and heritage attractions, 2,800 of which are included in the site's database. Also featured are regular news and exhibition stories and numerous links.

Table 3.3 – Art – key web addresses and contact details

Company	Web address	Email	Phone	Type
Agnews	www.agnewsgallery.co.uk	agnews@agnewsgallery.co.uk	020 7290 9250	Dealer
Art Fairs Worldwide	www.karaart.com	n/a	n/a	Other
Art Sales Index	www.art-sales-index.com	info@art-sales-index.com	01784 451145	Data
Artprice	www.artprice.com	info@artprice.com	n/a	Data
Bonhams	www.bonhams.com	info@bonhams.com	020 7393 3900	Dealer
Christie's	www.christies.com	info@christies.com	020 7839 9060	Dealer
Contemporary Art Society	www.contempart.org.uk	gill@contempart.org.uk	020 7612 0730	information
European Fine Art Fair	www.tefaf.com	info@tefaf.com	31 411 64 50 90	Information
Londonart	www.londonart.co.uk	info@londonart.co.uk	020 7738 3867	Dealer
Mei & Moses	www.meimosesfineartinex.org	n/a	n/a	Data
NuMasters	www.NuMasters.com	enquiries@NuMasters.com	020 7592 0880	Dealer
Phillips	www.phillips-dpl.com	inquiry.desk@phillips-dpl.com	020 7318 4010	Dealer
Photographers Gallery(The)	www.photonet.org.uk	Numerous on site	020 7831 1772	Dealer
Poster Classics	www.posterclassics.com	bruce@posterclasics.com	011 33 450 772052	Dealer
Sotheby's	www.sothebys.com	On site	020 7293 5000	Dealer
The Art Newspaper	www.theartnewspaper.com	feedback@theartnewspaper.com	n/a	Publisher

The following is a short list of some of the major public art galleries throughout the UK. Apart from permanent and temporary exhibitions many offer short courses and workshops.

Ashmolean Museum	www.ashmol.ox.ac.uk
Baltic Gateshead	www.balticmill.com
Birmingham Museums and Art Galleries	www.bmag.org.uk
British Museum	www.thebritishmuseum.ac.uk
Courtauld Gallery	www.courtauld.ac.uk
Dulwich Picture Gallery	www.dulwichpicturegallery.org.uk
Institute of Contemporary Art	www.ica.org.uk
Hunterian Gallery	www.hunterian.gla.ac.uk
Liverpool Museums	www.liverpoolmuseums.org.uk
National Gallery	www.nationalgallery.org.uk
National Portrait Gallery	www.npg.org.uk
National Galleries of Scotland	www.natgalscot.ac.uk
National Museums and Galleries of Wales	www.nmgw.ac.uk
Queens Gallery	www.royal.gov.uk
The Royal Academy	www.royalacademy.org.uk
Tate Britain	www.tate.org.uk/britain
Tate St Ives	www.tate.org.uk/stives
Tate Liverpool	www.tate.org.uk/liverpool
Tate Modern	www.tate.org.uk/modern
Walker Art Gallery	www.thewalker.org.uk
The Wallace Collection	www.the-wallace-collection.org.uk
Whitechapel Gallery	www.whitechapel.org
Whitworth Gallery	www.whitworth.man.ac.uk

GKR Bonds

Unit 4, Park Farm, Inworth, Colchester CO5 9SH, UK
Established 1979

GKR Bonds Ltd was established in 1979 and trades internationally carrying stock from most countries. Geoff Metzger, the Company's co-founder, has been a stockbroker for over 35 years and, prior to their redemption, specialised in Russian, Chinese & other defunct bonds.

The day-to-day management is in the hands of Hazel Fisher, who is always ready to give advice to new collectors. We are always interested in purchasing unusual items whether it be in quantities or single pieces.

For further information and a free catalogue contact us on 01376 571711 or log on to our website at: www.gkrbonds.com

Banknotes and Scripophily

This chapter groups together two collectable areas that are close cousins.

While you might think that banknotes are considered alongside coins (see chapter seven), they are a distinct superhobby area in their own right. Scripophily is the study and collecting of old bond and share certificates.

The key relationship between them is that they both employ security printing. Both are made of paper and elaborately printed to stop forgery. Both banknotes and old bond and share certificates also sport signatures that can, in some cases, add significantly to their value.

British banks began issuing notes in the 1600s. Few of the early notes survive. Most collections begin later, typically in the late 19th century. Scripophily dates back to the establishment of joint stock companies in the 17th century. Certificates from that era are rare. Most collections only include certificates from the 19th century onwards.

They have something else in common too. As with most collectables, condition is very important indeed when determining value. And as paper items, they have a fragility that can be something of a problem. Superhobbyists in both areas need to guard against degradation of their collections; many of the same means of storing collections are used in both areas.

Rather than write separate short sub-chapters on each item, what follows uses the same broad format of other chapters, but considers both banknotes and old scrip in turn in each section.

Banknote and Scripophily basics

Banknotes

History

The Chinese developed paper money in the 8th century as a temporary solution to a copper shortage, which limited the ability to mint coins.

Marco Polo brought the idea of paper money from China to a sceptical Europe in the late 13th century. The scepticism meant that paper money did not start out in Europe until the late 15th century. Then, as in China earlier, it was only used as an emergency measure. Banknotes were only issued on a regular basis from the 1660s onwards. Sweden was the first to try out the idea. The Bank of England and Bank of Scotland followed it in the late 17th century. Several other countries quickly followed suit.

Fundamental to the appreciation of banknotes for collectors and superhobby investors is knowledge of the different printing processes used.

The earliest banknotes were printed from woodcuts. Most notes now are produced using intaglio engraving. This is a process where the design is etched on a metal plate and printing done at high pressure. A new banknote produced by this process has a slightly raised surface on the face of the note. This detail is discernable to the touch, and matching it is a slightly indented surface on the back of the note. As the note is used, wear erodes this detail.

Banknotes inevitably attract forgers. This has led to a range of security devices being adopted by banknote printers. Countermeasures include an intricate amount of detail in the engraving, use of high quality paper, watermarking, numbering, micro lettering on the note that is visible only under a magnifying glass, anti-scanning and photocopying designs, security strips and holograms.

Condition

Condition is important. Poor condition detracts considerably from the value of an item. There are several issues to consider.

Banknotes need careful handling. Notes are normally kept in protective holders made from a neutral plastic material. This will preserve the note and avoid introducing any extraneous chemical change.

Some early banknotes had large dimensions. Once in circulation they were inevitably subject to folding and creasing. More recent issues will fit flat in a wallet and therefore many may be available with only slight evidence of folding.

Counting of new notes used to be done by hand. So even an uncirculated note would have some slight folding. Notes are now counted mechanically or electronically prior to circulation. This leaves little or no evidence of handling. Older items, even if they were uncirculated, may have some evidence of handling that is unavoidable and to be expected. The superhobby investor has to be satisfied in having a note in the best possible condition for a note of its age and type.

Terms used for the condition of banknotes are fairly standard across countries and are summarised in the table:

Banknote condition - standard terms		
Term	**Abb.**	**What it means**
Uncirculated	UNC	Perfectly preserved, firm paper, no folds or creases, original sheen
About Unc.	AU	Only minor handling, light folds at centre or corner, no creases.
Extra Fine	EF	Light handling, max of three light folds or one strong crease
Very fine	VF	Relatively clean but with more evidence of handling and wear
Fine	F	Many folds and creases, minor tears, colour clear but not bright
Very good	VG	Well used but intact, folds, creases, stains, pinholes and tears
Good	G	Heavily used, as above plus dirt, discoloration, holes, graffiti
Fair	F	Limp, dirty and well-used, with tears and bits missing
Poor	P	Severe wear, staining, graffiti, holes, pieces missing.

In addition bank note graders use the term 'about' to distinguish items that fall between two categories. So 'about very good' would be somewhere between good and very good, but nearer the latter. Notes graded 'poor' are really only acceptable as collectors' items if they are the only known example of a particular issue.

Price differences between grades are tending to increase as the number of collectors grows. Most collectors, and especially those collecting with an eye to superhobby investing, collect only those notes in 'very fine' condition or better. Even here, the difference in price between a note classed as 'very fine' and one classed as 'uncirculated' could be a ratio of 4:1. A VF example could exceed a VG one in a ratio of 2:1 or even 3:1.

As with stamps, scrip and other similar items, banknotes showing any evidence of cleaning or tampering should be avoided.

Currency terminology

Banknote collectors often have an interest in the names of currencies and how they originated.

Many names represent weight. Dirham probably equals dram, or gram. Peseta means 'little weight', Lira is a derivation of the French livre (pound), and from which comes the stylised letter 'L' that represents the Pound Sterling. The Livre was yet another high profile casualty of the French Revolution, replaced by the more proletarian Franc.

Using weights to signify currency names dates from those long-gone days when money was backed by a specific weight of precious metal. Their names lived on even when fiat currencies - backed by nothing more than faith in the note issuer - took over.

Other conventions for naming currencies were used too. In Portugal, the word Escudo signifies the coat of arms of a city, from a similar root to the English heraldic term escutcheon. The best guess is that the former Portuguese currency dated from the time when currencies were issued by cities rather than nation states.

Some other names are even more obscure. Drachma means 'handful', Forint and Zloty and Guilder mean 'golden' or 'gilded', Rouble means 'cut-off', Rupee means 'beauty' or 'shape' and Kuna means 'marten', which dates from when Croatians used pine marten skins as money. The 'cut-off' signified by Rouble dates from when money was comprised of pieces cut off from a bar of silver. Hence also 'pieces of eight'.

The Romans bequeathed currency names on the countries that fell under their imperial influence. In pre-decimalisation Britain, the letters l.s.d denoted pounds, shillings and pennies. Pennies took the letter 'd' from denarii, small units of currency in Roman times, from which also derives Dinar, currencies still used in many Middle Eastern countries to this day.

South American currencies often have more exotic derivations. Simon Bolivar may be one of the few political leaders to have seen his name live on in his country's currency. In Brazil, the Cruzeiro was the unit of currency for many years, until hyperinflation forced the change to the Cruzado and then the Real. The Cruzeiro is said, rather romantically, to have echoed the stars of the Cruzeiro do Sul, or Southern Cross, that great Southern hemisphere constellation.

In Ecuador, the Sucre might be thought to reflect the importance of sugar in the economy. In fact, as in Bolivia, it carries the name of a popular 19th century leader, Antonio Jose de Sucre.

Perhaps the prize for the most unusual derivation goes to the Cedi, the currency of Ghana. This appears to derive from the local word for cowrie. Cowrie shells were used in parts of Africa as currency and, to prove the point, cowrie shells feature on Ghana's coins even now.

And the ubiquitous Dollar? The explanation is mundane. It comes from the word 'taler' (sometimes written as 'thaler'), itself a contraction of Joachimsthaler. The meaning is that a thaler was a piece of specie from the silver mine of the same name located in Joachim's valley, now Jachymov, in the present day Czech Republic. How the name got from central Europe to the United States is unclear.

Collecting themes

Once the would-be banknote investor has assimilated all of this, it's time to select a theme for collecting.

As with stamps and coins, the best theme may be to stick to what you know. Most people collect banknotes from their own country. So for UK would-be investors, one of the best may simply be to collect British banknotes of a certain age or older, including those issued by private banks.

Another interesting theme is errors, the small quantity of banknotes printed with some form of mistake in the printing process, such as non-matching serial numbers, missing signatures, mistakes in cutting, or other flaws. Other themes include collecting older, large size banknotes.

Often historical events may dictate collecting themes. In the US, for example, as well as areas such as the above, collectors sometimes look for Confederate states currency, banknotes from the colonial era, or those from the early 1800s with denominations of less than a dollar.

Scripophily

History

As a superhobby investment category, scripophily dates back to the early 1970s when doctoral research in Germany led to the cataloguing of bonds issued in pre-revolutionary China and Russia. Stanley Gibbons entered the market and began publishing price lists, later conducting auctions of material. Prices began to rise, and an unusual situation developed. Some of the bonds in question still had stock market listings, creating a 'double market'.

At the time there was considerable general interest in collectables. The advent of a whole new area for collectors meant that prices went through the roof. At one point a Chinese 5% 1908 Gold Loan sold for ten times its face value. The market crashed in late 1979 and the speculative bubble was largely purged.

Since that time, however, the numbers of collectors involved has risen. As in some other areas covered in other chapters, this collector base provides a source of liquidity for anyone wishing to pursue it from a superhobby investment standpoint. Remember, though, that the number of collectors is still much less than in more mainstream collecting areas like art, antiques or stamps.

I've had a passing interest in scripophily for nearly 30 years. My first purchase was a Chinese 5% Gold Loan 1913 which I bought for £5 in 1975. Since that time I've acquired several other certificates, including Penn Central, the US railroad that went spectacularly bust in the mid 1970s, and certificates for old French brewery companies, cinema chains, an old Chilean tobacco company, and most recently, an Enron share certificate.

In a way this shows something of the diversity of scripophily. You can find share and bond certificates for almost any country and industry. There's a bewildering choice. So when you start assembling a collection, you need to have some ground rules.

Collecting themes

There are very many different themes to choose from.

You can, for example, specialize in South American mining companies, US railroads, pre-revolutionary communist or former communist government bonds, or companies that have been the subject of scandals or spectacular bankruptcies. Dealers in the US are currently seeing a lot of interest in the share certificates of busted dot.com companies.

Those adopting the superhobby investment approach we are advocating in this book need first to find out the relative scarcity of the individual items in a particular collecting area. You must bear this in mind if you view having a complete collection as an end in itself.

Company, state and city records generally mean that there is good information about the precise number of certificates issued and therefore the ease of collecting the items can be easily determined.

There are, for example, only seven extant certificates of the scarcest Chinese bond among those issued between 1898 and 1937. If you wanted to collect bonds issued by Russian cities, the scarcest of all bonds has only 11 certificates issued. The Confederate States, another popular theme, issued more bonds, but the scarcest one has only about 50 certificates in issue. These numbers place an upper limit on the number of complete collections there can be in these genres.

Scripophily - some collecting themes

- South American Mines
- US Railroads
- Confederate states bonds
- Pre-1917 Russian city or Imperial Government bonds
- Pre-1948 Chinese city or state issued bonds
- Subjects of famous scandals
- Share certificates with famous signatures
- Defunct dot.coms

You may not want to pursue scarcity for its own sake. What you want is something that is valuable, but for which there will be a ready future market that extends beyond a handful of obsessive collectors. Some study is required to get a balance between scarcity on the one hand, and cost and availability on the other.

It used to be the case that the older the certificate the better. Certificates from the late 18th and 19th century were the mainstay of many collectors. This was especially true if they bore the signature of a prominent capitalist of the time. Predecessor companies of US Steel bearing the signature of Andrew Carnegie, or those of Standard Oil bearing a Rockefeller monicker have always been highly prized. Now, however, there is much more interest in modern (20th century) scrip and collecting from the inter-war era is no longer disdained.

Another scripophily quirk relates the way bond interest and stock dividends were paid. Many old certificates were issued in bearer form. That's to say they weren't registered to any one individual, but simply regarded as the property of the person who held them. Dividend and bond interest payments were claimed by clipping off a series of coupons attached to the certificate and posted to or presented at the company's bankers. This is important from a collectors' standpoint, but not quite in the way you might expect.

Is a certificate more valuable if it has an intact set of coupons? Not necessarily. Arguably the subtler and more valuable item is the certificate of a company which was nationalized or went bust and where the certificate has the coupons clipped until exactly the moment in time when it ceased to exist. Some term it as being like owning a frozen piece of business history.

The opening up of Eastern Europe in the last decade has led to the supply of old certificates increasing from these sources. These are often certificates that individuals might have held through the communist era, perhaps because they were family investments before the war. They are now emerging onto the market. This area is an interesting collecting theme in itself, although you probably need to take advice and some care when dealing with sellers.

You can, of course, regard old scrip as simply like a branch of art or antiques. Some call it 'the art of finance'. Unlike art and antiques, however, because certificates were often printed with elaborate designs - rather like bank notes - they are hard to forge and any tampering looks obvious.

Condition

As is the case with banknotes, one of the things that mark out a good scripophily investment from a bad one is the condition it's in. Some wear and tear is perhaps inevitable, but other things being equal, the better the condition the higher the price.

The conventional categories of condition for old scrip are as follows:

Scrip condition - standard terms		
Term	**Abbr.**	**What it means**
Extremely fine	EF	Clean, some folds, almost unused
Very Fine	VF	Some folds and creases, slight wear
Fine	F	Circulated and worn, but not damaged
Poor	P	Well used, with some damage

Price differences are considerable. 'Poor' certificates sell at around 15% of the price of those in extremely fine condition while 'very fine' might sell at 85-90%. Flaws in condition tend to be the result of unavoidable factors such as the poor quality of paper used, the frequency with which the scrip was traded and the certificate therefore moved from owner to owner, and its age.

Correct storage is important. A certificate purchased in EF condition could deteriorate if stored incorrectly. Framing, provided acid-free mounts are used, is one alternative. Remember, though, that the cost of the frame needs to be factored into the cost of the certificate. It is important either to do the framing oneself or to stress to the framer that the certificate should not be cut or pasted in any way. The framed certificate should be hung out of direct sunlight.

Otherwise the main rules are always to keep certificates (and banknotes for that matter) flat, to keep them dry, to avoid temperature extremes and to enclose them in an album or other container. Unframed certificates should be stored in clear sleeves made from an acid-free and PVC-free plastic material like Mylar. Over time PVC deteriorates and releases acids and gases that can damage paper items.

Repairs and cleaning of certificates are a tricky business and best left to a specialist. Only attempt it yourself on relatively inexpensive items.

Returns

Returns on banknotes vary considerably from category to category and hard data is difficult to come by. Specialists confirm, however, that returns in some of the better areas have been very respectable indeed.

English private banks - the forerunners and original constituents of today's clearing banks - used to issue their own notes and prices of the better collectors' items have risen perhaps 40-fold in 20 years, a compound annual return in the region of 20%.

The best older Bank of England material shows a return over the same period in the region of 12%.

Other good performers until recently (prices have retreated somewhat in the past couple of years) have been old Hong Kong and other Far East banknotes, where prices even now have appreciated to show a compound return over 20 years in the region of 17.5%.

Returns like this are examples of the best performing items in exceptional condition. Other items may not have performed as well as this and some items have even gone down in value over this period. There is no guarantee that returns like this can be repeated.

Returns from old scrip are hard to gauge because of the relative thinness of the market and because of the distortions introduced by the boom and bust in prices in the late 1970s and early 1980s.

Rarer, more expensive pieces tend to be the most reliable investments. Sought-after 18th century certificates have shown a steady increase, probably doubling in price over the last 10 years, compound growth in the region of 7% a year. Classic 19th and early 20th century Chinese and Russian bonds have been more volatile although they are a perennially popular collecting area and therefore a relatively liquid market.

Is it right for you?

In general terms, as with other collectable areas, the crucial variable in both banknotes and old scrip is the general well-being and affluence of the collector base. Other things being equal, prices should tend to rise as the general level of prosperity increases.

However, the two markets are not alike. Nor are they that similar to other collectable areas like coins and stamps. One big difference is that they are smaller, more specialised markets. There are an estimated 10,000 active banknote collectors worldwide and much fewer serious collectors of old scrip.

Scripophily is really a market for aficionados. Banknotes form part of the wider field of numismatics, and some collectors of coins will collect banknotes too. Banknotes are an active collectors market, and prices reflect that.

With all this in mind, let's look at the questions you need to answer to determine whether either of these areas merits a place in your wider portfolio of investments.

Are you investing for the medium to long term?

A long-term perspective is essential. The certainty of good returns increases the longer you hold investments like this. And it is essential to make sure that you don't start out investing when prices are artificially high. As with stamps, for example, there was a bubble in scrip prices in the late 1970s. This was less true of banknotes, and this latter market has had an underlying firm tone over many years.

Do you have adequate capital?

Prices of banknotes and old scrip are generally affordable. The scarcer the item the more expensive it will be, particularly if in pristine condition. But, in the case of banknotes, a glance at recent dealers' catalogues shows few items priced at more than £500 and many priced at well under £100. Scarcer items such as Victorian Bank of England notes can, however, cost well into the thousands in top quality condition.

Banknotes and scrip - right for you?

- Long term perspective essential
- Generally affordable in both areas
- Storage and insurance costs undemanding
- Seemingly unrelated to stockmarket movements
- Returns are variable, but probably better for banknotes

In the scripophily field much the same is true. One leading US dealer's web page shows the scarcest and most expensive item - a Ford Motor Company of Canada certificate issued on the day of the Wall Street Crash - priced at $2,000. Many other items are available for much less. Signatures of famous individuals, whether industrialists or other personalities add significantly to the value of the item. But prices compare favourably with other art genres, perhaps the most apt comparison.

Are you happy to pay storage and insurance costs?

You can, if you wish, hold the banknotes and scrip you invest in physically on your own property. As with many other alternative investments, you may need good security measures and to make sure that your collection is properly insured. However, rather like stamps, collectable banknotes and old bonds do not have a readily apparent value to the untutored eye.

It may be possible, to store a collection off-site at a bank or safe deposit facility, but it is very important to make sure that the conditions under which the items will be stored are conducive to preserving them in their original state. A temperature and humidity controlled vault is a minimum requirement.

Is portfolio diversification an objective?

Like stamps and coins, prices of banknotes should rise in line with economic growth and inflation. In the case of old scrip, the same is probably true, although there are other factors at work that could affect the value of a certificate or a collection. One example is the actions of governments wishing to return to the international capital markets. This can affect the value of previously defaulted bonds. It makes redemption by non-collectors more likely, and the remaining bonds become scarcer and more collectable.

As we noted in the case of stamps, banknotes and old scrip may have the edge over coins in the sense that they are less durable, and hence there are fewer examples of top quality 'extra fine' items.

Other than from the standpoint of old bonds and possible redemption, there is no reason to expect that prices of banknotes or scripophily items will be particularly affected by movements in world stockmarkets. As such, they represent solid diversification.

Do you have an interest in history and business?

Collecting banknotes and old scrip is essentially about history, although enthusiasts would add that it takes in economics, geography, politics, and art. Many of the more collectable certificates have attractive vignettes usually depicting a classical scene or something relevant to the issuer.

A detail from an attractive 'vignette'

Banknotes on the other hand, rather like stamps, are mementos of the economic history of a particular country, telling one of the rise and fall of dictators, monarchs and politicians.

How to buy and sell

The procedure for buying banknotes for investment purposes is much the same as for coins and stamps (see chapters seven and eleven). While some lower value items can be purchased over the web or by normal mail order methods, for higher value items you need to visit the dealer to satisfy yourself that the item and its condition is as described.

Some mail order banknote dealers offer a money back guarantee. If a dealer is a member of a reputable trade association, there is no harm in buying on this basis. Many collectors also buy and sell items at shows, which gather a lot of dealers together in the same place.

Auctions remain a popular way of buying, either face to face or by mail. Once again, being able to inspect the items beforehand is a sensible precaution particularly if they are likely to be of high value.

A similar route can be pursued with respect to old scrip. There are dealers (although arguably fewer than is the case for banknotes, where coin dealers often double up), collectors' fairs at which dealers congregate, and periodic auctions from the likes of Bonhams and others.

With smaller collectables markets of this type, however, you need to ask yourself, when you come to sell your collection, whether the auction route is the best or whether it is a safer route to simply place the collection in the hands of a trusted dealer who can release items over a staggered period to allow the market to absorb it without unduly affecting the price. There is no single best answer to this, and it is best to take advice from several sources.

Those starting out assembling a collection of, say, banknotes for investment purposes need to bear in mind that active collectors may be competing for the same material and they, as it were, need to 'join the queue' to be offered the scarcer and more desirable investment grade material by the large dealers.

Collectors who are pursuing their interest for pleasure may be prepared to pay more than a particular note is worth in objective terms at that particular time simply to have it in their collection. This makes navigating the market difficult for those whose objective is to earn a worthwhile return.

The usual rules apply: get to know the market first; find a dealer you can trust; buy something you like; and buy the best you can afford.

Table 4.1 - Banknotes and Scripophily – key web addresses and contact details

Company	Web address	Email	Phone	Type	Type
Adam Historical Shares	www.adamshares.de	AdamShares@aol.com	n/a	Dealer	Scripophily
Baldwins Auctions	www.baldwin.sh	auctions@baldwin.sh	020 7930 9808	Dealer	Auctions
Bonhams (Glendinings)	www.bonhams.com	andrew.litherland@bonhams.com	020 7468 8256	Dealer	Scripophily
Dix Noonan Webb	www.dnw.co.uk	chris@dnw.co.uk	020 7499 5022	Dealer	Banknotes
Galerie Numistoria	www.numistoria.com	gcifre@numistoria.com	33 1 4927 9271	Dealer	Scripophily
GKR Bonds	www.gkrbonds.com	gkr4@hotmail.com	01376 571711	Dealer	Scripophily
Old Shares	www.husi.ch/hwp	n/a	n/a	Dealer	Scripophily
International Bank Note Society	www.ibns.it	On Site	n/a	Other	Banknotes
International Bond & Share Society	www.scripophily.org	chairman@scripophily.org	01225 837271	Other	Scripophily
Scripophily.com	www.scripophily.com	service@scripophily.com	n/a	Dealer	Scripophily
Scripophily.nl	www.scripophily.nl	molen@worldonline.nl	31 50 5348795	Dealer	Scripophily
Scott Winslow	www.scottwinslow.com	onlinesales@scottwinslow.com	n/a	Dealer	Scripophily
Society of Paper Money Collectors	www.spmc.org	On site	n/a	Other	Banknotes
Special Stocks	www.specialstocks.com	n/a	n/a	Dealer	Scripophily
Spink Banknote Dept.	www.spink.com	info@spink.com	020 7563 4000	Dealer	Banknotes

Where to go for more information

In the banknote area, a good starting point is Spink (www.spink.com). This old-established London firm holds about five auctions each year for banknotes. They have sold many world famous collections. They also sell online and a list of available stock is on the site.

Spink sells banknotes

Dix Noonan Webb (www.dnw.co.uk) is a specialist London auction house dealing in coins, medals and paper money. A list of forthcoming auctions is on the site together with a searchable database. The site also includes prices realized at auction and news and articles. Registered users have a special area on the site where online valuations can be requested and bids submitted for forthcoming auctions.

Baldwin's Auctions (www.baldwin.sh) hold paper money auctions in London, details of which can be found on the site together with prices realized.

Banknotes.com (www.banknotes.com) has a searchable list by country of notes for sale. The site also has much useful information on collecting including grading, printers and mints plus thousands of images of banknotes worldwide.

Coincraft (www.coincraft.com) also has a stock of banknotes. Based in Bloomsbury, it sells online as well as to personal buyers. The site has useful information on collecting banknotes plus a searchable database of banknotes for sale. Coincraft's monthly catalogue 'The Phoenix' can be subscribed to online.

If you are looking for information independent of dealers, the International Banknote Society (www.ibns.it) is a non-profit making organisation with members worldwide. The site has useful information on the grading and history of banknotes together with images of over 7,000 notes. Members receive a journal, a list of contacts and dealers and many other benefits.

The Society of Paper Money Collectors (www.spmc.org) may be of use for those interested in US notes. The site has brief general comments on the worth of US notes plus links to US clubs, societies and periodicals. A newsletter is published quarterly for members.

Dealers in scripophily are less numerous than those involved with stamps and coins. Some have taken to the web, but many of the more prominent ones have not. Herzog Hollender & Phillips, for example, are only contactable by telephone on 0207 433 3577 or by email at hollender@dial.pipex.com.

Fortunately there are others who are more 'new media' savvy. Adam Historical Shares (www.adamshares.de) based in Berlin is an online dealer with a database searchable by industry, country and date. The site also has a worldwide auction and show a calendar and numerous links.

The Bonhams subsidiary Glendinings (www.bonhams.com) holds periodic auctions of old bond and share certificates.

GKR Bonds (www.gkrbonds.com) based near Colchester, sells a wide range of old shares, bonds, and also maps, and has a free catalogue available. The firm can be contacted by email on gkr4@hotmail.com.

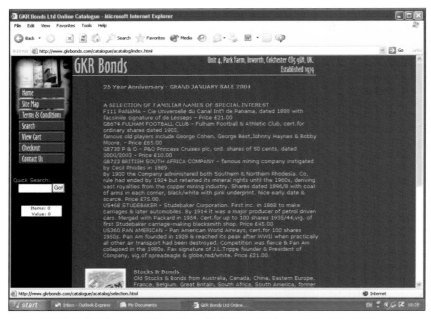

GKR Bonds sell all types of bond and share certificates

Old Securities (www.husi.ch/hwp/) is a particularly good site for Swiss bonds and shares but has many worldwide certificates on offer. Prices are in Swiss francs or euros. The site features an online catalogue with an email query facility for would-be purchasers.

Scott Winslow (www.scottwinslow.com) is a US dealer who sells actively via his web site and over the eBay auction system.

Scripophily.com (www.scripophily.com), based in Virginia, is a leading provider of collectable stock and bond certificates and has been in business on the internet since 1996. The site has a searchable database. It can also be viewed by category. Categories include entertainment, energy, frauds and scandals. Most of the items on offer are related to the USA and only a limited number for the rest of the world. Shipping is worldwide.

Scripophily.nl (www.scripophily.nl) has a catalogue of 2,000 items ranging across many countries and is fully searchable. Elsewhere in Continental Europe, Galerie Numistoria (www.numistoria.com) specialises in French bonds and those of a range of other countries.

SpecialStocks (www.specialstocks.com) lists items by country of issue with prices in American dollars. They will ship worldwide.

Probably the best starting point for serious scrip collectors is the International Bond and Share Society (www.scripophily.org). The society was founded in 1978 and has members in 50 countries. Its site has a useful overview of scripophily, numerous links and a gallery of the most popular collecting themes. It also has details of society membership, the benefits of which include a directory of collectors and dealers, a quarterly magazine, collectors meetings, a bibliography of over 80 publications and the opportunity to take part in mail auctions at low commissions.

There are several books about banknotes and scripophily that are well worth perusing. These are reviewed briefly below.

Banknote Year Book Token Publishing

This is a UK price guide and collector's handbook. As well as valuations the book includes a wealth of other information advice for beginner collectors, technical information and a directory of dealers, and fairs.

English Paper Money Vincent Duggleby

This is a standard work on the subject of English banknotes, which is useful to collectors for identification and valuation purposes.

Standard Catalogue of World Paper Money Shafer and Cuhaj (Editors) Krause Publications

This is a three volume series covering specialised issues, 1650-1960 and 1961-2003. It contains hundreds of illustrations with current values. Reference information includes international grading terms, foreign exchange rates and numerous historical facts.

Scripophily Keith Hollender Ward Lock 1982

This book is written by a founder director of Herzog, Hollender & Phillips, an international dealer in old scrip. Hollender [NB sp] says he was prompted to write the book by a lack of literature on the subject. This is still the case and although written more than twenty years ago it is still relevant today. The book is divided into three parts: general background and history; collecting themes and developing a collection with advice on looking after a collection; and how and where to sell and what to look for and avoid.

Scripophily: The Art of Finance (Krause Publications) is a more recent offering from the same author.

5 | Books

Writing this chapter was a labour of love. I have been interested in books from an early age. But the value that a collection of rare and collectable books can acquire was only recently brought home to me.

A book collector friend of mine who lives in Australia recently sold a small part of his collection for tens of thousands of pounds. The rest of his collection, including many signed copies and letters from authors, is probably worth a small fortune.

This prompted a re-examination of the large number of books we have accumulated over the years. There are those that my wife and I have purchased, and review copies from publishers. When we moved house two years ago, all of the books were packed in boxes and subsequently gradually unpacked. We unearthed all but the last two boxes a few months ago.

As we unpacked them, we systematically looked at our dust-jacketed hardbacks and discovered to our pleasure that we had a number of first editions. These include modern fiction and some classic books on finance. Out of around 1,600 books in all there were only a handful of them, but enough at least to form the start of a collection.

This is probably how many book collectors start. Transforming a collection like this into a superhobby portfolio of investment grade quality is a different matter. Indeed some prominent book dealers scorn the very idea of using books as an investment medium.

While there are 'used and rare' book dealers nationwide, finding a dealer that specialises in the area in which you choose to collect may take a little more effort. But the advent of the internet has made the process of locating dealers and books easier and less time consuming than it once was.

Good quality material may be harder to find, however, and the trend in prices of collectable books is less well documented than in some other areas included in this book, such as coins or stamps.

Rare book basics

History

Collecting books is as old as the libraries of great universities. Country house libraries flourished in the 16th and 17th centuries, and in the Victorian era book collecting spread to the educated middle classes.

Yet while many avid readers have large collections of books, few make the jump into the serious collecting of sought after items. Fewer still have devoted time to investigating book collecting as a superhobby investment proposition.

This is not to say that you can't pursue book collecting this way. But what it does mean is that, with a smaller serious collector base and with book collection diffused over hundreds of different themes, it is a less liquid market than, say, stamps and coins.

The advent of the internet has helped to improve the situation. It has allowed collectors to scour the world for the books they require, using specialist newsgroups and web sites. Sites like eBay have allowed books to be auctioned to a customer base of millions of potential purchasers.

The subject of buying and selling through online media like eBay is covered in chapter fourteen. But remember that with eBay you are buying 'sight unseen'. Condition is important for books, and some would argue that you need to see and handle a book to verify that what is being offered is a true first edition, that it is in the advertised condition, and that a signature, if there is one, is genuine.

This reservation aside, the web has made it easier for specialist booksellers to advertise their stock and new acquisitions, in turn making it easier for collectors and would-be investors to locate the book they require from a source within an acceptable travelling time from their home. On the downside, the chances of finding bargains in out of the way flea markets and antique shops have probably diminished.

According to some purists in the book trade, the internet has ushered in the era of speculative buying of books. They appear to deplore the spread of book collecting to a wider market. My guess is that this attitude is simply the self-interest of long standing booksellers and collectors, who want to keep the rare book market a well-kept and profitable secret. They tend to look down their noses at the hoi polloi latching on to the idea that it could be rewarding to buy books for investment purposes.

Investors and collectors alike are always likely to buy with an eye to the future potential value of a book. While some may claim to collect a particular genre for its own sake and to keep in perpetuity, the salerooms are full of the books of those who are happy to realise the value of a collection and move on to a new area.

What to collect and invest in

The short answer to this question is to collect what interests you. If you have an interest in a particular type of literature or book category, then the chances are you will keep yourself informed about it.

There are, however, several obvious genres that are naturally popular.

Modern first editions:

How you describe 'modern' depends on your taste, and perhaps your age, but most would date modern as being from the early part of the 20th century. Maggs Bros., the rather grand bookseller in London's Berkeley Square, starts its modern category at 1800.

Literary merit and popular appeal is another variable. Writers who become prolific sellers may not prove to be the best investments, although first editions of their first novel, before their popularity became evident, would probably have had small print runs and therefore be scarce.

Even established writers of acknowledged quality go out of fashion. While Hemingway, and Faulkner and others are always collected, John Galsworthy has gone out of fashion and Steinbeck is currently fading in popularity. Ultimately you have to take a view that an author you wish to collect - take Graham Greene as an example - will stay in favour or become more popular.

Another valid approach is to adopt a 'buy low' scattergun approach of buying a first edition of a first novel (or a second or later novel from a relative unknown) shortlisted for a literary prize.

> ### What to collect
> - 'Modern firsts'
> - First novels
> - Crime
> - SF, fantasy and horror
> - Sporting classics
> - Children's fiction
> - Military books
> - Travel and voyages

The key is that the author's work has a low initial print run. By doing this, as a reader you have the chance to enjoy new work. As a collector cum investor, you have the chance that the author will become popular and repay the investment many times over.

An example from our own collection is a first edition of Monica Ali's book 'Brick Lane', which was shortlisted for the Booker Prize in 2003 and has subsequently sold very well.

Collecting books of this nature also increases the chance of getting hold of a signed copy, which can add to the value of the item. Collecting at the short list stage is the only practical way to do this. Once the winner is announced the print run increases and the scarcity value evaporates.

Children's books:

Classic children's authors like JM Barrie, Charles Kingsley, Beatrix Potter, Arthur Ransome, Roald Dahl, Captain WE Johns (of 'Biggles' fame) and, of course Terry Pratchett and JK Rowling, are a popular and extremely active market. Books in good condition from authors like this can fetch a considerable amount.

Crime:

Crime is a popular genre for many collectors. Books from authors such as Dashiel Hammett and other American stalwarts of detective fiction are an obvious starting point, as is Agatha Christie and then more modern authors like Ruth Rendell, PD James, Ian Rankin and Colin Dexter. Gollancz crime novels with their distinctive yellow dust jackets are a genre in their own right, as are 'The Saint' novels of Leslie Charteris. Though not strictly crime, first editions of Ian Fleming's James Bond books are eminently collectable.

Science Fiction, Fantasy and Horror:

This genre is also popular and spans writers from the 19th and early 20th century through to the present day. Collectable authors range from Jules Verne, Edgar Allen Poe, Edgar Rice Burroughs, Kurt Vonnegut, Arthur C Clarke and Isaac Asimov to writers like Frank Herbert, Peter Hamilton, Stephen Baxter, Ray Bradbury, HP Lovecraft and Stephen King, the latter said to be the most collected living author.

The early work of a writer like Dean Koontz, who does not fit precisely into this genre, is also widely collected. First editions of his newer work have large print runs and are only worth having to keep a larger collection up to date.

Military:

Books about military campaigns are popular, with collectors focusing on books about key events in history ranging from WW2 back to 1066, and from the English Civil War to the American Civil War. In the US, the Civil War is the most popular area and items pertaining to the Confederacy are highly sought after.

Sport:

This is another specialist area, with collections based around early works relating to classic sports such as hunting, shooting, fishing, motor sport and golf. Signed sporting memorabilia is also a major area of interest for many collectors, too large to be included within the scope of this book.

Travel:

Many book collectors believe that voyages and travel represent a classic area that will never lose its popularity, particularly since many books of this nature are lavishly illustrated with maps, photographs and drawings that enhance the appearance of the book.

Identifying a rare book

This really comes down to identifying a first edition, although for some scarce books, this is not the be-all and end-all. A reprint of a particularly scarce book could have considerable value in its own right.

The term first edition is itself a somewhat confusing one. What all collectors and investors alike are seeking is books that are 'first edition, first state', in other words the very first print run of a published book. Often this print run of a book will be small, especially if it is an author's first novel or the early work of an author who has only subsequently become popular.

Only when the popularity of the book has been gauged will a second larger print run be made, sometimes with some errors in the original removed. This book will still be a first edition, but much less collectable because it is less unusual and produced in much greater quantity. This together with the condition of a book (see next section) is normally the reason for wildly disparate prices for what are seemingly more or less identical books.

On modern books a number system will normally help identify whether a book is a true 'first edition, first state' copy or not. On the page of the book containing the copyright information (or sometimes on the page at the very back of the book) will normally be a series of numbers either in ascending or descending order thus:

10 9 8 7 6 5 4 3 2 1

or: 3 4 5 6 7 8 9 10

or else: 1 3 5 7 9 10 8 4 6 2

The presence of a 1 in the series indicates a first edition first state copy. So the sequence in the top and bottom examples would be such a book. The second example would actually be the third printing of the book (the lowest number is a 3).

One big exception to this (although not the only one) among well-known publishers is Random House. It will state 'First Edition' in a first edition and yet have the list of numbers beginning with 2.

This is not, however, a foolproof way of identifying a book. Many publishers have more idiosyncratic ways of identifying first editions, sometimes by printing the words 'first edition' on the copyright page, others in more arcane ways. If it is not obvious, then you need to consult an expert or a reference book to establish the situation beyond doubt.

The website Bookaway (www.bookaway.com) has a useful section on identifying first editions from publishers' marks. The book 'A Pocket Guide to the Identification of First Editions' by Bill McBride takes a more comprehensive look at the subject.

Bookaway's guide to identifying first editions

Another point worth remembering is that in the case of some modern books, a small number of proof copies may have been issued to reviewers. Because these tend to be even fewer in number than first editions, they can also be collectable and may even fetch more than a conventional first edition.

On the other hand, collectors need to take care that they buy the first edition of the country in which the author was first published, on the assumption that editions of a popular UK author published, say, in an American edition (or vice versa) would come later, have a larger print run, and therefore be less collectable. In my collection for example I have an American first edition of a fairly scarce book by Ian Rankin, acquired for a much lower price than the UK first edition would fetch.

Key collecting points

- Check 'number line' and copyright statement
- Publishers' first edition conventions vary
- Foreign editions may be less collectable
- Signatures add value
- Associations with other authors or notables add value

There are other points to watch for. Some publishers like Cassell, Collier, Tower and others are known only for publishing reprints, and their books, with a few exceptions, are not collectable. The same goes for book club copies, which are generally worthless to collectors and investors. The only exception to this is books published in numbered and signed limited editions or those authors whose first editions were only published under a book club imprint.

The signature of an author, with or without an inscription, can add considerably to the value of a book, particularly if the author has since died. By the same token, the inscriptions of previous owners in books, unless well known in their own right, actually detract from the value of a book. Books of one famous author owned by another and inscribed as such, or books dedicated and signed by one author to another are particularly valuable.

So a first edition of F Scott Fitzgerald's 'The Great Gatsby' owned and signed by former US president Herbert Hoover would be a valuable collector's item. One signed by the author and inscribed with a dedication to his friend Ernest Hemingway is the sort of book most collectors would kill for, since it is probably quite simply one of a kind.

Some living authors will sign copies of their books, either on the book itself, or on a bookplate. You need to contact the author via their publisher to see if this is possible. Some well-known authors charge for signatures. A flat-signed (ie directly onto the title page) copy is better than a signature on a bookplate, but either is better than no signature at all.

Opinions differ about whether or not a bookplate should be pasted into a book. My own view is that keeping a signature separate in a protective sleeve is the best policy. Signatures and autographs are a collectors market in their own right, so keeping a signature separate makes sense. It may be possible to acquire the signature of a dead author to place with a book. Autograph dealers and fairs are the place to seek these out.

Condition

The most important single additional aspect governing a book's value is its condition, and particularly whether or not a dust jacket is present.

What makes a book in good condition or not is obvious. For investment purposes, you need to avoid buying books that have cracked or torn spines, cracked or loose hinges, mildewed or worm-eaten pages, ink or pencil marks on the pages other than an author's signature or inscription, loose or missing pages, and so on.

Condition and grading terms, and the effect they have on prices, are shown in the table:

Table 5.1- Books - Price variations according to condition

Mint	Fine	VG	Good	Poor
200.00	180.00	150.00	80.00	10.00
150.00	135.00	125.00	70.00	8.00
100.00	90.00	75.00	40.00	5.00
75.00	65.00	55.00	30.00	4.00
50.00	45.00	40.00	20.00	3.00
40.00	35.00	30.00	18.00	2.50
30.00	27.00	22.00	13.00	2.00
25.00	22.00	18.00	10.00	1.50
20.00	17.00	15.00	8.00	1.00
15.00	13.00	11.00	7.00	1.00

The table shows prices relative to those paid for a mint copy.

Mint = Indistinguishable from a new unread book. DJ as new.

Fine = Some evidence of ownership. DJ slight rubbing.

VG = As fine, other than slight foxing or fading. DJ rubbed but colour good.

Good = Complete but obviously 2nd hand. DJ fairly clean; some marks and small tears.

Poor = Warped, missing pages, damaged spine. DJ tatty, dirty, marked, creased, or torn.

Source: Adapted from a similar table in 'Book & Magazine Collector'

The presence of a dust jacket is, however, the biggest single item that enhances the value of a book. The better the condition of the dust jacket the better, but any dust jacket is preferable to none.

The difference in price between first editions with dust jackets in good condition and those without is considerable. The table shows the difference in price for some well known collectable first editions with and without the dust jacket present.

Table 5.2 - Difference in prices of first editions with and without dust jacket

Author	Book	With DJ (£)	Without DJ (£)
Arthur Conan Doyle	Hound of the Baskervilles	80,000	5,000
Virginia Woolf	Jacobs Room	25,000	1,000
JRR Tolkien	The Lord of the Rings	25,000	3,000
Graham Greene	Brighton Rock	30,000	700
Ian Fleming	Casino Royale	15,000	1,000
Arthur Ransome	Swallows & Amazons	15,000	2,000
Kenneth Grahame	Wind in the Willows	50,000	6,000

You can see from this table that the difference in value is anything from eight to fifteen times, and sometimes more. The reason is that the dust jacket is easily destroyed, damaged or removed. Therefore copies with a dust jacket, especially one in good condition, are scarcer and fetch more from collectors.

At some stages of the 20th century, it was a fashion to remove dust jacket. Books from that era - those by Virginia Woolf are an example - are rarely found with dust jackets. If one is available with a dust jacket, it will attract considerable interest.

Is it right for you?

Investing in rare and collectable books, generally taken to mean first editions or other scarce material, as with many of the superhobby investment categories in this book, should be able to provide you with a hedge against inflation.

Prices of books like this as a whole tend to rise over time. Like stamps, books are perishable if not cared for properly. This means that the supply of good quality material can contract. In many instances the first editions of some books were not produced in large quantities and can be quite scarce. The depredations of time and the actions of those who are not collectors can result in a valuable book being lost forever as a collectors' item.

Rare books, particularly modern first editions (normally taken to mean authors from the beginning of the 20th century onwards), are subject to fads and fashions that affect their value. To build a collection of investment quality that will stand the test of time necessitates collecting the classic authors that are perennial favourites, and avoiding temporary fads. Even then some authors go out of fashion. John Galsworthy first editions took a hit in the wake of the Wall Street Crash and have never really recovered.

Let's look at some of the other questions you need to answer to determine whether rare books could form a place in your wider portfolio of investments.

What is your time horizon?

Few people get involved in book collecting simply to make money. It is possible to assemble a solid collection of books and sell it for appreciably more than you paid for it, but probably only after some time has elapsed. Like most of the superhobby categories in this book, a period of at least ten years probably needs to go by before significant increases in value can be achieved.

There are exceptions of course. Some authors achieve phenomenal popularity in a much shorter timescale and the value of their first editions increase dramatically. The best example of this is perhaps Harry Potter author JK Rowling. A first edition of the original book 'Harry Potter and the Philosopher's Stone' cost a few pounds when first published in 1997 and now sells for £25,000.

Examples like this are, however, a rarity and if you are fortunate enough to possess a book like this, it makes sense to take advantage of an author's temporary popularity to realise profits to reinvest in more classic items. Another recent example is that even second-rate examples of JRR Tolkien's 'Lord of the Rings' trilogy have been fetching silly prices, and dealers have been cashing in accordingly - generally selling to the less well-informed buyer.

Do you have adequate capital?

Throughout this book we explain that using tangible assets as part of your investment strategy means that what you invest in this area should represent perhaps 10-15% of the total amount you have available for investment. If you have, say, £200,000 invested in the stock market, then an alternative asset portfolio totalling £30,000 is probably appropriate.

> ## Right for you?
>
> - Best returns over long time horizons
> - Affordable - prices start at under £100
> - Insurance, security and periodic valuations required
> - Prices not volatile, so good diversification
> - Time needs to be spent on maintenance, research, signatures etc.
> - Interest in literature required

If you choose books as one of your favoured superhobby investing categories, what you spend can be tailored to your pocket. Books, even from eminently collectable authors, can be found at all price ranges. Worthwhile collections can be built up spending less than £100 per item, rounding off the collection with a scarce work that might cost £1,000 or more. You can start off your book portfolio with a modest amount, and then build up as your knowledge increases and you develop an idea for a collecting 'theme'. Buying first editions of newly published authors costs less, but try and get a signed copy if you can, as this will hold its value better.

Are you happy to pay the cost of insurance?

Books are relatively bulky items and it is impracticable to store them in a safe. This means they need insuring to protect them from fire and theft. You need to make sure that your home contents insurance is sufficiently comprehensive to cover your collection, and to keep receipts for your purchases in a safe place (perhaps a fireproof lockable cabinet) in case you need to make a claim. A periodic valuation for insurance purposes is a good idea.

Can you devote time to the care of your books?

Books need careful location and display, in particular to avoid the risk of damp and fire. You need to have a dry room, with no dampness or overhead water or central heating pipes, a minimum of curtains and upholstered furniture and, for preference, a fire retardant carpet. Books should be kept in such a way that they are not damaged and that features such as dust jackets are preserved from damage and from direct or strong sunlight.

Excessive humidity and excessive dryness and heat should be avoided. Books need to be checked periodically for damage from insects, and if damage is found an appropriate treatment applied. Proper storage, in rigid bookshelves is essential. Books need to be handled carefully, especially old and leather bound volumes, whose value may be adversely affected by scratching and scuffing.

Repairing very old books is best left to a professional bookbinder. Modern books with defects such as cracked hinges and torn spines may be able to be repaired carefully at home. Leather books need periodic treating with leather dressing every six months. This treatment replaces the animal oils in the leather, which can dry out as time passes.

Care of dust jackets is vital. Buy from a good bookseller and dust jacketed copies will most likely already have the dust jacket protected by a clear plastic sleeve. New first editions you buy from a normal bookshop will not be protected in this way. Plastic sleeving can be bought by the roll and it is a matter of a few minutes work to do the job yourself.

All of this takes time but is time well spent if it preserves and even enhances the value of your investment. If in doubt on points of repair, it is best to seek the advice of a professional before attempting anything radical.

Is portfolio diversification an objective?

There is probably less documentary evidence surrounding rare books than there is for similar types of collectables like stamps and coins.

Apart from certain classic authors, writers can come into and go out of favour quickly for no apparent reason. A favourite of mine, 'The Herries Chronicles' by Hugh Walpole, a five-volume set covering the history of a fictional Lake District family, does not merit a mention in most booksellers' catalogues, while Virginia Woolf, James Joyce and other authors writing around the same period, are all the rage. John Steinbeck, once a collectors' standby, is now decreasing in popularity.

Some books seem to share a similar level of medium term price volatility as the stock market, but classics, the blue chips of the book world, climb inexorably in price. You need to decide whether your primary reason for buying collectable books is for the pleasure they bring you, or for long term gain. The two are not mutually exclusive. Some of my personal favourites - Charles Dickens, George Orwell, Graham Greene, Ernest Hemingway and a number of others - are all collectable blue chip authors. One expert calculates that a pristeen first edition of Dickens' 'Bleak House', generally regarded as his best book, would have returned 4% a year over the last 30 years.

Even among alternative asset categories, some form of diversification is worthwhile. It probably doesn't make much sense to have too many of the same style of alternative investments in your portfolio. By this I mean that stamps, banknotes and coins are essentially similar - well documented and dependent on the spending power of the collector base.

Books are too, but what ranks as classic literature, and is therefore collectable, is constantly shifting. Rather as with art, it is a more subjective judgement than it might be to identify what makes a classic investment-grade coin or stamp. In these latter cases, scarcity is measurable and unvarying. So books can make a good counterweight to other superhobby investing areas.

Do you have an interest in literature?

The final indispensable item is to have an interest in literature and subject you are collecting.

If this sounds obvious, remember that it is possible to regard some other alternative investments, like stamps and coins, as an 'off-site' financial investment that you can leave securely in a bank or a dealer's vault.

Books are going to sit in your home, and the pleasure of handling them is part of the collecting and investment process. A love of, and knowledge of books and literature is a vital part of the process, as also perhaps is a love of browsing round bookshops and a tolerance of the sometimes odd characters that frequent the book trade.

Returns

Unlike with stamps and coins, with books there is little systematic organisation of the price information from dealers and auction results that might allow you to calculate returns with reasonable accuracy. However, we can make some estimate from current prices of the sorts of returns that would have been made had a particular book been purchased new in the past.

The method we've adopted is to use the obvious idea that a hardback book purchased new will have cost a different amount depending on when it was first published. We assume, as a rough guide, original prices as follows: 1900-10: £1; 1911-1920: £2; 1921-30: £3; and so on up to the present day when a new book might be had for around £11. Using this method, and factoring in recent auction results to get the present day price for a particular item, the returns from some modern first editions work out approximately as follows.

Table 5.3 - Returns from jacketed first editions bought from new

		Year	Price then (£)	Price * now (£)	Compound rtn % pa
Arthur Conan Doyle	Hound of the Baskervilles	1902	1.00	80,000.00	11.8
James Joyce	Ulysses	1922	3.00	40,000.00	12.4
Virginia Woolf	Jacob's Room	1922	3.00	25,000.00	11.8
JRR Tolkien	The Lord of the Rings	1954	6.00	25,000.00	18.5
Graham Greene	Brighton Rock	1938	4.00	20,000.00	14.0
Ian Fleming	Casino Royale	1953	6.00	15,000.00	16.9
Arthur Ransome	Swallows & Amazons	1930	3.00	15,000.00	12.4
Kenneth Grahame	Wind in the Willows	1908	1.00	50,000.00	12.1
Beatrix Potter	Tale of Peter Rabbit	1902	1.00	10,000.00	9.6
John Fowles	The Magus	1966	7.00	250.00	10.2
Zadie Smith	White Teeth	2000	10.00	125.00	132.1

* Source: Sotheby's

This is clearly only a guide, but it does seem obvious that annual percentage returns in the low to mid teens can be expected for a book that is or becomes a classic, if you buy it from new. This argues for a very long-term view of collecting for investment purposes. At the same time there are the whims of fashion to watch out for.

Zadie Smith's 'White Teeth' in first edition first state would currently fetch around £125 compared to a purchase price in 2,000 of around £10, whereas a set of John Galsworthy's 'Forsyte Saga' is currently fetching only £350, a very low return for a book published in the 1920s.

First editions of the first 'Harry Potter' book have fetched as much as £25,000, a phenomenal return over the six years since publication because only 350 copies were printed in this first state. Subsequent first edition print runs have been massive, so that sets will not fetch commensurately more and subsequent books in the series will probably be virtually worthless to collectors or investors.

The golden rule remains, therefore, when it comes to modern or ultra-modern authors to collect what you like and books that have been well reviewed. For books published in the 20th century the best returns will be from those authors no longer alive that have stood the test of time - Graham Greene, George Orwell, William Faulkner, F. Scott Fitzgerald, Ernest Hemingway, and others. The jury is still out on some living literary lions like John Updike, Norman Mailer and Philip Roth. In Mailer's case, for example, at present it is only his first two or three books that are really collectable.

Further back, classic authors like Charles Dickens, Jonathan Swift, Conan Doyle, the Bronte sisters, and Jane Austen are likely to make good investments. Look for the perennially popular giants of literature and avoid paying top price for today's current favourite.

How to buy and sell

American bank robber Willie Sutton was asked why he robbed banks, replying 'because that's where the money is'.

Paraphrasing Sutton it is perhaps just stating the obvious to say that you buy books at bookshops, but that is the truth of it. Antique shops, flea markets, book fairs and the like are other good sources of books, but the astute superhobby investor has to have a theme in mind, and to be opportunistic, and be able to spot a good value book when he sees it.

With many 20th century authors who do not fall into the 'classic' category, you have to take a view, much as you would with any sort of investment. Are Galsworthy or Walpole on the up; are Zadie Smith and JK Rowling overpriced. The rule about buying is to buy what you enjoy, in the best condition you can find, without paying over the odds.

Canny buying and selling

- Opportunism required when buying
- Collections may be best sold through a trusted dealer
- Sell overpriced new authors to reinvest in classics
- Beware of film-driven price bubbles (eg Tolkien)
- Pursue signatures to add long-term value

Selling is another matter. If you have built up a collection you may find it hard to part with. If you have built up a relationship with a book dealer he may be the best outlet for your collection rather than the risky route of the auction house. On the other hand many dealers will try to buy a book as cheaply as possible and it is only where you have a complete and desirable collection that a dealer is likely to offer a competitive market price.

Though auctions may seem expensive, you are at least guaranteed a more perfect market than a single dealer, even though you may have to pay commission of 15% of the hammer price. Placing a realistic reserve price is vital. See chapter fourteen for more about dealing at auction.

The table opposite has details of booksellers, auction houses, relevant publications and how to find them.

The next section has more information on the various forums for buying and selling. By far the best option initially is to build up relationships with a network of local booksellers and contact them regularly and let them know the type of material you wish to buy.

If you wish to locate signed copies of newly published first editions and avoid paying a premium, it may be necessary to make frequent visits to large Central London bookstores. Firsts in Print (www.firsts-in-print.co.uk), a UK bookseller based in the Isle of Wight, specialises in signed and unsigned first editions of newly published titles and has many signed copies and limited editions available.

The final chapter of the book goes into more detail of buying and selling using dealers and online auctions and salerooms.

Where to go for information

The book trade, which some mistakenly regard as stuffy, has in large measure taken to the internet like a duck to water.

There are exceptions, of course. But like many other areas of collecting, the ability the web offers a bookseller to reach a much wider base of customers, the ease with which customers can search for a title, and the ability it offers to buy and sell online have all made the medium a natural.

The following is a selection of sites that we have found to be useful, together with some brief notes on books and publications relevant to book collecting and investing.

Table 5.4 – Books – key web addresses and contact details

Company	Web address	Email	Phone	Type
Abebooks	www.abebooks.co.uk	info@abebooks.co.uk	n/a	Dealer
Addall	www.addall.com	n/a	n/a	Dealer
Alibris	aol.alibris.com	On site	n/a	Dealer
Antiquarian Book Review	www.antiquarianbookreview.com	On site	01494 562266	Publication
Antiquarian Booksellers Association	www.abainternational.com	admin@aba.org.uk	n/a	Association
Any Amount of Books	www.anyamountofbooks.com	charingx@anyamountofbooks.com	020 7836 3697	Dealer
Bibliofind	www.amazon.com	n/a	n/a	Dealer
Bibliology	www.bibliology.com	n/a	n/a	Links
Biblion	www.biblion.com	onsite	020 7629 1374	Dealer
Blackwells Rare Books	www.rarebooks.blackwell.co.uk	rarebooks@blackwells.co.uk	01864 333555	Dealer
Bloomsbury Auctions	www.bloomsburyauctions.com	info@bloomsburyauctions.com	020 7495 9494	Dealer
Bonhams Book Dept.	www.bonhams.com	books@bonhams.com	020 7393 3900	Dealer
Book and Magazine Collector	n/a	janice.mayne@dpgsubs.co.uk	0870 732 7070	Publication
Book Guide (The)	www.thebookguide.co.uk	n/a	n/a	Links
Bookaway	www.bookaway.com	n/a	n/a	Information
Bookfinder	www.bookfinder.com	On site	n/a	Dealer
Christie's Book Dept	www.christies.com	On site	020 7839 9060	Dealer
D&M Books and Packaging	www.bookcovers.co.uk	daniel@care4books.com	01924 495 768	Dealer
Exedra Booksearch	www.exedra.co.uk	info@exedra.co.uk	020 7731 8500	Dealer
Francis Edwards	www.francisedwards.co.uk	sales@francisedwards.co.uk	020 7430 2535	Dealer
HD Bookfairs	www.hdbookfairs.co.uk	exhibitionteam@aol.com	020 8224 3609	Dealer
Int'l League of Antiquarian Booksellers	www.ilab-lila.com	onfo@ilab-lila.com	n/a	Association
Maggs Bros.	www.maggs.com	enquiries@maggs.com	020 7493 7160	Dealer
Provincial Bookfairs Association	www.pbfa.org	info@pbfa.org	01763 248400	Links
Robert Frew Books	www.robertfrew.com	shop@robertfrew.com	020 7580 2311	Dealer
Scottish Book Collector	www.essbc.demon.co.uk	jennie@essbc.demon.co.uk	0131 228 4837	Publication
Sotheby's Book Dept.	www.sothebys.com	On site	020 7293 5050	Dealer
Spink Book Dept.	www.spink.com	info@spink.com	020 7563 4000	Dealer

Dealers and Markets

Abebooks Europe (www.abebooks.co.uk) is part of the Abebooks empire which professes to be the worlds largest marketplace for second hand, rare and out of print books. If a book is not listed a search request can be left which will be checked against new titles updated daily until the book is found. The database can be searched to provide UK results first. The site also features a useful glossary of book terms such as size, condition and common abbreviations. A monthly newsletter features special offers and news of bestsellers.

Alibris (aol.alibris.com) is a US site selling new, hard-to-find and out-of-print books, music and films. The site features a searchable database and a glossary of book terms plus an email newsletter with special offers, news and promotions.

Bookaway (www.bookaway.com) has a useful guide which covers frequently asked questions about rare books and values. There is also a section on the terms used in bookselling, an author list and online bookstore courtesy of Abebooks.

Any Amount of Books (www.anyamountofbooks.com) in Charing Cross Road London has online catalogues searchable alphabetically and also to download. For personal shoppers the shop is open seven days a week and stocks books from £1 upwards. If you are looking for something special, a 'wants' service is available with items featured on the site.

Any amount of books in Charing Cross Road

Bibliology (www.bibliology.com) is a UK site linking to numerous dealers. The site also includes news and comments, links to sites such as bookbinders and a list of UK book fairs.

Biblion (www.biblion.com) is an online marketplace with three million items from hundreds of dealers in rare, antiquarian and second hand books. The site has many useful features including links to literary societies, dealers and auctions, libraries and booksellers associations. For personal callers Biblion also has a shop in London with a wide range of stock from over 100 sellers.

D&M Books and Packaging (www.bookcovers.co.uk) specialise in old and rare children's books, annuals and comics and also offer a complete range of book supplies such as covers for dust wrapper protection, packaging and accessories such as book adhesive etc.

Bookfinder (www.bookfinder.com) based in California links to 50,000 sellers of new, used, rare and out of print books worldwide. The site has a searchable database and for those seeking further assistance specific requests can be posted on the many bulletin boards or the producers of the site can be emailed directly.

The Book Guide (www.thebookguide.co.uk) has information on shops, fairs, auctions, binders etc.

Exedra Booksearch (www.exedra.co.uk) specializes in finding out of print, second-hand and rare books in all subjects. Books can be requested on the site and the requests will be kept live for a year. Once the book is found you will be contacted but there is no obligation to purchase.

HD Bookfairs (www.hdbookfairs.co.uk) hold large, regular book fairs in the south of England for collectable, rare, second hand, antiquarian and out-of-print books.

Mentioning individual dealers is possibly invidious so the following are cited as examples only - with no recommendation for or against attached.

Blackwell's Rare Books (www.rarebooks.blackwells.co.uk) has been selling books in Oxford since 1879. Apart from personal callers, Blackwells sells online via a searchable database.

Francis Edwards (www.francisedwards.co.uk) has its main shop in the world famous Hay Cinema Bookshop in Hay-on-Wye, with two smaller establishments in London. Books are available on all subjects from 50p up to £5,000. All the stock can be purchased online. Some 40 mail order catalogues are published each year and these can be requested by email.

Maggs Brothers (www.maggs.com) was established in 1853 and is one of the world's largest antiquarian booksellers. Although based in Berkeley Square in London some of their stock can be bought online via a searchable database. There are detailed, authoritative entries on many of the books available. Maggs also makes a point of finding unusual items, like annotated proof copies and the like. Books are available over a wide price range and can be shipped to anywhere in the world.

Associations

The Antiquarian Booksellers Association (www.abainternational.com) is the trade association for dealers in rare and fine books, manuscripts and allied materials and has a searchable database of members. The site includes a useful glossary of terms, book fairs and numerous useful links.

The Provincial Booksellers Association (www.pbfa.org) provides a regular London shop window for dealers outside the capital. Apart from those held in London each month, fairs are held throughout the year in various venues around the country. The site features a fair calendar, publications for sale and links to members throughout the country.

Auctions

Bloomsbury Auctions (www.bloomsburyauctions.com) holds sales every two weeks and is the only auction house in England devoted entirely to the sale of books and manuscript material. The sales cover a wide range of subjects and vary in price from £50 to £500,000.

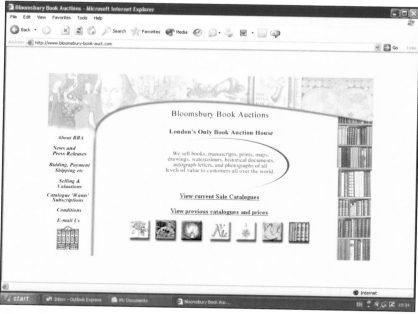

Bloomsbury Auctions

The site features future auction dates, press releases, information on bidding, selling valuations and information on catalogue subscriptions. There is also a 'wants' list service for those with interest in a particular field whereby the collector receives a full catalogue description of up to 35 lots per auction or a complimentary copy of the catalogue if more than 35. The annual subscription for this service at the present time is £25. Bidding is either in person or by email, telephone, fax or post.

Bonhams (www.bonhams.com) holds twelve book auctions each year in London and the regions. A catalogue is available online one month before the sale.

Christie's (www.christies.com), the leading auction house, has been responsible for selling many of the world's finest single owner collections. An example was the sale of the library of William Foyle for £12 million in July 2000. The site features an online searchable catalogue where images and specifications can be viewed up to two months in advance of sales. Absentee bids can be left online on items in Christie's auctions round the world.

A so-called LotFinder Assistant will search sales for specific items for a year and notify by email as new results are found. Christie's also handles less renowned but still collectable books ranging from children's books to modern first editions. Exploration and Travel is a distinct section within the book department, with its own auctions held 3-6 times a year. These sales typically feature items relating to the travels of world navigators and explorers such as Captain Cook, Ernest Shackleton and David Livingstone.

eBay (www.ebay.co.uk), the online auction site, has everything from modern signed first editions to antiquarian books and other collectables.

Sotheby's (www.sothebys.com) has a book department divided into six areas of specialism: Americana, music, general books and manuscripts, mediaeval illustrated manuscripts, natural history, travel and atlases, and Oriental manuscripts and miniatures. All the specialists can be contacted by email. An overview of books for sale is on the site. For more detail a catalogue can be purchased online. All the items for sale can be viewed a week prior to the sale at Sotheby's premises in Bond Street. For details of future auctions and events, Sotheby's News can be subscribed to online.

Publications

Three publications stand out as essential reading for a would-be superhobby investor in the book field:

Book and Magazine Collector is a monthly publication that contains a range of interesting articles on various aspects of book collecting. Of interest to collectors is a large classified section at the back of each issue where dealers advertise their current stock (with information on condition and price) and books they are seeking for clients. The publication as yet has no web presence. Contact details are in the table on page 101, and the publication is available from leading newsagents.

Antiquarian Book Review is a monthly publication with articles of general interest to collectors. It has no classified section, but does contain detailed listings for fairs and auctions.

Scottish Book Collector (www.essbc.demon.co.uk) is published four times a year and can be subscribed to online. The magazine features interviews with major authors, information on rare and collectable books, reviews, salesroom reports and a section on Scottish History. A list of reasonably priced second hand Scottish books is issued to subscribers.

Books about books

Breese's Guide to Modern First Editions Martin Breese Books (1999)

This is a resource for collectors of British first editions with profiles of authors and values at the time of writing.

Collecting Children's Books Book and Magazine Collector (2003)

The book contains references to 12,000 titles by 330 children's authors and illustrators with current values.

Guide to first edition prices Ray B. Russell Tartarus Press (2001)

The title speaks for itself.

How to find, buy, and sell used and rare books Ian C. Ellis Perigree (2001)

This book mainly deals with first editions of modern books. The various chapters include buying and selling on the internet, auctions, catalogues and avoiding beginner's mistakes.

Miller's Guide to Collecting Modern Books Miller's Publications (2002)

This is a guide to collecting British and American books from the late 19th century to 2002, explaining the factors that influence value. There is practical information on collecting, together with a glossary of technical terms.

Official Price Guide to Collecting Books Tedford and Goudey House of Collectables (2002)

This book contains values for thousands of collectable books in all genres with prices in American dollars. Information is also included on topics such as the care and repair of books, a look at the book trade, what to collect and a review of the book market.

Used and rare: travels in the book world Lawrence and Nancy Goldstone Griffin Trade Paperback (1998)

A readable and well written book, which tells the tale of how an American couple's search for a hardcover version of War and Peace led to a lifelong passion for book collecting. The pleasures and pitfalls of collecting are narrated along the way.

6 | Classic Cars

If you are the sort of person who likes the idea of owning an asset you can be seen in, classic cars could be the superhobby investment medium for you.

Like many alternative asset categories, classic cars have been prone to periodic cycles. Some makes and model of classic cars enjoyed a brief, if rather speculative, price bubble in the course of the late 1980s. The bubble burst, and prices of many cars like this are still recovering. But recovering they are. Many enthusiasts have found to their pleasure and surprise over the last few years that the classic or veteran car under wraps in the garage may have held its value rather better than most stock market investments.

Like many collectors, classic car enthusiasts have a particular image. It is divided roughly into two types. One type is the oil stained, overall-wearing, bobble-hatted enthusiast inspecting a dilapidated Morris Minor on a windswept showground. The other is a toff in a deerstalker competing on the London-Brighton run. But neither image is wholly correct. Many enthusiasts are just ordinary individuals with a love of motoring history. Owning a piece of history in the form of a car is one way of giving expression to that interest.

Some wealthier individuals take their interest a stage further. Affluent collectors may own cars with a view to participating in rallies and concours d'elegance, or competing in historic races, or else going to Royal Ascot or Glyndebourne in a particular type of car simply 'to be seen'. Affluent collectors and superhobbyists may own one or more cars appropriate to each type of activity: a Jaguar D-type for the historic race; a vintage Bentley for the 'concours d'elegance; and an old Rolls Royce for the Glyndebourne picnic.

That side of owning a classic car isn't really what interests us for the purpose of this book. What we can say is that when it comes to buying and selling, it is more than likely that superhobby investors in the classic car market will be buying from and selling to enthusiasts rather than other investors.

So how do cars stack up as investments? What are the pluses and minuses? And how have investors in classic cars fared over the years?

Basics

The obvious rules that apply to all forms of superhobby collecting apply to classic cars, but with an extra twist.

Scarcity and condition are a key determinant of price, but not the only one. Fashion and even press comment also dictate prices to a much greater degree than in some other alternative asset markets. Would-be car investors also need to bear in mind that, unlike stamps, coins and art, for example, the investment is in a mechanical item that has running costs associated with it. This has some tax benefits, but it has some other drawbacks too.

Car genres

Let's begin at the beginning with some basic definitions. There are several recognised categories of classic car. Cars built before 1930 are, by common consent, called 'vintage' cars. Cars built between 1930 and WW2 are often called 'post vintage'. Some of the more fanciful writers on the subject sometimes call them 'post vintage thoroughbreds', although the distinction - to me at least - is a little obscure. Those cars built in the post-war era fall under the general epithet of 'classic cars', even if they are as little as, say, 20 years old.

Some enthusiasts also dub cars of more than ten years old as 'modern classics', even if they were not considered particularly distinguished ones at the time. It depends on your point of view.

Cars featured in films - VW Beetles, Mini Coopers, BMW M3s and so on - are a good starting point for working out which motors might attain this 'modern classic' status. In many instances, though, the term reflects nothing more or less than the opinions of motoring journalists about which cars might attract a fan club following as time goes by. They may or may not prove to be right.

> **Car genres**
>
> - Vintage - pre-1930
> - Post vintage - 1930-1945
> - Classic - 1945-1973
> - Modern classic - 1973- 1988

One important watershed recognised by all car enthusiasts, however, is that classic cars are zero-rated for road tax if they were built before 1st January 1973. Originally the idea, first mooted in the days of a Tory government, was that any car older than 25 years would be placed in this category. Under Labour, the 1973 date has been fixed for some time. Note that the time cut-off relates to when the car was built, not when it was registered.

Balancing all this up is difficult but, as Rick Jones of the web site Oldclassiccar.co.uk notes: 'the term classic car is now accepted as applying to any car over, say, 15 years of age that has some fan base to draw upon'.

It is also worth noting that many of the hardened collectors of classic cars also collect other motor vehicles, such as old motorcycles, and even old commercial vehicles. Car auctions sometimes include commercial vehicles such as old 'Routemaster' buses, charabancs, lorries, pick-up trucks, tractors and the like, as well as motoring memorabilia of one sort or another. I have even been to a car auction where the most enthusiastic bidding of all surrounded a die cast model toy tractor dating back to the 1950s.

The motives that drive collectors to acquire particular cars can be a complex mixture. Tim Schofield, classic cars expert at Bonhams, has isolated ten one-word reasons why collectors buy. They are: nostalgia; engineering; prestige; symbolism; fantasy; design; obsession; patriotism; affection; and rarity.

But as with stamps, coins and other alternative assets, there can be a difference, when it comes to choosing a car, between picking something you like and picking something that will prove to be a good investment.

In general for investment purposes we can forget buying cars that need major restoration jobs to achieve their optimum value - unless you are prepared to do all the restoration work yourself and ignore the opportunity cost of the time devoted to it.

While an old Jaguar or Morris Minor picked up in a country auction or rescued from a breakers yard might seem a tempting project, restoration is time consuming and the costs of the work unpredictable. This means that identifying and guaranteeing your return is a much more difficult prospect, unless the car in question is extremely rare.

Why collectors buy

- Nostalgia
- Engineering
- Prestige
- Symbolism
- Fantasy
- Design
- Obsession
- Patriotism
- Affection
- Rarity

A car bought for £5,000 as a restoration project may only be worth £20,000 in mint condition, but restoration work could easily cost £40,000-50,000, leaving the would-be investor out of pocket. Only in the case of the few very rare cars that could be worth £500,000 in mint condition and where the owner has £100,000 or more to spend on restoration can a return be guaranteed.

The example I know personally where this type of restoration work has been successfully done was on a wrecked old Jaguar saloon. The only drawback was that the owner was the scion of a large family-owned motor dealership and repair shop and was able to put mechanics to work on the job, when other work was slack, at no cost to himself.

So what do you need as a precondition for pursuing classic car investing on a serious basis?

More than just an interest in cars and a liking for driving them, that's for sure.

Maintenance

Unless you are wealthy enough to employ a chauffeur-cum-mechanic, you need basic mechanical expertise to be a serious classic car collector. This is because you may need to identify minor (or even major) faults that crop up from time to time. You have to be able to rectify them yourself without necessarily having to call in expensive outside help. Any outside help you do bring in, if it is from a commercial entity like a garage, is going to cost money and deplete your return.

It is also vitally important that you have a secure dry place to store and work on any vehicles you buy as an investment. If this isn't possible, remember that storing a car under a so-called protective cover is not advisable. It will simply trap rust-causing moisture on the bodywork and hasten the car's demise.

Remember too that cars also need to be used regularly if they are to stay in reasonable working order. If they are not given a few outings each year, it is quite likely that the brakes and clutch will seize up and cost money to put right. The corollary is that if the car is to be used, it needs to be maintained in a roadworthy condition, insured and licensed.

Maintenance in general is a big subject, but there are a number of issues that need to be addressed. It starts from the day you contemplate buying the vehicle.

At this point, quite apart from giving a car a good check-over in the company of an expert, you need to know several other items of information. For example, has the car has been adapted by its previous owners to run on lead-free petrol? How easy is it to get basic spare parts for the car, especially spare body parts? And how easy or otherwise is it to find matching paint?

The last point is important. Bodywork deteriorates and may need replacing or repairing, and in turn this will necessitate a paint job. Some colours have been long discontinued and may be difficult to match. An unpopular colour may also be one reason why a car is offered at a discount to the price you might expect. If you buy it despite this, remember that it may be hard to move when you want to sell it.

While it is probably naïve to expect to find a 25-year old car in its original condition, crude and obvious modifications to the car, such as a new or radically different engine type from the original, should be avoided. This is because they may limit the resale appeal of the car when the time eventually comes to sell it. Many cars converted in such a way are, according to experts, worth little more than half the price of ones that are largely in their original form and colour.

Collecting themes

The collecting theme or genre you choose to adopt depends in large measure on the amount of undercover workshop and storage space you have at your disposal. It will also reflect the capital you have available to allocate to your investment.

The basic rules of any form of serious collecting apply here too: buy the best you can afford and look for the best combination of condition and scarcity value.

The classic car market is made up of many different strata, each with their own price brackets and devoted band of enthusiasts.

Supercars

At the top end of the superhobby investing market for cars are the classic 'supercars' like Ferraris or Maseratis. These have also been made in strictly limited quantities because of their high price when new. Here it is the combination of power and glamour that cars like this exude, as well as their exclusivity, that makes them an investment proposition.

Would-be investors should be warned, however, that it has been this area that in the past has attracted most speculative money, almost to the point that places on the waiting list for particular cars were traded like options. You need to beware of buying at this end of the market if bubble-like conditions seem to be prevalent.

Vintage cars

Cars from the early years of motoring may be interesting as collectors items but are often less attractive as investments. Many of the classics, like Model T Fords or 1930s Morris saloons, were made in such quantities as to lack any scarcity value and therefore tend to have prices that remain relatively stable over long periods. That said, some commentators detect a pick-up in interest from cars made in the very early days of motoring that are now more than 100 years old and this suggests interest in the cars of the 1920s and 1930s may gather pace over the next decade or two.

> ### Key collecting themes
>
> - Supercars
> - Vintage cars
> - Sports cars
> - Post-war classic saloons
> - Commercial vehicles

Sports cars

One area that attracts persistent interest is the sports car market, if only because many affluent collectors, invariably male, think back to the times when, in their testosterone-charged youth, they might have liked to own one of these cars but were unable to afford it. On a more rational basis, owning a sports car is probably simply something aspirational. Later models are more easily driveable, with handling closer to that of their present day equivalent.

One plus point for many classic sports cars is that they are generally quite well served for spare parts and have sizeable owners clubs around the world. This is actually an important general point when it comes both to buying a classic car and selling one. Owners' clubs can be a source of a great deal of advice for potential buyers and sellers of the make and models in question.

Back in the sports car market, the best placed from the owners' club standpoint is understood to be the T series MG. Later versions and analogues of classics like this - the MG Midget, MGB and Austin Healey, for example - are also eminently collectable and in reasonably ready supply. The same is true of cars like the Morgan, and even modern classic performance cars like the Saab 99 Turbo and, believe it or not, the Ford Capri.

Post-war saloon cars

Among saloon cars, there is a range of vehicles which were made for the mass market and which qualify as classics. Examples include the Austin A40, Austin Cambridge, Rover 3500, Ford Popular, Ford Anglia, Ford Prefect, Mark 1 Ford Cortina and Corsair, the Triumph Herald, the old-style VW Beetle, the DAF, the older-style Volvo 'Amazon', and the Citroen 2CV, as well as the ubiquitous and much loved Morris Minor. The trick is finding mass-produced cars like this in collectable condition, since many of them were not built to last.

Commercial vehicles

Commercial vehicles present their own particular difficulties, not least because of the difficulty of storing them and also because spares may be hard to come by. Even in the case of small vans, for example, contrary to what you might imagine, parts are sometimes not interchangeable with those of the saloon version on which were based.

Small vans fetch better prices than larger lorries. Large lorries have major upkeep and storage issues that put them outside the reach of normal collectors.

Is it right for you?

Let's look at the questions you need to answer to determine whether classic cars might have a place in your wider portfolio of investments.

Are you investing for the medium to long term?

Like many other categories of superhobby investing, classic cars generally fulfil their potential over the longer term. However, be warned. The market is much more cyclical than other forms of tangible asset investing, with the possible exception of some segments of the art market.

This is a two-edged sword. If you buy the right model at the right price, perhaps when prices are depressed, your return could come relatively quickly, with a decent uplift over 3-5 years. High-end cars like Ferraris and Aston Martins, for example, have almost doubled in price over this period. They are now returning to the prices reached at the height of the boom in the late 1980s, but this time largely on the back of genuine demand from collectors rather than speculators.

Pay a premium price just before an economic downturn brings out forced sellers and you could be left with an asset that drops sharply in value and costs money to maintain.

Not only do you have to invest long term to get your return in the classic car market, but you also need to be savvy enough to cope with the market's volatility.

Do you have adequate capital?

There is no minimum or maximum investment involved in the classic car market, but like most things, you get what you pay for. Your capital dictates the type of car you can go for, and also whether or not you can buy more than one to spread your risk. You need to choose your make and model carefully and decide whether you want to risk all your available capital on one particularly good example, or buy two or three different models to diversify.

The price range in classic cars is huge. I recently saw a beautiful 'Inspector Morse' style Jaguar saloon sell for £6,000 at a provincial auction, at what I would judge to be a pretty good price for an example that seemed in superb condition.

These days you could pay £300,000 for a 40-year old classic Ferrari or less than £1,000 for a Ford Popular of the same vintage. Some cars that lack scarcity will sell for hundreds rather than thousands. A budget of £10,000 should allow you to own two or three moderately priced classics. Serious collectors can spend appreciably more.

Are you prepared for storage and maintenance costs?

This is one of the drawbacks of collecting classic cars. You need to have a dry, secure garage or garages in which to keep your collection. The cars need care and attention, including some routine maintenance. There are running costs to bear in mind, although these are generally less onerous than for a new modern car. Spare parts, where they are available, are often of a simpler design and lower price than their modern equivalent. Insurance is often available relatively cheaply from specialist providers, reflecting the fact that insurers recognise that collectors take considerable care of their cars. There may be a mileage restriction written into the insurance policy. But maintenance and running costs must be factored in and deducted from any return when the investment is realised.

> **Right for you?**
>
> - Prices can be volatile
> - Prices from £100 to £100,000+
> - Storage and maintenance costs can loom large
> - Cyclical price movements mean poor diversification
> - Need to be interested in cars
> - Wasting asset - so no CGT

Is portfolio diversification an objective?

The jury is out on whether or not classic cars outperform the stock market or run counter to it. Common sense, and past history, suggests that classic car prices are susceptible to the economic cycle and it is a matter of record that prices have experienced periods of boom and bust in the past - the last boom having been deflated in the early 1990s at the same time as the last serious property crash. Timing and selection is everything in the classic car market, making it not that dissimilar to the stock market and therefore perhaps less than suitable for diversification purposes.

Do you have an interest in cars?

I have to confess personally to having little interest in old cars. I am not mechanically minded and regard a car as a lump of metal simply designed to get me from A to B. Moreover, I don't possess anywhere near sufficient storage space to start a collection of classic cars. However, if you are interested in tinkering under a car bonnet, have a knowledge of cars and what makes them tick, and possess sufficient knowledge to recognise a good example from a bad one that could fall apart once you get it home, then this avenue of investing could be for you.

Are there tax considerations?

The short answer to this question is 'yes'. One of the big plus points for investing in classic cars is that they are rightly considered a wasting asset by the Inland Revenue and therefore, provided you do not buy and sell them often enough to be regarded as a dealer, there is no capital gains tax levied on any profit you make buying and selling them.

Whatever you do, however, don't let the tax status blind you to the fact that these are inherently risky investments. More so, perhaps than other areas, like antique clocks and watches, that share the same tax status but are less troublesome to maintain and store.

It is difficult to point to consistent returns from classic cars that would be enhanced by their tax-free status. So to some degree the tax question is a bogus one. It might prove difficult to make consistent money investing in classic cars, in which case their tax status is neither here nor there.

Prices and returns

It is a mistake to assume that classic cars are one big homogeneous market that delivers uniform returns to investors. Even leaving aside questions of condition and the sharp difference in prices that can result from it, there are trends in the classic car market that are down to national differences and to sentiment.

For instance, the US classic car market is separate and distinct from the UK and European ones. Different makes and models of cars have different associations and resonance with buyers, and therefore prices and collecting or investment habits cannot really be compared.

One point that has been noticed, however, is that prices paid even for British cars in the US market have been exceptionally firm of late. An auction in Scottsdale, Arizona at the beginning of 2003 saw 90% of the 800 cars on offer sold on the day. This is a statistic that might amaze those used to attending some car auctions in the UK, where it is not uncommon for a significant percentage of cars to fail to reach their reserve price. An exceptional British example at this Arizona auction was a Morris Minor Traveller, which fetched roughly three times what might have been considered the best price then obtainable in the UK.

This may be due to quirks of the British market. In the UK, it is frequently argued, a sizeable percentage of the collector base is obsessed with condition, while sellers expect unrealistic prices from the cars they offer onto the market. In the US the market may be driven more by a 'money no object' mentality, a pumped-up auction atmosphere and sellers prepared to accept the judgement of the market rather than quibble unduly.

However, the example is evidence of one trend in the market. It is that, while some British collectors may be parochial in their view, in general at the serious collecting and would-be investor end of the classic car arena, the market is an international one.

Returns
- Size and pattern is uncertain
- Prices still recovering from aftermath of 1990 bubble
- Maintenance and running costs deplete returns
- Long term returns around 6.4% pa
- Wide variation in returns from different segments of the market
- Condition is vital

There are other trends at work too. According to a recent article in the Financial Times, the overall long-term return in the prices of classic cars since 1981 has been a very modest 6.4% per annum. This estimate is according to data from Art Market Research. But this conceals some very different trends between different categories, with the more modern sports and performance cars of the 1960s gaining significantly, while older cars from the 1920s and 1930s, which you might think would be scarcer and therefore more valuable, seeing prices little changed.

Even prices of more opulent cars - Rolls Royces and Bentleys - from the immediate post war period have gained little, perhaps as little as 1-2% a year from 1981 to the present. By contrast classic Ferraris and Aston Martins have shown respectable growth, with gains in the region of 10% or more per annum over this two-decade period.

The other facet of the market that needs to be factored into the equation is the cyclical nature of classic car prices.

I have alluded already to the fact that there was a major boom in the market in the late 1980s and prices peaked in 1990, and then quickly halved after the bubble burst in late 1990.

There may have been technical factors behind that price action. This period in the UK coincided with recession, a property collapse and negative equity. Many cars may have been forced sales by customers who needed to placate nervous bankers. In addition it is known that there was a considerable amount of speculative money chasing prices of the more prestigious marques, notably Ferraris.

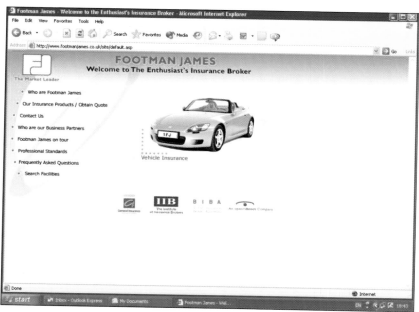

Insure your classic car through Footman James

If returns look impressive since the last bubble burst, the information can be taken two ways. The optimists might argue that it could mean that the market is gathering itself for another leap forward, or else that price speculation is likely to be confined to the higher priced items, out of reach of all but the most affluent investors. In fact what the data shows is that investing in classic cars is a highly subjective business. Some models seem to do well - the Aston Martin DB6 and the humble Morris Minor - but many do not.

How to buy and sell

Buying a classic car is deceptively easy. There are plenty of magazines devoted to the hobby, all with classified advertising. Magazines such as Classic Cars, Classic & Sportscar, The Automobile, and Practical Classics all fall into this category.

It may be possible to locate a car over the web, using auction sites, although the problem here may be inspecting the car prior to purchase. A visual and hands-on inspection, 'kicking the tyres' to use a well-worn expression, is a sine qua non when buying mechanical items whose condition is vitally important.

If you have a particular make and model in mind, another route is joining the relevant owners' club even before you buy. This could allow you to access details of cars for sale that never appear in the press and are simply passed around among enthusiasts.

Another benefit of being in an owners' club is that it can help with an inspection, since there will be experts on hand who are prepared to help you assess the mechanical condition of your target and how much it might be worth paying for it.

Canny buying

- Auctions not necessarily poor value
- Prices easy to check
- Get a second opinion on a vehicle's condition
- Owners' clubs can help

Beyond this, the oldclassiccar.co.uk web site has a checklist of items to watch for when performing a check on a car, including instructions on how to check for rust. You probably also need to assess the spare parts situation before you buy, including the cost and availability of spare body panels when you do so, as these are often the hardest to find. This may affect the price you are prepared to pay.

Obviously the usual cautions apply to the mechanical condition of the vehicle. You need to start it up and listen for ominous sights and sounds, and take it for a test drive. Be wary if the engine is warm when you arrive for your inspection. This may indicate the car has already been warmed up before you arrive and could conceal cold starting problems.

Auctions are another way of buying and are not necessarily a particularly expensive route either. Many auctions are held each year and buyers can afford to be choosy, which opens up an avenue for an opportunistic purchaser with capital to spend to get a bargain.

Selling a car is the same process in reverse. The choices of outlets are the same and the same ground rules apply. Cosmetic touches like buffing up the tyres and polishing leather upholstery can help sell a car, and some cars, like convertibles, may sell better in the spring and summer when their virtues can be shown off to best advantage.

Unlike in other areas, auctions are not necessarily the best route to the best selling price (except perhaps at the top end of the market where money is no object). This is simply because they are now so common as to allow would-be buyers to pick and choose and because the market is well served by mass circulation publications with classified advertising.

Sellers also sometimes forget that going the auction route sometimes involves extra costs with some auction houses charging 15% sellers commission on the hammer price and even applying this to the reserve if the car doesn't sell.

As with other collectable areas the best advice is to go for quality, for something that has an iconic quality, and to buy the best you can afford in top quality condition.

Where to go for more information

There is no shortage of information on classic cars, from the various magazines already mentioned through to specialist web sites. Here are a few web-based sources of information and places to buy and sell.

Bonhams (www.bonhams.com) motoring department sells vehicles at auction from the 1890s to the present day. Sales are held throughout the year across the UK, sometimes associated with a motoring event such as the Goodwood Festival of Speed. Descriptions of lots for sale are on the site when they become available.

The Complete Automobilist (www.completeautomobilist.co.uk) sells vintage and classic motoring parts. Parts can be ordered online and the site features an online catalogue. A printed version can be ordered online.

'Rusty Ricks' Old Classic Car (www.oldclassiccar.co.uk) run by a classic car enthusiast is a comprehensive site covering all aspects of running classic or vintage cars. The site includes articles on choosing, buying and running a classic car, photographs, images and postcards of cars from both the UK and USA, information on choosing possible future classics and much more.

'Rusty Rick's' old classic car site

The Ugliest Cars in Britain (www.uglycars.co.uk) according to the site owners is 'a totally pointless web site' featuring the most hideous cars past or present.

Vintage Supplies (www.vintagecarparts.co.uk) are specialist mail-order suppliers of classic car parts, fittings and accessories with the emphasis on veteran and vintage car parts. The catalogue can be viewed online or a printed version ordered by email.

Collectors of American cars might find Classic Car (www.classiccar.com) of interest.

Classic Cars (www.classiccars.co.uk) has links to dealers throughout the UK and Worldwide plus information of auctions, news and events.

Classic cars web site

Paradise Garage (www.paradisegarage.co.uk) of Sloane Avenue, London SW3 is a specialised dealer in collectable cars. The site features a virtual showroom with email contact for further information.

J.D.Classics (www.jdclassics.co.uk) of Chelmsford, Essex, specialise in selling, buying and maintaining classic Jaguar racing cars.

Gregor Fisken (www.gregorfisken.com) of Kensington caters for all budgets and tastes. The site features an online newsletter.

Insurance broker Footman James (www.footmanjames.co.uk) has a specialised vehicle department dealing with all classic motor vehicles.

Table 6.1 - Classic Cars - key web addresses and contact details

Company	Web address	Email	Phone	Type
Bonhams	www.bonhams.com	cars@bonhams.com	020 7393 3900	Auction
Car Collector	www.carcollector.com	editorial@carcollector.com	n/a	Information
Classic Car	www.classiccar.com	news@classiccar.com	n/a	Links
Classic Cars	www.classiccars.co.uk	On site	n/a	Links
Classics and Customs	www.classicsandcustoms.com	On site	n/a	Links
Complete Automobilist	www.completeautomobilist.co.uk	orders@completeautomobilist.co.uk	0177 842 6222	Dealer
Footman James	www.footmanjames.co.uk	On site	0845 458 6782	Insurance
Gregor Fisken	www.gregorfisken.com	cars@gregorfisken.com	020 7584 3503	Dealer
JD Classics	www.jdclassics.co.uk	On site	01245 400060	Dealer
Oldclassiccar	www.oldclassiccar.co.uk	dodgenut@4onthefloor.co.uk	n/a	Information
Paradise Garage	www.paradisegarage.co.uk	sales@paradisegarage.co.uk	020 7584 0660	Dealer
Ugly Cars	www.uglycars.co.uk	On site	n/a	Information
Vintage Car Parts	www.vintagecarparts.co.uk	info@vintagecarparts.co.uk	01692 650455	Dealer

Chapter 7 | Coins

In chapter ten, which covers investing in gold, we are going to see that it's possible to buy gold coins like South African Krugerrands and Australian Koalas. It's simply a way to buy bullion.

If you want to invest in gold coins and those made from other precious metals, it pays to distinguish between bullion coins like Krugerrands, which are minted regularly, and rare gold coins - like sovereigns. Rare coins may have some bullion content, but investors and collectors value them for different reasons - primarily their rarity and condition. In this case, the bullion content of the coin is, if not irrelevant, usually far outweighed by the scarcity value of the coin.

Prices are set differently too. Present day bullion coins have a value that is 99% determined by the value of the weight of metal they contain. That price is set every day. But rare coins, which also include coins other than those made of gold or silver, have a price that varies according to condition and is usually determined by annual coin catalogues, dealers' lists and above all auction results.

Rather like stamps, which we look at in chapter eleven, you can both collect coins and invest in them. The two activities are not mutually exclusive. Some collectors become investors as they gradually upgrade their collections by selling the more common items to buy a smaller number of rare pieces. Some of those who start off as investors may get 'hooked' and develop an interest that goes way beyond mere consideration of investment returns.

Like stamp investment, assembling a collection of investment quality coins is a similar process to investing in the stock market. Certain coins move in and out of favour, and like stamps, demand for coins is broadly linked to the state of the economy and the spending power of the underlying collector base. In both cases the collector base is international.

> ## Coin investing - the essentials
>
> - Different from bullion coins
> - Prices set by dealers, not metal markets
> - Portfolio approach, similar to stock market
> - Spending power of collector base provides liquidity

Superhobby investors in coins can pick a portfolio of ten or twenty items to avoid undue dependence on any one particular coin, and can buy additional items if they wish as they go along, adding to their portfolio over time.

As is also the case with stamps the coin dealer can play the role of an advisory broker, drawing attention to possible new portfolio additions, and perhaps highlighting the potential to take a profit in an item that has risen too far in value relative to the rest of the market.

As a stock market investor, you should be pretty relaxed with this approach, because it is similar to the one you should have adopted for your stock exchange investments. Like stamps, coins form an easily understandable, well-researched and documented investment category. The sizeable collector base provides liquidity.

Coin basics

Coinage was first introduced in Ionia around 650BC. This long history means there is infinite variety in the types of coins that can be collected for either aesthetic or investment purposes. In turn this means that you probably need to pick a theme or series of themes around which to base your superhobby portfolio, avoiding those areas that are temporarily fashionable and picking those that have long term potential.

Coins are split into two broad types: the older hammered variety and the more modern milled type. Hammered coins were produced by hitting two interlocking pieces of iron or bronze with a hammer. On the inside, the bronze or iron dies contained the imprint for each face of the coin. These were typically the head of the monarch on one side and the coin's denominations and some other pattern on the other.

The two parts of the die were slotted together after inserting a blank coin after which a hammer blow imprinted the pattern simultaneously on both sides of the coin. This is clearly a slow and cumbersome way of creating coins and prone to error.

Milled coins, produced in large quantities from the mid 17th century onwards, are machine made. Milled coins have much more precise definition and uniformity.

The machining of coins also enabled the introduction of milled edges and inscriptions, which prevented the coins being clipped.

Coins were clipped, especially in the days when they were backed by silver or some other precious metal, so that small amounts of metal removed from a number of coins could be used to make another one, thus yielding the clipper a profit.

We'll come onto the condition of the coins you buy later. This is a separate subject in its own right, and vitally important to the value of a coin.

Typically coin collectors will look to collect the coins of one country or group of countries, coins from a particular historical era or geographical region, or else coins that have something unusual about them - either commemorative sets, or those with errors, or the same or similar coins with different varieties of die.

A common collecting theme is to collect a set series: one coin of each type for each year the coin was minted during the reign of a particular ruler and including any design variations that may have been introduced, or those originating from different mints.

Some coin collecting themes

- Ancient or 'modern', hammered or milled
- All the coins of one monarch's reign
- Coins from all monarchs' reigns
- Coins of different countries
- Oriental coins
- Proof coins and errors

As a general rule, it makes sense to collect and invest in the coins of the country where you live because the chances are that you will be more aware of its history and better able to judge what makes a particular coin special.

From a more practical standpoint, it also makes sense for UK collectors to collect British coins for another reason. It is likely that the biggest volume of coin dealing and largest number of collectors of this type of coin will also be in the home market.

The goal of having a complete set of say, the coins of Henry VIII is within the reach of most collectors or investors: remember that millions of examples of the coins in question were produced and unlike stamps, for example, coins are much more durable and almost never discarded. So, unlike scripophily for example, there are no limits on the number of complete collections of this type that can be assembled.

This brings us on to the factors that go to make up the price of a rare coin. In reality it's simply common sense. The value of a collectable coin depends primarily on its date and design, on its precisely graded condition, on its mintmark, and on the supply and demand for that particular type of coin at any one time. The coin's condition, that's to say its state of preservation is of paramount importance in determining price and saleability.

One way of making sure that the coins you buy for investment have a scarcity value is to collect only those of monarchs with a short reign, and who are not known to have debased the currency to a greater than normal degree. So for example, Eadred (946-955), Richard III (1483-85); Edward VI (1547-53), Mary and Philip (1553-58), the Commonwealth (1649-1660) and so on, may make good subjects for coin investment. On the other hand, the chances of finding coins like this in sufficiently good condition to warrant investment may be harder.

Some collectors go for more ambitious targets, at least in terms of the potential size of a collection. One interesting theme is to attempt a collection of all the coin issues during the years of Victoria's reign. While there is plenty of material like this around, there are also plenty of collectors of it, and hence potential buyers and sellers.

Another wrinkle is that, for a long-reigning monarch, several different styles of coinage may have been issued, each with a different representation of the monarch, some of which are more collectable than others.

As we'll also find out in the chapter on stamps, condition is the single biggest factor governing its price. The next section looks in more detail at how to grade the condition of a coin, and how to keep it in that condition once you have bought it.

Condition

As with many superhobby-style assets, condition is crucial to its value. But it isn't as simple as it might seem.

Coins are sometimes called 'proof' or 'prooflike' if they have particularly sharp definition. This is a special category of coins, collectable in its own right, but not to be confused with the grading that is applied to coins in general.

'Proof' coins are struck from specially prepared dies as samples of new coinage. They frequently have plain edges, rather than milled ones, and a mirror like finish that comes from the highly polished dies from which they are struck. 'Prooflike' coins are the first examples of new coins for circulation struck from these dies.

The table opposite shows the variations of condition that are generally accepted for coins in the UK. The US has its own slightly different terminology. At the margin the variations in condition may only be detectable under a magnifying glass, although some will be more obvious.

To a degree this terminology of the grading given to a coin is subjective and some dealers are more cautious than others in the grade they give. This argues for going to a reputable and long established dealer whose gradings are consistent and reliable. Less expert dealers may tend to overgrade coins.

UK grading terms for coins	
FDC	'Fleur de coin'. Perfect mint state.
BU	'Brilliant uncirculated'. Used of modern coins. Full lustrous mint condition.
UNC	'Uncirculated'. Some loss of lustre due to exposure to air.
EF	'Extremely fine'. Magnification shows wear on high points, fine scratches.
VF	'Very fine'. Clearly in circulation, but clear detail.
F	'Fine'. Noticeable wear on high points, details faded.
Fair	Worn, but with features and legend clearly distinguishable.
Poor	No value to a collector.

Note: American terms describe 'poor' coins as 'fair', and 'fair' as 'very good'.

The tone of the coin is also important. Tone signifies a coin that has, with time, acquired a colour that is deeper and richer than the original. The importance of toning usually applies to older coins. Most collectors and investors prefer more modern coins to have their full lustre, as though they had just been minted. But a brown or green patina on ancient bronze and copper coins is said to increase their value substantially.

Tones are also evident on old coins made from precious metals. Silver can have a golden tone ranging through to an almost black or plum colour. Tone can also affect the raised parts of the coin differently from the rest. While to some degree the attractiveness of the tone can be subjective, an attractively toned coin could add as much as 40-50% to the value of a coin over and above one that has no tone.

The legend on a coin can have an impact on its value, especially in cases where the monarch's name has been misprinted or abbreviated. This is not uncommon on older coins where the literacy of those making the coins may not have been high, making occasional mistakes more likely. Mintmarks on the coin, usually a single letter to indicate where it was made, are also a distinguishing feature and can have a significant effect on value.

The edges of a coin are also important to its value. Edges that have been knocked or damaged in some way warrant a discount to the price of those that don't have this sort of imperfection.

Some dates are much rarer than others. In the UK, a 1933 penny is scarce. The same is true of an 1804 dollar, an Australian 1919 shilling and a Canadian 1921 50 cent piece. These capture the public's imagination, but the date alone is rarely the basis for a good investment.

Though there is a temptation to do so, coins should not be cleaned. This is because most methods of cleaning will result in some abrasion to the coin's surfaces and the removal of what may otherwise have been a valuable patina or lustre. According to dealers any form of treatment of this sort can more than halve the value of the item, and the risk is just not worth taking. An expert can easily detect treatment of this sort.

Key factors in value

- Scarcity
- Condition
- Tone
- Legend
- Mintmark

Protecting your coin portfolio once acquired is a separate subject in itself. We have already alluded to the need to store coins securely in a safe or safety deposit box if your collection is of considerable value. Insurance is also a good precaution, though sometimes neglected.

Most important, if you have your coin collection on the premises is to take great care in storing and handling them. Coins are sensitive to moisture, and dropping them will cause damage and affect their value. Even handling them carelessly will make a difference. Wear gloves when handling coins. The human finger contains a corrosive salt that will damage copper and bronze coins and tarnish silver ones.

It is essential as far as possible to store items in an airtight, moisture free seasoned hardwood box (mahogany is a popular choice). Coins should be stored out of sunlight, in a storage system made from inert material. You should not place items in contact with each other or with any other metal object.

Is it right for you?

Investing in coins, as with many of the superhobby investment categories in this book, can provide you with a hedge against inflation. Coin prices tend to rise as the general level of prices rise. This is because, as is also the case with stamps, the general well being and spending power of the collector base is all-important.

Let's look at the questions you need to answer to determine whether coins could form a place in your wider portfolio of investments.

Are you investing for the medium to long term?

Investing for the long term is crucial. The May 2003 auction by Spink of the Slaney collection of British coins suggested that the optimum period for investing in coins could be as long as 50 years. The sale of Lord Hamilton of Dalzell's collection in 1979 also contained coins acquired over a 50-year period. Holding a portfolio of coins for this length of time may not be necessary to achieve good returns, but the certainty of achieving excellent returns probably increases the longer you hold them.

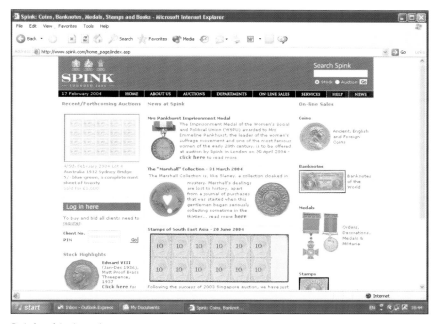

Spink - big in coins

Do you have adequate capital?

Whether or not you feel able to afford an investment in coins depends on the scale of your other assets, and what other superhobby investments you are contemplating. However, would-be investors need not be put off by the high headline prices fetched by some coins in the Slaney sale.

The very first lot in the Slaney sale, a coin dating from the reign of Henry VIII, sold for £900. Many coin dealers have stock dating from this era and earlier priced at a few hundred pounds. This enables those with modest amounts to invest to assemble a small but diverse portfolio for as little as £5,000, much as one might collect investment-grade stamps or Victorian watercolours. Those with more to invest can have their choice of individual coins ranging into thousands and tens of thousands of pounds. The most expensive coin in the Slaney collection was sold for £138,000. A Henry VIII gold sovereign might sell for £15,000.

Are you happy to pay storage and insurance costs?

As we will see in the later chapter dealing with stamps, you can if you wish hold your superhobby coin portfolio physically on your own property. But if you do, you need to invest in both insurance and security measures. One obvious measure is to install a safe. Safes designed for collectors can cost anything up to £1,000 plus VAT including installation. Unlike stamps, whose value is not readily apparent to the untutored eye, rare coins, especially gold and silver ones, would have obvious value to a thief. This means they probably do need a bit of extra special protection.

Right for you?

- Long term view essential - 25-50 years
- Coins available from £100 upwards
- Factor in cost of safekeeping
- Prices linked to economic wellbeing, not contracyclical
- Interest in history essential

Whether or not you wish to invest in security measures depends on whether or not you wish to have the coins available and on view at home, or whether you are content to have them stored in a bank or at a dealer's premises. Firms like Spink offer secure storage facilities for coins bought through them. Fully alarmed safety deposit boxes can be had for as little as £100 a year in Central London. Outside of London, a local branch bank may offer such a facility for less.

The decision you choose to make on the security standpoint really depends on the size of the collection you intend to build. If the collection is likely to be just a few high value items you want to see only occasionally, then a safety deposit box may be the best answer. If you want to have a larger collection at home, then a fireproof safe large enough to store your coin cabinet is essential.

Is portfolio diversification an objective?

Prices of rare coins should rise in line with economic growth and inflation. But unlike bullion coins like Krugerrands, they may not protect your wealth particularly well in the case of a severe economic downturn.

In short they have rate of return characteristics similar to some parts of the stock market, but without the volatility normally associated with day-to-day investment in shares. They are not true diversification in the sense that, say, gold is. Their prices move in line with, rather than against, the general trend in the stock market.

Paradoxically stamps, though flimsier, may have the edge over coins. They are less durable; so fewer good examples of top quality stamps exist. On the other hand, stamp history only goes back to the first half of the 19th century: coin collecting can stretch right back to the pre-Christian era.

Do you have an interest in history?

Numismatics is essentially about history. Enthusiasts would add that it also takes in economics, geography, heraldry, metallurgy, politics, art, and military history. Coins are essentially 'pictorial' historical items. They tell us about the conditions of the time they were issued, in both the good and bad senses of the word. Coins hint at war, revolution, currency debasement, human corruption, and even engineering prowess. While it is not essential to have an interest in this to buy coins for an investment, it helps.

Returns

Prices of coins are well documented and periodic auctions make it fairly easy to calculate returns.

Taking the Slaney auction at Spink in May 2003 as a benchmark, for example, we can see that the prices realised by this collection confirmed that there are highly respectable rates of return to be had in long-term quality coin investments.

A selection of 50 coins from the collection, acquired during the 1940's and 1950's at an aggregate cost of £2,350, fetched £460,000. If we assume the mid-point of the acquisition period for these items was 1950, this represents a compound return of 10.5% a year over the 53-year period involved.

The most spectacular result from the auction, the sale of a Charles II Pattern Crown from 1663 (known as the Petition Crown) produced a not dissimilar return. This was purchased in 1950 for £450 and sold in 2003 for £138,000 versus a pre-sale estimate of £40,000 to £50,000. The price realised represents a compound return of 11.4% per year.

The sale of Lord Hamilton of Dalzell's collection in 1979, again built up over a fifty-year period, appears to have resulted in a return of something in the region of 8.7% per annum.

By any stretch of the imagination these are respectable returns, but many investors will not want to wait for that length of time before cashing in their investment. Using the 1997 prices from the Seaby's coin catalogue edition for 1998 (see end of chapter for more details on this invaluable publication) and the latest Spink numismatic circular for end-2003 prices, we can see how the prices of 'very fine' coins have increased over this five-year period.

This is shown in the table below:

Table 7.1 - Changes in coin values over five years

Monarch	Coin	Cat. No	Value 1997	Value 2003	Compound return % pa
Addedomarus	?	202	430	1,800	27.0
Vep Corf	?	410	850	1,400	8.7
Early Anglo-Saxon	?	768a	1,250	2,500	12.3
Charles II	Shilling	3143	450	1,500	22.2
Cromwell	Crown	3226	1,850	3,250	9.9
Cromwell	Halfcrown	3227a	1,100	3,750	22.7
Charles II	Crown	3359	1,000	1,500	7.0
George I	Halfcrown	3642	500	1,100	14.0
George III	8 reals	3765a	150	1,000	37.2
George IV	Crown	3805	350	850	15.9
William IV	Proof shill.	3835	250	1,250	30.8
Victoria	Crown	3883	475	1,150	15.9

Note: Coins chosen for their significant current value. Price variations may reflect slight differences in condition.

All coin examples are VF or EF in both cases.

How to buy and sell

As with most of the categories in this book there are a number of different ways to buy coins for long-term investment purposes.

While those collecting for the purposes of a modest pastime may be content to buy smaller value coins by mail order or from dealers at fairs, those who are approaching the task from the standpoint of a serious superhobby investor need to be more cautious.

Buying 'sight unseen' is an absolute no-no. It is safe enough if you buy from an ultra-reputable dealer like Spink, Baldwins or Noble Investments (UK). But that is not the issue. Even then, it is surely important to view the coin before buying, especially if the resulting purchase is then going to be locked away in a safety deposit box.

Coin exhibitions are a good way of meeting a number of dealers clustered in the same place, and the competition helps to keep prices fair. Coinex, which takes place each year in October in London, is a good place to start.

Canny buying and selling

- Don't buy 'sight unseen'
- Use a reputable specialist dealer
- Coin exhibitions a good source of information and material
- Material in antique shops and sales may be suspect
- If selling at auction, set realistic reserves

Auctions of antiques, country house sales, flea markets, craft fairs and the like may be a source of material, although it is often the case that coins displayed in sales like this are overgraded, sometimes unintentionally and sometimes deliberately. Some dealers use sales like this to sell problem coins to uninformed buyers. Items on display at antique shops need careful examination for the same reason. A reference guide such as Seabys, as well as a magnifying glass, is an essential adjunct to any purchase.

The ideal way to buy is through a trusted and highly reputable dealer with whom you have a good relationship. If you are serious about building up a portfolio of coins, the dealer will realise that you are likely to represent a considerable source of future business and treat you accordingly.

Purchasing coins over the web falls foul of the strictures over being able to inspect the coins, although it is useful as a way of making contact with other collectors who have coins they wish to sell. You can then arrange to meet in person to view the coins and make a trade. We deal elsewhere in the book with the advantages and disadvantages of using online auctions like eBay.

Would-be coin investors should note that some well-known auction houses now permit internet bidding for coin auctions, although this should be a last resort. There is no substitute for being in the saleroom for gauging the right level to pitch a bid.

Selling a collection to harvest your returns may be the last thing on your mind as you begin your coin investing. Depending on the strength of the market the auction is probably the most favoured exit route, since it will attract a considerable number of buyers and potentially allow competitive bidding to drive the price up to an optimum level.

Setting realistic reserve prices (or even no reserve at all) is very important and bear in mind that your realisation will also be net of the saleroom commission. Getting a realistic estimate of your portfolio's value before submitting it to auction is also a good idea. Setting a reserve price can cost extra. Issues like this need thrashing out with the auction house before you commit yourself to a sale.

The table on page 138 sets out a list of coin dealers and auctioneers.

Where to go for information

As with many other areas of superhobby investing, the web has made some considerable difference to the business of coin dealing. The changes are arguably less marked than with stamps or books, since the three dimensional nature of a coin is harder to render on a web page than a two-dimensional stamp. Nonetheless dealers provide information and price lists on the web, and much coin dealing is done by mail order, notwithstanding the importance of seeing and examining coins before you buy.

The following are some comments on some useful web based sources of information, and print publications that can help with background information and prices.

Dealers and auctioneers

Baldwins (www.baldwin.sh) are a traditional family firm based in London. An online catalogue is featured on the site. A separate branch of the firm, Baldwins Auctions, holds auctions in London, Singapore, the Gulf States and New York. Forthcoming auctions and prices realized are both on the site.

Coincraft (www.coincraft.com) is a family firm based in the Bloomsbury area of London. The site has information on collecting as well as detailed information about the available stock. The 'Phoenix' newspaper is published monthly and contains a list of items for sale. This publication includes banknotes as well as coins. Special mailings are sent to favoured collectors.

The Coin Dealers Directory (www.numis.co.uk) is a list of coin dealers in the British Isles and has information on magazines, associations, clubs and other resources. The site includes a useful section on how to identify and value coins.

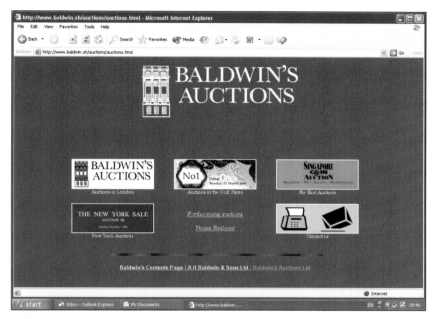

Baldwins, a specialist auctioneer for coins

The London auction house Dix Noonan Webb (www.dnw.co.uk) professes to have the largest online numismatic database in the world with over 40,000 coin and medal entries. All forthcoming auction catalogues are uploaded to the site a month before the sale. The site also features prices realized at auction, an auction calendar and news and articles. Members can request online valuations, submit bids for forthcoming auctions etc. A wide range of numismatic books is also on offer.

Glendining's, a division of Bonhams (www.bonhams.com) has been selling coins (and banknotes and scrip) at auction since the 1990's. An online catalogue is available on the site together with an auction diary.

The auction house Morton and Eden (www.mortonandeden.com) was set up in 2001. Its principals are two former Sotheby's directors. It still maintains a close association with Sotheby's. Catalogues of forthcoming and past sales are available on the site.

Table 7.2 – Coins – some key web addresses and contact details

Company	Web address	Email	Phone
Baldwins	www.baldwin.sh	coins@baldwin.sh	020 7930 6879
Bonhams (Glendinings)	www.bonhams.com	Andrew.Litherland@bonhams.com	020 7393 3900
Coincraft	www.coincraft.com	info@coincraft.com	020 7636 1188
Dix Noonan Webb	www.dnw.co.uk	chris@dnw.co.uk	020 7499 5022
Morton and Eden	www.mortonandeden.com	info@mortonandeden.com	020 7493 5344
Noble Investments	n/a	igoldbart@aol.com	020 7581 0240
Simmons Gallery	www.simmonsgallery.co.uk	simmons@simmonsgallery.co.uk	020 7831 2080
Spink	www.spink.com	info@spink.com	020 7563 4000

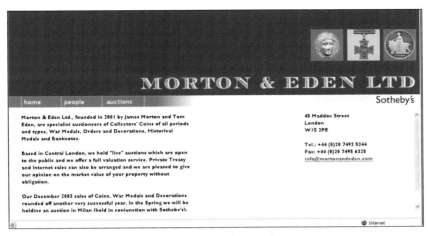

Morton & Eden - a relative newcomer to the market

Noble Investments (UK) is currently the only quoted coin dealer. It is run by Dimitri Loulakakis who, as owner of Chelsea Coins, has had some 40 years experience in the international coin market and has an excellent reputation for strict grading and fair dealing. Fellow director Ian Goldbart is an erstwhile coin collector of many years standing. The firm has recently recruited Helen Papaefthymiou, who has specific and highly regarded expertise in ancient Greek and Roman coins.

Simmons Gallery (www.simmonsgallery.co.uk) runs the London Coin Fairs. It also deals in coins and tokens online.

Spink (www.spink.com) was founded in 1666 and has been dealing in coins (and banknotes, medals and stamps) since 1703. The company is now in Bloomsbury close to the British Museum. Auctions are held frequently and a list is available on the website together with prices realized at previous auctions. The site also features a searchable database of available stock for sale online or in person. Past catalogues can also be viewed. The Spink Numismatic Circular is published six times a year and has details of coins for sale and articles on various numismatic topics.

The firm also publishes reference books on numismatics and carries a stock of major works on the subject together with rare and out of print books.

Information

British Coin Collector (www.britishcoincollector.co.uk) specialises in providing information on British coins and tokens from the Celtic period to the present day. The site includes coins for sale, news, books, and links to dealers, collectors and online auction sites.

The British Museum (www.thebritishmuseum.ac.uk) houses one of the world's finest numismatic collections, with about one million objects. It covers the entire history of coinage from the seventh century BC to the present day, and has a quantity of related material like moneyboxes and tokens. The site has a brief summary of the collection plus links to numismatic societies and museum collections in the UK and worldwide.

The Royal Mint (www.royalmint.com) has a wide range of information on both collectable and present-day coins. Although its primary purpose is to provide UK coinage, more than 100 countries have entrusted the striking of their coinage to the Royal Mint, such is its reputation. The site also includes links to other mints worldwide, an online British Royal Mint Museum tour and an online shop with coins and related articles for sale.

Coin News (www.tokenpublishing.com) publishes three yearbooks and two monthly magazines together with a range of other titles. 'Coin News' features a 'what's on' section with details of fairs, societies, and auctions. The magazine also has saleroom reports and book reviews.

Coin Resource (www.coinresource.com) is a US site with a 'Coin Encyclopedia' of American coins - with facts, photographs and history. Among the site's many other features are a beginners guide to collecting, articles on coins and numerous links.

Cornucopia (www.cornucopia.org.uk) is a searchable database of museum collections throughout the UK.

The Fitzwilliam Museum site (www-cm.fitzmuseum.cam.ac.uk/coins) is useful for background information. There is an online database of Greek coins in public and private collections in the British Isles plus links to numismatic projects and collections.

Societies

The American Numismatic Association (www.money.org) is useful for background information on the basics of coin collecting together with detailed information about American coins. The site also features virtual exhibits and collections.

The British Association of Numismatic Societies (www.coinclubs.freeserve.co.uk), based at the Manchester Museum, is the national organization for numismatic societies throughout the UK. Apart from links to societies the site has details of publications and video lectures by prominent numismatists, together with details of conferences and lectures.

The Oriental Numismatic Society (www.onsnumis.org) serves collectors of all types of oriental coinage, from North Africa to the Far East. The society publishes a newsletter four times a year with information and articles about individual coins, problems of dating them, and several other topics.

The Royal Numismatic Society (www.rns.dircon.co.uk) and The British Numismatic Society (www-cm.fitzmuseum.cam.ac.uk/coins/britnumsoc) are the leading academic numismatic societies in the UK. Both websites have details of their publications, prizes, history and events.

The British Numismatic Trade Association (www.numis.co.uk) has 70 member firms throughout the British Isles. These are listed on the site together with website links if available. The BNTA organise 'Coinex', the London coin fair, which takes place each October at the London Marriott Hotel. Details of the next forthcoming fair can be found on the site.

Books

Coincraft's Standard Catalogue of English and UK Coins (Coincraft)

This is a handbook of English and UK coins from 1066 to the present, with historical information, prices, a section on hammered and milled patterns and collecting tips plus other detailed information. It is printed in large size (A4) format with over 740 pages.

Coins and Investment (A Consumer's Guide) J.Pearson Andrew (Spink 1986)

This is a useful book covering all aspects of coin collecting from an investment point of view. Areas discussed include the various factors that determine the price of a coin, the coin market past and present, forgery, and a dictionary of coins and their history.

Coin Year Book (Token Publishing 2003)

This is a price guide and collectors handbook for UK coins. Articles include valuation for UK coins, a collector's review of the previous year, a guide to the latest auction prices, the storage of coins and much other useful information.

Seabys Standard Catalogue of British Coins (Spink)

This book is considered by many to be the 'bible' for coin collectors. It has been published regularly since 1929 and is a complete catalogue for British coins, providing an invaluable tool for collectors. The book also contains a useful beginners guide to coin collecting, with advice on buying and selling coins and detailed information on minting processes and condition. It is universally called 'Seaby's', after the original publishers, even though it has been owned and published by Spink for a number of years.

Standard Catalogue of World Coins Krause and Mishler (Krause Publications 2003)

Published annually, this has complete coverage of coins from 1601 to the present day, in four volumes, each covering a century. Each volume is lavishly illustrated and the four volumes in total comprise nearly 6,000 pages. Coins are priced in five grades of condition and include the mint number and date. The book also includes a guide to identifying coins, a coin sizing chart and international numerics and much more. As this is a US publication prices are given in American dollars.

8 Film and Theatre

All of the chapters in this book so far have dealt with investments that can be touched and admired, whether a work of art, antique, coin or car.

Investing in film and theatre is different. Investments like this have an aesthetic value, but less tangibility and permanence. A film or play may become a classic, and you may be lucky enough to invest in one. But this doesn't alter the fact that its value depends on its ability to attract members of the public to pay and see it. It isn't inherent in the production itself.

In some respects the same could be said of a work of art or an antique, but these have prices that are well documented and established regularly by competitive bidding at auction. This isn't true of film and theatre productions. Once a stage play closes, the future value of an investment in it is zero.

Furthermore unlike truly tangible assets, investments like this have no scarcity value. Hundreds of film proposals are put forward every month, and few have much chance of real commercial success, let alone of becoming a classic.

Forget about the glamour involved in the film industry. What you need for successful film investment is a grasp of how the tax system works - or someone who can advise you on it - and the ability to think long term. The first night parties and tickets for the premiere may be part of the deal, as might the supposed perk of being an extra on the film you invest in, but if you think these are important, you probably aren't approaching the investment in the right frame of mind.

That is not to say that investing in film and theatre is a waste of time, as we will find out. But we need to distinguish between two distinctly different types of investment. Investing in film finance, for example, can be done in a way that has limited risk and useful tax benefits.

> ## Film and theatre characteristics
>
> - Aesthetic value, but no tangible qualities
> - No transparent valuation
> - Once closed, zero value
> - Returns of some investments enhanced by tax relief
> - Invest in finance or productions?

Investing in film and theatre productions - where investors have equity-style exposure - is quite different. It is a much higher risk activity even than most normal stock market investing, but it can be done in ways that reduce the risks involved. Investing in film productions, however, has tax benefits that investing in theatrical productions doesn't.

Rather than look at all of these activities together, we have to recognise their substantial differences, and adopt a slightly different approach to that followed in other chapters. So we will look at film 'sale and leaseback' schemes first, then at investing in film productions, and then at investing in theatrical productions. At the end of the chapter we will look at how you can access information on all three main types of investment.

Film partnerships - 'Sale and Leasebacks'

Film partnerships use tax breaks that were originally introduced to encourage the production of British films. These enhance the returns to film partnerships considerably. Most film partnerships are unregulated collective investment schemes. Because they are unregulated they cannot be actively promoted to the general public, although many accountants and IFAs are fully aware of the advantages they confer. They take three main forms:

- 'Sale & leaseback' partnerships, which involve minimal commercial risk

- 'Production partnerships', which depend on the film's success for their returns

- 'Hybrid partnerships', which contain differing elements of both.

The basic attractions of film partnerships are that they have offered the opportunity to shelter (strictly speaking, to defer) unlimited amounts of current tax. Recent tax proposals have made some schemes unviable, but basic traditional sale and leaseback and production schemes are unaffected.

In this section we'll look at the sale and leaseback style of partnership, before going on in a subsequent section to look at those that derive a greater part of their return from the commercial success of the film or films involved.

'Sale and leaseback' film partnerships have received the lions' share of investor money in recent years and have been actively used by large firms of chartered accountants to shelter tax for wealthy clients. At its peak it was estimated that around £1.7bn of income and capital gains was sheltered in this way. Since then there has been some tightening of the tax rules relating to schemes like this.

So how do they work?

A film sale and leaseback scheme can be used to defer tax for up to 15 years.

Investors in a partnership have to make an upfront payment of around 20% of the amount they wish to shelter, and the rest is borrowed.

Film sale and leaseback summary

- Substantial upfront tax relief
- Need large amount of tax to shelter
- Best tax concession expires in 2005
- Tax deferral not tax offset
- Requires disciplined investment approach

When all the funds have been assembled the partnership buys a number of films and immediately leases them back to the producers. The producers agree to make lease payments over the remaining 15 years of the partnership's life.

What normally happens is that the film producers take a cut of around 12-15% of the purchase price of the films, and then put the balance of the money received from the partnership on deposit with a recognised financial institution. Interest from this deposit services the lease payments.

In the first year the partnership records a tax loss, because there has been no revenue but the film portfolio has been purchased from the producer. Investors are thus able either to defer current tax, or claim refunds of tax already paid.

Because the investor has paid only 20% of the cost of the investment in cash and borrowed the rest, but receives - assuming he is a top rate taxpayer - a tax refund based on 40% tax on the full amount invested (including the bank loan), there is an immediate positive cash flow benefit equivalent to around 20% of the total amount invested.

Receipts from the lease payments provide most of the funds required to pay interest on the 80% loan taken out in the beginning and to fund later tax liabilities in the partnership. This does, however, assume the investor can earn a reasonable so-called 'hurdle' rate of return on the cash that he has received from the tax rebate.

Schemes like this work particularly well for those whose earnings are expected to reach a peak early in their careers and then tail off. Footballers and other sportsmen, and those working in the entertainment industry, are among those who have made use of schemes like this, but they work equally well for anyone potentially with top rate tax liabilities (either in income tax, capital gains tax or inheritance tax) to shelter.

The crucial point about schemes like this is that they function quite independently of the merits of the films that are part of the package sold and leased back. If the films do badly, the way the finance is structured means that everyone continues to benefit. If they do well, it is the producers and not the investors that reap the extra return.

In effect what investors in pure sale and leaseback partnerships get is an interest free loan from the Inland Revenue over the life of the partnership, normally 15 years.

Let's look at a brief example.

- An investor has £100,000 of tax to shelter.

- He makes an investment of £20,000 in February 2004, and borrows £80,000.

- He receives a tax rebate of £40,000 in July 2004, and then pays no tax on partnership revenue for two years.

- From 2006 to 2019 he faces a gradually rising tax liability as lease payments are received: payments start at £600 annually and rise to around £3,000 annually by the end of the partnership's life.

- If however he invests the net amount of £20,000 received up front at 5% a year, he receives £1,000 a year that can be used to defray the future tax liabilities as they build up as well as the interest on the loan.

- Remember, though, that the future tax liabilities generated by the scheme relate only to the large amount of prior year tax relieved at the start of the partnership. They are on top of any other tax that might become payable on other 'normal' income and capital gains during the period from 2004 to 2019.

- Remember this is only a guide. All film partnerships differ, as does the 'hurdle' rate of return (5% in the previous example) you need to earn on the cash received upfront.

Is a sale and leaseback partnership right for you?

There are several considerations you need to take into account when investing in a film partnership. They are not good schemes for everybody. But if you have the right profile they can be a very effective and remunerative investment.

Do you have enough tax to shelter?

This is pretty obvious. The minimum investment in a film partnership is in practical terms around £100,000 - or at least that is the example quoted most often by the firms that construct them. Some schemes have a minimum investment of £50,000. This means you need to have at least that amount of taxable income, likely to be taxed at the highest rate (currently 40%), in the year in which you invest.

Prior year tax liabilities can also be sheltered but you need the advice of an accountant on how best to do this and obtain the maximum relief. If you don't fall into this tax bracket, or don't have sufficient income in the top tax bracket to shelter, then sheltering tax in this way is not a sensible option. Film partnerships can also be used to shelter inheritance tax.

Are you the right age?

Film partnerships tend to run over 15 years. The tax shelter obtained is only a deferral, not a write-off so, while the partnerships tend to be self financing, it is probably wise to make sure that you are still earning a reasonable level of income as the partnership comes to an end and the tax liabilities involved in the scheme rise. Individuals who have reached their peak earning period, but who still have at least 15 years to go to retirement typically use partnerships like this.

Do you have good financial advice?

Irrespective of whether you are employed, self-employed or retired, entering into a film partnership means that for tax purposes you are a self employed trader in this respect.

> ## Film sale and leasebacks - right for you?
>
> * Top rate tax bracket
> * £100,000 tax to shelter
> * Need an accountant
> * Significant fees
> * 15 year commitment
> * No early exit

You can have a full time job and be self-employed in this way at the same time. There are, however, several issues that need to be addressed that relate to self employed status. These include national insurance contributions, as well as the paperwork involved in claiming the tax rebates generated by the partnership investment. This means that a film partnership investment only makes sense if you have an accountant who is already well versed in your tax affairs.

Are you prepared for the long-term commitment?

Investing in a film partnership is not a 'fire and forget' investment. In fact it isn't really an investment at all, but rather a way of deferring tax.

You need to be assiduous in investing the cash you release through the tax refund in order to provide funds to repay the difference between your borrowing costs plus the rising tax liabilities through the life of the partnership, and the cash received from lease payments. The tax rebate should not be spent, and disaster awaits those who do.

What about fees?

Remember that the financial firms that create film partnerships are not working for free. They will charge annual management fees (typically 1.5% of the gross amount invested - i.e. including borrowing). They also offer commission to IFAs introducing clients to the scheme. These commissions can be as high as 3.5% initially and 0.5% a year on a regular ongoing basis. You need to factor these fees into your cash flow calculations.

Do you have a confident view about future tax rates?

One of the problems with a film partnership relates to future tax rates. Film partnerships only defer tax. The tax you would have been liable for at the outset has to be paid towards the end of the life of the partnership. It will be assessed on the tax rates in force then. If the top rate of tax rises in the meantime, you may end up deferring tax that would have been paid at one rate, and end up paying tax at the end of the deferral at a new higher rate. So you have to be prepared for this risk, or view it as unlikely.

Can you move quickly?

The tax regime that has allowed film sale and leaseback tax deferrals to flourish is due to expire at the end of the 2004/2005 tax year. The regime that replaces it will probably make schemes like this less attractive. If you want to enter a scheme like this and it makes financial sense for you to do so, you need to do it before April 5th 2005. We explore this in more detail in the next section.

The taxation issues

The same taxation regime applies not just to the sale and leaseback style of film partnerships, but also to those that invest in film productions with the aim of sharing in their success or failure. There are hybrid partnerships that combine the two.

So before we go on to look at these other types of film vehicle, let's just have a look at where the tax relief involved originates from, and the rules that have to be followed.

Official encouragement for homegrown film production through the tax system goes back more than ten years. It isn't simply a function of New Labour's links to leading 'luvvies'. In fact, changes in the last few years have simply added complexity for investors.

The tax breaks only apply to 'British qualifying' films. You might think this means that a film has to be made by British producers, in Britain, with a British cast. But this isn't the case.

Co-production treaties with other countries means that even a film shot in, say, Luxembourg or the West Indies can qualify. Normally 70% of the production costs of a film have to be spent in the UK for it to qualify, but where a co-production treaty is involved this drops to 20%. Co-production treaties are in force with Australia, Germany, Italy, Norway, New Zealand, Canada, France, Ireland and some other territories.

> ## Film partnerships - taxation issues
>
> - Section 42 and Section 48 relief
> - Section 48 expires in 2005
> - British qualifying feature films only
> - Co-production treaties broaden scope
> - Tax changes have fostered hybrid vehicles

Once a film qualifies, the tax breaks come through Section 41 and 42 of the Finance (No.2) Act 1992 as amended by Section 48 of the Finance (No.2 Act) 1997. These are normally shortened to Section 42 and Section 48.

Recently there have been several twists in the story. One is that the rules on film sale and leasebacks were more tightly defined in the 2002 Budget. The change excluded from schemes like this productions that were made for TV. Prior to the change, film partnerships could be used to finance normal TV soap opera episodes. To qualify now, however, films have to be intended for theatrical release in the commercial cinema. This change meant something of a reduction in the product available for use in sale and leaseback schemes.

To give an idea of what a difference this made, the amount of tax being sheltered was around £1.7bn a year before the change went through. The change to the rules meant that initially only around £600m a year could be sheltered, because there were simply not enough films being produced to cater for the demand. This situation has now rectified itself to some degree, but there is still probably excess demand. Industry pundits reckon that the 'natural' demand for sale and leaseback style vehicles is probably around £1bn a year.

The size of the tax shelter money chasing those vehicles that are available has meant that producers have been able to extract more favourable terms, and investors need to achieve higher hurdle rates to make the exercise self-financing. Producers' fees have typically risen from 10% to 15% of the amount raised, while hurdle rates have climbed to over 5%.

As explained earlier, the hurdle rate is the amount you need to earn on the initial net cash rebate to recoup the difference between the lease revenue on the one hand and the cost of the built-in borrowing in the partnership together with the stream of future tax payments on the other.

The shortage of sale and leaseback product also resulted in the creation of hybrid vehicles that combine some elements of both sale and leaseback and production schemes. We'll look at these in more detail later, but in brief, some provide partial exposure to the upside of a film production scheme, but with a minimum level of return built in. Others offer a sale and leaseback style of structure, but with a kicker built in that increases lease payments and therefore reduces the hurdle rate if the film is successful. Some just bundle together sale and leaseback returns with production risk.

One key issue for film partnerships in the future is that the 100% first year tax deferral allowed under Section 48 of the Finance (No.2) Act 1997 expires in July 2005. After this date, under Section 42 of the same Act, full tax deferral could only take place over three years. This reduces the upfront cash flow benefits of sale and leaseback schemes, and will make them harder to sell to investors.

Film partnerships - production schemes and hybrids

Film sale and leaseback schemes are more a risk-free tax deferral vehicle than a conventional investment, and so we haven't even considered them in terms of the more normal risk and return criteria that we've looked at in many of the other superhobby style investments profiled elsewhere in this book.

Film production partnerships are more akin to a conventional investment that has both risks and rewards.

'Normal' production schemes - the basics

These are film partnerships that utilise similar tax breaks to those available in sale and leasebacks, deferring tax for a period of years, but also sharing in the success or failure of the film in question.

It is possible, though risky, to use a film production partnership to invest in a single film. But many vehicles like this use a portfolio approach, investing in several films to reduce the risk. They also reduce risk by investing only in films where there are significant pre-sale commitments. This means that film distributors have committed themselves, prior to it being made, to taking the film for distribution.

Even where there are commitments like this, this should not blind any investor to the fact that production partnerships are high-risk vehicles. The reason is that gearing is introduced into the pot in the form of production loans.

The partners' investment typically represents 25% of the film or films' budget and production loans amount to 75%. Partners are liable to repay the production loans if the film is a turkey.

What sort of returns can be made? It's hard to say.

The typical returns from film productions vary considerably. Most financiers however, work on the basis of the returns being something as follows:

Income returns on production costs

'Hit'	7 times costs
'Good'	2 times costs
'Breakeven'	1 times costs
'Turkey'	0.7 times costs or less

A typical portfolio of 10 films might fall into one of three possible scenarios:

	Hit	Good	Breakeven	Turkey
Profitable	1	2	5	2
Breakeven	0	2	5	3
Loss-making	0	0	5	5

It is however worth making the point that the way the deals are structured tends to mean that a fund will recoup its investment in a film before all of the production costs are covered. A film has to do very badly for the fund to face substantial losses, although from time to time these do occur.

In broad terms a £100,000 investment would generate about £125,000 of tax rebate but a contingent liability - if the worst happens - of £250,000. In the worst case you could find yourself losing £350,000 in total and eventually repaying over a period of many years £125,000 in deferred tax.

There's another tax aspect too. Tax refunds are granted to the partners on the basis that the film will not make any money, but any money the film does make is taxable, so the incidence of tax liabilities is much less predictable than in the case of a sale and leaseback.

If a film does well, partners may need to reinvest the proceeds in another film or series of films to avoid being hit with a big tax bill. However, returns typically come through fees from distributors once the film is screened, and with the subsequent sale of rights to the film for video and TV.

The table gives a brief example of the cash flows generated by a moderately successful film.

Table 8.1 - Illustration of film production scheme cash flows

Item	Year 1	Year 2	Year 3	Year 4	Year 5	Total
Initial capital contribution	-100000	0	0	0	0	-100000
Tax relief	0	120000	0	0	0	120000
Final distributions less tax	0	0	0	0	58820	58820
Sale of rights less tax	0	0	0	0	72243	72243
Success fee	0	0	0	0	-266	-266
Net cash position for partner	-100000	120000	0	0	130797	150797
Cumulative cash flow	-100000	20000	20000	20000	150797	

Note: The example assumes the film returns 112.5% of budget and has a library value of 25% after 6 years.

The example shows that, with the film recouping 112.5% of production costs and the rights being sold for 25% of the budget after five years, the investor will make a 50% return on the initial £100,000 invested over the five year period.

Many films do not achieve this level of success, one reason for taking a portfolio approach and entering into a partnership that invests in several films.

They work in a broadly similar way. Here's an example. In 2003, London stockbrokers Teather & Greenwood launched 'Take 6', a film production partnership with an intended five-year life. As its name implies this was the sixth in a series of such vehicles, set up to invest in a portfolio of films, and offering investors the opportunity to participate for a minimum investment of £10,000.

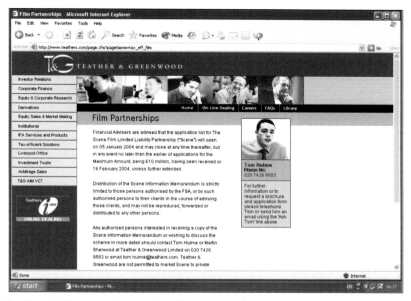

Teather & Greenwood organise film partnerships

Features of the 'Take 6' partnership were that it would only invest in films with an average of at least 75% pre-sale commitments. Any one film would have pre-sale commitments of at least 65%. All of the money raised was intended to be spent in the first year and any income received from successful productions in the first four years of the partnership would be carried forward to invest in further productions, providing ongoing tax deferral. Rights to all films would be sold after five years.

Production loans were secured against pre-sale commitments. Doing this substantially reduces the risks to individual partners. The partnership also tended only to invest in films that have already secured substantial financing. This means that the partnership, in providing the final crucial piece of funding, is often able to dictate the terms on which it will invest.

It insisted (as do other such vehicles) that some recouping of the amounts invested occured at each stage as film receipts were received. In effect, by doing this, the fund could recoup its investment ahead of other participants, such as the producer. Typically a fund like Take 6 will break even on its investment when around 75% of production costs have been covered by revenue.

> ## Film production schemes - characteristics
> - Portfolio approach limits risk
> - Tax rebate offsets initial capital investment
> - Potentially large contingent liability
> - Exit problems if successful

As with previous partnerships in the 'Take x' series, the partnership was advised by Baker Street Media, a specialist film finance house. This firm has been responsible for several award winning and commercially successful films, the latest and best known of which was 'I Capture the Castle'.

Baker Street Media

Most film production partnerships, where they invest in a portfolio of films, function in broadly similar ways. Close Brothers Investment, for example, has also launched a series of film partnerships - along similar lines to the Teather & Greenwood ones - but advised by Visionview, another prominent film finance specialist.

Hybrid Schemes – the basics

The shortage of conventional sale and leaseback products that came about as a result of the tightening of the rules governing qualifying British films brought with it an upsurge in other types of film investments. These newer variants combine some elements of both the safety-first sale and leaseback type of investment, with those of the riskier film production ones. These hybrid vehicles are constructed so as to provide some element of relatively risk free deferral together with a proportion of riskier production based investment as well.

According to one expert 'they are saying that if you want to have the sale and leaseback concept, then you have to take some film production risk as well'.

At the moment there are at least four broad types of hybrid vehicle.

Conventional production schemes that nonetheless involve significant release of cash upfront.

Equity sale and leaseback. These provide extra lease payments to investors linked to the success of the film or films concerned.

Production and distribution schemes with downside protection. These do not release cash upfront, but aim to provide a positive return regardless of the success of the film, but with an extra return if films are successful.

Straightforward *combination of sale and leaseback and production* in roughly equal proportions.

There is not much to be gained from going into the intricacies of these concepts as each new scheme contains its own different quirks and variations on the theme. It's also worth recording that none has proved as popular as the straightforward sale and leaseback or the 'production portfolio' approach. It should also be noted that the recent changes governing tax relief on some of the more ingenious schemes have removed their attractions.

Are they right for you?

There are a few relevant questions that need to be asked at the outset and that ought to govern whether or not you invest in normal production schemes or hybrid schemes like those described above that also have a production element.

Do you have an accountant?

Investing in vehicles like this needs to be done involving your accountant every step of the way, as he or she will need to take certain steps on your behalf to maximise the benefit you get from the investment. If you do not already use an accountant, the chances are you will derive minimal benefit from investing in a scheme like this.

Do you have enough capital?

Minimum investment levels vary but can be anything from £10,000 to £100,000. You need to have sufficient tax to shelter the gross amount invested.

What is your time horizon?

Film investment schemes that are successful can represent an ongoing investment. The normal life of production related schemes is five years, but if significant profits have been made, then it is likely these will be rolled over into a new scheme to maintain the momentum of tax deferral.

There is no early exit. You are not usually able to sell your participation during the life of the scheme, which will be wound up and the profits distributed to partners at the end of its life. Trying to exit from the scheme early will incur adverse tax consequences.

Is your main purpose to invest in films or defer tax?

If it is the latter, then there is only merit in a hybrid scheme if it has a significant sale and leaseback element and has only limited production risk. Equity sale and leaseback might be interesting in this context because the extra lease payments received if the films are successful reduces the hurdle rate of return appreciably.

Is the structure wholly new or has it been tried and worked before?

You should probably, if there is a choice, give preference to the structure that has been tested in the market before. Schemes that 'push the envelope' in tax terms are being targeted by the Treasury and Inland Revenue.

What is the quality of the backers and their advisers?

This is probably one of the most important features. Reputable film financiers with a track record of innovation in structuring partnerships like this are probably a better bet than those who have only recently burst on the scene. Good advisers are essential, because they get to see the best scripts and have the best contacts with producers.

Have you factored in the fees you will pay?

All collective schemes like this have fees - see the previous page for some examples - that are taken at the beginning and end of the scheme, and during their life. These need to be taken into account when calculating your likely return.

▌Are you comfortable that the returns you expect to get are, however, not secure?

There is little independent published information available on returns from film partnerships and the returns will differ with each individuals particular tax position. No portfolio schemes have been going for a sufficiently long period to have definitive information available about their returns.

▌Remember your own input is secondary

Lastly, you may be investing in a scheme like this partly because you have an interest in the movie business. However astute a film buff you consider yourself to be, remember that you have no input in selecting the investment portfolio. You may get tickets to the premiere of a 'portfolio' film and meet the stars, but that is about as active as your involvement will be.

Investing in film production through EIS schemes

In the past there have been instances of money being raised for film productions through the Enterprise Investment Scheme. EIS investment involves buying shares in a company normally set up to establish a new trading venture, and gives an immediate tax deduction of the amount invested. Any subsequent gains in the price of the shares - usually quite rare - are free of capital gains tax.

Amounts usually raised through EIS issues are generally too low for the average film budget, but there have been some past instances of issues that have been mounted successfully.

Investments of this type have largely been superseded by film production partnerships. Though partnerships involve only a tax deferral rather than a permanently reduced liability, they have a number of more attractive characteristics, not least the ability to take a portfolio approach and the ability to shelter much larger sums.

You also need to remember, that from the standpoint of an investor, investing in an EIS scheme has uncertain liquidity. As I know to my personal cost, investors in EIS schemes can be stuck with shares long beyond the three-year period needed to qualify for tax relief. Investors have to rely on the EIS company to create an exit route through which they can sell their shares, via a takeover, a stock market listing, or some other mechanism.

Table 8.2 - Film Investing - key web addresses and contact details

Company	Web address	Email	Phone	Type
Allenbridge Group	www.taxshelterreport.co.uk	n/a	0800 3399 99	Adviser
Astute Money (Chambers IFA)	www.astute-investor.co.uk	info@astute-investor.co.uk	01225 428444	Adviser
Civilian Capital	www.civilian.com	info@civilian.com	323 938 3220	Dealer
Close Investments	www.closeinvestments.com	info@cbil.com	020 7426 4000	Dealer
Future Film Group	www.futurefilmgroup.com	stephenn@futurefilmgroup.com	020 7434 6600	Dealer
Horwath, Clark, Whitehill	www.horwathcw.com	wolfj@horwath.co.uk	0161 214 7500	Adviser
James Baxter	www.jamesbaxter.co.uk	enquiries@jamesbaxter.co.uk	020 7939 9600	Adviser
Kreis Consulting	www.kreisconsulting.com	n/a	n/a	Dealer
Matrix Group	www.matrixgroup.co.uk	jh@matrix-film-finance.co.uk	020 7292 0899	Dealer
McCann Fitzgerald	www.mccann-fitzgerald.ie	n/a	353 1 8290000	Adviser
Offshore-Onshore	www.lowtax.net	marketing@lowtax.net	01494 474480	Adviser
Park Caledonia Associates	www.parkcaledonia.biz	dgoldberg@parkcaledonia.biz	020 8 543 8882	Adviser
Revenue Ireland	www.revenue.ie	jbarry@revenue.ie	n/a	Adviser
Teather & Greenwood	www.teathers.com	tom.hulme@teathers.com	020 7426 9583	Dealer

> ## Film Investment via EIS
>
> - Immediate tax deduction - not deferral
> - Largely superseded by film partnerships
> - Limited number on offer
> - Minimum three year holding period
> - Exit can be difficult

Film producers have also generally resisted going down the EIS route except as a last resort because, although EIS was seemingly tailor-made for small film producers, it does involve shares being issued to the public and consequently has to meet what some would regard as the onerous requirements for drafting a prospectus and complying with the strictures of the Financial Services Act.

Because of this it tends only to be used as a last resort or in special situations where a prominent producer/director might command a public following. Among the films produced in this way has been 'Paradise Grove', which raised £250,000, 'Mr Bean' and Oscar Wilde's 'An Ideal Husband'. More recently Close Brothers Investment raised £8m through an EIS to finance the making of an animated film based on the comic book superhero Captain Scarlet.

Would-be investors should remember in general terms EIS schemes are a much riskier route to getting exposure to film production returns than the portfolio approach adopted by Teather & Greenwood and others. They are more like the investment that 'angels' make in theatrical productions, which is covered in brief in the next section.

Investing in theatrical productions

Investing in commercial theatrical productions is high risk.

For every production like 'Cats', which has taken £1.4bn around the world, there are many more flops where the curtain comes down shortly after the opening night. Only one in five West End shows make a profit. One in five breaks even. The other three vanish into oblivion, eating up a lot of cash along the way.

For theatre lovers the main advantage of being an 'angel' - the traditional term for financial backers of theatre productions - is that it provides a way of being involved in a production directly, one level above just being a member of the audience. Angels may have the opportunity to attend first nights and first night parties, meet the cast and be part of the glitz and glamour of the West End.

Many producers have their own list of angels who have backed both successes and failures and who are given the first option to invest in a new show. Andrew

Lloyd Webber would be unlikely to invite you to invest in his next project, unless you were one of his original backers.

Strange though it may seem now, back in 1980 traditional theatre investors wouldn't touch 'Cats'. Enter Cameron Macintosh, who agreed to produce it and encouraged theatregoers to invest £750 each to raise the £450,000 needed. The rest is history.

Every £750 invested produced a return of £42,500 and heralded the start of a rejuvenation of British musicals that has arguably seen the West End eclipse Broadway.

'Cats' had staging by Trevor Nunn, music by Andrew Lloyd Webber and choreography by Gillian Lynne. With that sort of pedigree it would be hard to fail. Unfortunately, in the fickle world of theatre, even a big name line up does not guarantee success. 'The Beautiful Game' with music by Andrew Lloyd Webber and a script by Ben Elton, cost £1.5m to stage. It closed after a year's run because it was losing money.

How to invest

There are two main routes into an investment in theatre productions.

Traditional angels

As inferred earlier, the majority of producers have their own private lists of angels and will offer investment units for both plays and musicals with investment contracts being exchanged with each angel individually.

Most West End plays cost in the region of £250,000 to mount. An angel would be expected to invest a minimum of £5,000, either as an individual or as part of a consortium. The normal understanding is that the investors will share in 60% of the production profits pro rata to the amount of their respective contributions. The other 40% goes to the producer.

Theatre investment - key points

- Only 20% of productions profitable
- Big returns if successful
- Access to good potential productions restricted
- Industry secretive
- EIS schemes problematic
- Can approach more enlightened producers direct

Even if a production is ultimately a winner it may take a considerable time for the angel to see a return on his or her investment. Apart from the initial start up costs, regularly weekly bills have to be paid such as theatre hire, paying on- and off-stage staff, advertising, paying for publicity and royalty fees.

A return on an initial investment will only be repaid if there is a sufficient surplus of box office revenue after all these projected running expenses have been met.

The Stage newspaper website (www.thestage.co.uk) has a useful section on theatre investment. They advise limiting the risk by spreading investments over a wide portfolio, such as five to ten productions with a limited amount in each.

Leaving EIS schemes on one side for the moment (see below), there is nonetheless some tax relief available for losses sustained by traditional angels. Investors have two choices, either full loss relief against capital gains from other investments, or setting the loss off against profits from other theatre productions.

Theatre EIS Schemes

Some angels invest through EIS schemes. Here, you need to check exactly what type of deal is on offer.

An EIS investment structure gives you a full tax deduction when you first invest, but you are required to maintain your investment for at least three years and, if the show comes off before the three years is up, you may have no alternative but to roll over your investment into a new production or else forfeit all or part of your initial tax relief.

Some producers also avoid EIS schemes because of the need to produce a prospectus and satisfy City regulators.

Finding opportunities

Finding information on forthcoming productions that may have investment units available is sometimes difficult.

The Society of London Theatre (SOLT), the trade association for theatre managers, owners and producers of shows in the West End, has a confidential list of angels.

Only those producers who are SOLT members can send details of productions to the Society, which then forwards them to angels on their list. How this works in practice is difficult to evaluate, as the whole process is shrouded in secrecy. How individuals get on the list is not entirely clear.

Some producers who are not members of SOLT can be contacted individually to see if they have angel opportunities available. Although this may sound straightforward, in practice finding out which producers have productions in the pipeline is not an easy matter for an average member of the public with no insider theatrical contacts.

One producer who has seen the light is Marc Sinden. Details of his productions are posted on the web. Details of his forthcoming productions can be found on his website (www.sindenproductions.com), with contact details for those interested in becoming an angel.

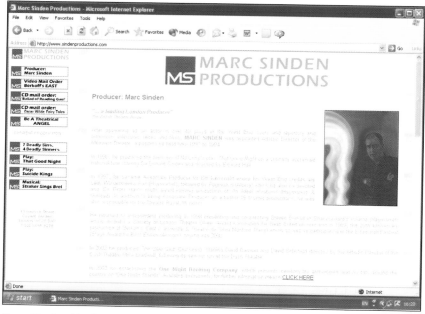

Marc Sinden Productions - seeking 'angels'

He believes in personal contact with his investors and appears to treat them well. Mr Sinden sees himself as the theatrical equivalent of a chef who needs to get all the ingredients right for a successful production. Being from a theatrical background helps: his father is the well-known character actor Donald Sinden. He also spent many years as an actor, and his knowledge and experience of the theatre is extensive.

Table 8.3 – Theatre Investing – key web addresses and contact details

Company	Web address	Email	Phone	Type
Box Office Data Report	www.officiallondontheatre.co.uk	n/a	020 7557 6700	Data
Denton Wilde Sapte	www.dentonwildesapte.com	info@dentonwildesapte.com	020 7242 1212	Adviser
Harbottle & Lewis	www.harbottle.co.uk	neil.adelman@harbottlecom	020 7667 5000	Lawyer
Marc Sinden Productions	www.sindenproductions.com	mail@sindenproductions.com	020 8455 3278	Producer
Society of London Theatres	www.solt.org.uk	susanne@soltma.co.uk	020 7836 0971	Association
The Stage	www.thestage.co.uk	n/a	n/a	Publication
Theatrical Management Association	www.tmauk.org	n/a	n/a	Association

Where to find more information

One essential prerequisite before embarking on investment in any of these areas is professional tax and accounting advice. While investing in both film and theatre productions sounds exciting and can have fringe benefits, they are essentially high risk, high return endeavours even when the investments are structured to allow you to diversify.

There is a fair amount of information about film production and investments schemes available, but a relatively small amount on the theatre.

The following are a number of the most useful sites.

Advice, analysis and scheme providers - film

Allenbridge Group (www.taxshelterreport.co.uk). This site is primarily a research resource for professional advisers. As such, it has limited information for private investors on its site. You can subscribe to receive research for a fee of £295, which is refunded if you subsequently invest £10,000 through the Allenbridge Group.

Astute Money (www.astute-investor.co.uk), in association with Chambers IFA, has a general summary of film partnerships on the site. There is direct email access to the Film Partnership Enquiry Centre together with telephone contact numbers.

Baker Street Media Finance (www.bakerstreetfinance.tv) specializes in the co-production and financing of British feature films. The company works alongside Teather & Greenwood in raising funds for its projects. There is a brief summary of film partnerships on the site together with information on the films it has recently financed.

Close Investments (www.closeinvestments.com), like Teather & Greenwood, mounts a range of tax efficient collective investment schemes, including film partnerships. It has only a very brief summary of film partnerships on its site, with email and telephone contact details for further information.

Horwath Clark Whitehill (www.horwathcw.com) is a firm of chartered accountants with branches throughout England. They advise on all aspects of tax planning, including film partnerships and sale and leaseback schemes. Basic information is available on the site.

Matrix Group (www.matrixgroup.co.uk) is a finance house with a specialised tax section. Information on film partnerships is only available to IFAs. Past and future films in which Matrix has been financially involved are listed on the site, which may be of interest to investors as background.

Nielsen EDI (www.entdata.com) has box office statistics for the UK and other territories including box office takings since the 1980's.

Offshore-Onshore (www.lowtax.net) reviews tax incentive schemes in high tax countries and has a comprehensive summary of film partnerships on its site.

Pact (www.pact.co.uk) is a UK trade organization that represents the commercial interests of independent production companies involved directly in the production and distribution of films. Membership is only available to commercial organisations but some information is available to private individuals on subscription. An email contact address is provided for questions and queries relating to the film industry.

Teather & Greenwood (www.teathers.com) is a city stockbroker with a dedicated 'tax-efficient solutions' department. Information on film partnerships is only available to IFAs, but there is a link to its adviser Baker Street Media Finance for further information.

General Information - film

The British Film Institute site (www.bfi.org.uk) has everything you need to know about the British film industry, including statistics on cinema admissions and the top ten films of all time, plus information on distribution rights and current news and events.

The Irish Revenue (www.revenue.ie) has detailed information for Irish investors on film investment in the publications section of the site, together with an email address for further information.

Screen International (www.screendaily.com), Screen Digest (www.screendigest.com) and Screen Finance (www.informamedia.com) all have box office data and analysis.

The Tax Efficient Review (www.taxefficientreview.com) has published a guide to film partnerships that is available to financial advisers and 'qualified investors'. It contains a review of tax issues, the pros and cons of different partnership structures and a review of the independent film sector.

The UK Film Council (www.ukfilmcouncil.org.uk) has weekend box office charts.

Theatre - general information

The Society of London Theatre website (www.officiallondontheatre.co.uk) is a mine of information on the London theatre scene with up to date news, information on current productions plus a regular free email newsletter. It publishes a range of reports and publications including The Box Office Data Report, which provides detailed information on attendances and audience trends for the previous year, and The Wyndham Report, which was the first ever, detailed analysis of the industry.

Harbottle and Lewis (www.harbottle.co.uk) is a firm of lawyers specialising in the media, entertainment and communication industries. Its site has an interesting article on raising finance for commercial production, previously published in Prompt.

Marc Sinden Productions (www.sindenproductions.com) has information concerning present and future productions, together with an email contact address for further information for potential angel investors.

KD Management and Productions (www.kdmanagement.co.uk) also has information about past and future productions together with an email contact address for further information for potential angel investors.

Books and publications

The British Film Business Baillieu and Goodchild, John Wiley 2002

The book explores the development of the industry from the beginning to the end of the 20th century including both successes and failures. The role of government intervention is explored plus comments on recent and future developments.

Prompt, published by the Theatrical Management Association (www.tmauk.org), is a quarterly magazine for theatre managers and anyone involved in the performing arts in the UK. It includes a summary of audience figures and business news, plus news from managers, producers and administrators. It costs £15 per year for four issues but some information is available free online. Links are provided to theatres and producers nationwide.

The Stage (www.thestage.co.uk) is the world's longest established theatre trade weekly and is full of news, reviews and features, a selection of which appear on the website. There is also a summary of theatrical investment for private investors in its 'Legal Eagle' section covering some of the contractual issues involved.

9   Forestry

Forestry has been an investment medium for private individuals for about fifty years. But it is surrounded by misconceptions - not least that it is only for the very wealthy. Many wealthy individuals have invested in woodland because of its tax benefits. In recent years, however, the interest in it has widened. To cater for this, some collective investment plans have been devised to appeal to those investors who wish to invest modest amounts.

The basics of forestry as a long-term investment are pretty easy to understand. They centre on one simple fact. Trees grow and become more valuable the larger they get. Buy a parcel of young forestland, and if you sit on it for long enough the trees on it will grow and its value should increase. Eventually you will be able to harvest some of the trees and sell the timber. Or you can buy an already mature plantation and harvest the crop from day one.

The attractions of forestry as an investment are enhanced by the tax advantages it possesses, which we'll go into later in this chapter. Suffice to say at this point that forestry can be used to mitigate inheritance tax, and also to generate tax-free income and capital gains. It is effectively a tax-free investment.

In the rest of the chapter we'll look in more detail at the basics of forestry and why you should invest in it, the tax advantages, the long-term returns you can make from it, and some of the pitfalls you need to avoid.

Forestry basics

The UK was once covered with forests, but the industrial revolution and subsequent eras led to wholesale clearance of forestland. This proceeded to the point where, at the turn of the 20th century, only about 5% remained under woodland. The figure now is around 12%. Much of this reafforestation has occurred since WW2, as successive governments have tried to encourage the commercial timber industry. The state-owned Forestry Commission dates from 1919.

Most of the private sector forestry established since the war is in Wales, northern England and Scotland. It is predominantly of Sitka spruce, a perennially productive and hardy species. The investments of that period were made because investment in forestry then attracted an immediate income tax deduction, rather as do Enterprise Zone Trusts and Enterprise Investment Schemes now. This concession ended in 1988, although sizeable tax benefits remain. These include grants originally designed to compensate investors for this loss of income tax relief.

Forestry Commission

The size of the forest market potentially available for outside investment was also boosted from 1980 onwards when some Forestry Commission properties were sold off, although this source of supply has now dried up.

The current UK figure of 12% for forest coverage compares with an average of 31% afforestation across the EU and much higher percentages (around 60%) in countries like Finland and Sweden.

The EU currently produces only 25% of its timber requirements, compared to abundant self-sufficiency in food, although the enlarged 25-member EU will be 95% self-sufficient. The EU and individual member governments support the forestry industry with tax breaks and grants, recognising that there is both an economic case for supporting forestry and to encourage its role of sustaining rural development.

Interestingly, forestry falls outside the scope of the Treaty of Rome: most EU grants derive from the environmental benefits conferred by forestry, or from taking land out of conventional farming.

Scandinavia is indelibly associated in people's minds as the home of forestry, but in fact the climate for growing trees in the UK is superior to Scandinavia and among the best in the world. It is on a par with Chile and bettered only by New Zealand. Trees in Scotland, for example, on average put on 16 cubic metres of growth per hectare per year, compared with around five cubic metres in Russia and Canada and seven or eight in Scandinavia and the USA.

It is this strong growth that underpins any investment in UK forestry. It does, of course, also underline that forestry is a naturally renewable resource.

The returns you can earn from forestry as an alternative investment are therefore reasonably predictable. They are a function of the maturity and quality of the woodland you own, timber prices, and the tax breaks and grants available.

Commercial timber in the UK takes about 40 years to mature fully. Where in this cycle you buy in governs the price you pay per hectare and the timing and scale of the income that can be extracted. Whether you buy an immature plantation or a mature forest depends on your time horizon and your investment objectives.

Forestry basics - key points

- UK's climate is ideal for forestry
- Timber takes 40-50 years to mature
- Once established, growth is predictable
- Yield varies by species, location, and site type
- Location (i.e. distance from sawmills) affects price

Forests are normally divided into four categories: young (up to ten years old); mid rotation (11-20 years old); semi mature (21-30 years old) and mature (31 years and older). They are also split into different yield classes. The yield class measures their general productivity in terms of the incremental growth per year and their consequent income-earning potential. Yield class in turn depends on species, soil fertility, rainfall, the topography of the site, and several other natural influences.

Because it is hard to predict early in their life how productive a particular new plantation is going to be, there is sometimes the opportunity to buy young potentially high yielding crops at 'average' prices. The investor may then benefit from an uplift in values as the yield class of the woodland becomes more evident.

Other factors affect the price of forests. The larger a forest, the cheaper it will tend to be per hectare. A typical difference might be £2,000 per hectare for a parcel under 50 hectares, but perhaps £1,600 per hectare for a forest of more than 200 hectares.

Small woodlands, classified as being less than 25 hectares (around 60 acres), tend to be valued also for their amenity value and sometimes for their sporting potential. Prices of small woodlands vary considerably by region. Prices are highest in the South East and Central England and lowest in South Wales.

Location and proximity to large markets also has a significant impact on the price of larger forest properties. The West Country, the Welsh Marches, Northumberland and Southern Scotland are favoured areas.

Finally, tree species go in and out of fashion. So you need to make sure that the forest you buy contains timber that the market will want when harvested. Sitka spruce, Douglas fir and larch are perennial favourites.

Tax benefits from forestry

The heyday of investing in forestry was between the end of WW2 and 1988. During that period higher rate taxpayers received an immediate tax deduction for investment in forestry, which made it highly attractive.

The benefit was similar to the tax concession that applies at present to investment in Enterprise Investment Schemes. But forestry then was more attractive than EIS is now, because returns from it were essentially more predictable.

The abolition of the Schedule D/Schedule B system in 1988 removed this benefit, but despite this, forestry can be an extremely tax efficient investment.

The current benefits from forestry investment come in several different areas.

Income tax: income from sales of standing or felled timber, and grants received from the Forestry Commission under the Woodland Grants Scheme, are currently free from income tax. Grants can be awarded for the maintenance and restocking of woodland as well as other activities such as deer control, recreational development and community work. What this means is that forestry can generate significant tax-free income. Moreover because of the flexibility inherent in forestry (more trees can be cut down one year, and fewer the next), this income can be used to form part of wider tax planning goals.

Capital gains tax: any increase in the value of standing timber in commercial woodlands is not subject to capital gains tax, although the land on which it stands, and any building in the property, does fall into the normal CGT regime. There may, however, be opportunities for rollover relief if new planting is being contemplated.

Inheritance tax: for many investors the biggest draw to investing in forestry is the exemption from inheritance tax. This arises because woodland managed on a commercial basis is eligible for 100% Business Property Relief from Inheritance Tax provided it is held for more than two years. Amenity woodland not managed on a commercial basis may attract Agricultural Property Relief although the scale of this relief depends on circumstances and could be as little as 50%.

The Inheritance Tax exemption is often the single biggest reason attracting investors to the forestry market. This is because the rise in the value of residential property has brought many more ordinary individuals into the inheritance tax bracket for the first time and so prompted a search for inheritance tax planning options that allow them to pass on their assets, untaxed, to their children.

While benefits like this are a potent attraction, it is also important not to get completely carried away by them. Other simpler means, such as trusts, can be used to minimise or eliminate IHT for those with relatively modest estates.

It is an old investment adage that you should not let the tax break 'drive' the investment decision. In other words, if you are thinking about forestry as a potential superhobby investment, make your decision based on its attractions as an 'alternative' asset and the returns it can make. Treat the tax breaks as a bonus on top.

Tax benefits - key points

- Don't let the tax break drive the investment
- Size of prudent investment needs to be measured against other assets
- Income from commercial timber sales is free from income tax
- Commercial forests are free from CGT
- Commercial forestry exempt from IHT after 2 years
- Remember the tax regime can alter; this could affect a forest's value

---

So factor the tax-free income into your calculations of potential returns and how an investment would stack up against other alternatives. But don't simply put money into forestry for inheritance tax reasons without taking account of whether or not the investment will make money over the longer term. A forestry investment needs to make sense in the context of the size of your other assets. A direct investment in forestry can take sizeable capital. Don't let it form a disproportionate percentage of your overall investment portfolio.

Do bear in mind also that tax benefits can alter. Although governments have consistently wished to foster forestry through the use of tax concessions, there is no guarantee that they will remain precisely as they are over the time horizon demanded by an investment of this sort. Remember that a later removal of a tax concession might affect the demand for the type of forestry in which you have invested and could therefore have an adverse impact on its value.

Having said that, the beauty of a forestry investment is that your ultimate exit route could simply be to fell the timber and sell it. And it's worth remembering that the IHT tax concession is not specific to forestry but relates to relief given on business properties as a whole, which it is most unlikely any future government would remove entirely.

Remember that the tax benefits in the main apply only to woodland that is operated on a commercial basis. Buying a few acres of woodland from your local farmer for amenity reasons will not produce the tax benefits described earlier. To derive the benefits, you need to demonstrate that it is a commercial operation, by having it professionally managed, keeping proper records, applying for and receiving grants, and registering for VAT.

All of this means that the capital outlay required to buy an appropriately sized parcel, and the administrative complexities of dealing with it, may be more than you had in mind. It may entail an investment that is too large relative to the other assets and investments you hold to be a prudent diversification. Only you can make the decision on whether or not this is the case.

Is forestry right for you?

Superhobby investing is, as we have said elsewhere in this book, very much a matter of finding categories that suit you, your interests and your tax position.

Forestry is no different. Much of the early private investment in forestry was driven by the generous tax breaks available. Though these have lessened somewhat, this remains the case. But if you are contemplating an investment like this, it helps to have an appreciation of woodland as an amenity and an interest in conservation to derive full satisfaction from it. The economics of the timber industry and the outlook for timber prices are important, if more mundane, considerations.

Let's look at all of these aspects in a bit more detail before moving on. Later we'll look at the supply and demand background underpinning forestry investment. We'll also look at how to invest - if you decide that forestry is for you.

For now let's take a look at the basic requirements you must have to make forestry investment worthwhile.

Have you got adequate capital?

Adequate capital is a must. While it is possible to invest in some collective investment schemes that have a small minimum investment level, most serious forestry investors buy a direct interest in a forest.

Broadly speaking you get what you pay for: an income generating forest will be worth more per hectare than an immature one where the trees have several years to go before some can be harvested. Location, access and soil fertility govern value as well. Forests can be bought for as little as £30,000 but prices of worthwhile investments are often much higher than this. You also do have to bear in mind that there are annual running costs to meet, although these are modest as a percentage of the total value of the investment.

Calculating the amount you have available to invest in this way depends both on the size of your conventional investment portfolio and also on the amount you might wish to put into other superhobby investment areas. You should aim for diversity, and not have one category dominating all the others. If you have an investment portfolio of £1m, then a forest worth £100,000 might be a sensible investment. If your total portfolio is worth less than £1m, then you may have to look to collective investment to get your stake in forestry.

Have you got confidence in timber prices?

A large part of the return you get from your forestry investment depends on the movement in timber prices. In general terms, timber demand usually exceeds supply on a global scale. Much of the UK demand for timber is satisfied from imports. Economic growth increases the demand. It follows that the price of good quality timber, an area in which the UK excels, should rise in the long term.

This is crucial. You need to have confidence that timber prices can increase over the longer term. This is not an investment you can make simply to take advantage of a short-term imbalance between demand and supply. If you are in forestry, you have to be there for the long haul, and an absolute minimum of five years.

Can you utilise the tax breaks?

Once you have held it for two years, putting some of your assets into forestry and keeping it there means you reduce your heirs' inheritance tax liability. For an investment in forestry to be worthwhile you therefore need to have, or expect to have when you die, an estate of at least £255,000, including the value of your house and any other stock market and tangible investments. Investing capital in excess of this figure in forestry in effect enlarges the exemption limit and minimises any future inheritance tax liability for the next generation.

Forestry can in certain circumstances also satisfy a requirement for tax-free income. This may be important if you are in, or close to, the 40% tax band already. Forestry can also yield grant income, which is tax-free, for maintenance works. The grant system is complex and differs by UK region. In general, grants are available for restocking, for opening up forests for public use, and for conservation.

Are you interested in woodland as an amenity?

Forestry is a great investment for those interested in conservation. There are few things more satisfying than planting trees and watching them grow. Trees absorb carbon dioxide, which is good for the planet. You probably need to have a feel for, and interest in these aspects to get the most out of an investment in forestry. The ability to visit and walk in your own piece of woodland should not be underplayed. It is tangible evidence of the quality of your investment.

Can you take the rough with the smooth?

High winds and forest fires can devastate woodland, although both of these can be insured against and are rare. Pests (such as the pine weevil, which attacks young trees) can be a problem, although attentive management of the woodland can minimise the risk of infestation. Most foresters will spray against pine weevil as a matter of course. If forests suffer storm damage there is no statutory obligation to restock. But if you suffer a forest fire, restocking is obligatory and if you are not properly insured you will need funds to cover this.

Have you got cash to fund annual costs?

There are also ongoing costs to fund in the form of annual management fees to cover the services of a forester and insurance. Management fees are generally in the region of £10 per hectare per year, but other maintenance costs can add a further £30 to £40 per hectare per year. Any planting costs may be offset by grants. Typically, a 100-hectare, 25 year old forest might cost £4,500 a year for management, insurance and routine work.

If you answered 'yes' to these six questions, then forestry could be the ideal superhobby investment for you. Read on to find out more about prices and potential returns from forestry investment.

Timber prices

Timber prices are a big factor in the returns from an investment in forestry. Having a forest that produces a decent amount of tree growth year by year is only one side of the equation. What you realise from selling harvested trees depends ultimately on timber prices. This governs the cash yield from your forest property and in turn the value of the property as a whole.

Since there are many areas around the world where timber is grown commercially, this is a function not only of supply and demand but also of sterling's value in the foreign currency markets.

> ## Timber prices - key points
> - Timber prices crucial to returns
> - Baltic states are low cost competitors, but EU accession may change this
> - Current glut of cheap timber is gradually receding
> - Recovery to previous best levels would be 50% or more

One big problem that forestry investors have faced in recent years is that timber prices in sterling terms have been very soft. One reason for this is the disintegration of the Soviet Union. This placed many forests in the Baltic States that were formerly in public ownership back in private hands, with a very low historic book cost. Forestry in countries like these has also benefited from low labour costs, so actually extracting the timber and getting it to market is cheaper than in the UK.

The result was that these countries, desperate for foreign currency, encouraged forest owners to harvest and sell this high quality timber without being too worried about the prices they realised. The resulting glut of timber has meant that timber prices have been declining for several years. Relative strength of sterling in the foreign currency market hasn't helped either. In turn these two factors have adversely affected the value of forestry plantations in the UK and elsewhere. Costs are, however, now increasing in the Baltic states and this may help the UK situation in a year or two.

In some ways, as a potential new investor in forestry this could be good news. Prices are relatively depressed right now, but they should recover strongly when the world economy rebounds from its current period of slow growth and recession.

A return to the best levels seen in the last six to eight years would provide an uplift of 50-60%, boosting forest freehold prices too.

Let's look in more detail at how timber prices have moved and their impact on total returns from forestry investment. Figures produced by IPD (see following table) show that returns reached a peak of around a weighted average of 10% in the 1993-96 period and then declined and started to show negative returns for successive three year periods from 1996 onwards.

Table 9.1 - Total returns from forestry and timber price movements

	Total rtn index	Timber pr change %	Timber pr index
1993	95.5	11.3	111.3
1994	104.9	21.1	134.8
1995	113.8	-5.6	127.2
1996	126.7	-7.5	117.7
1997	131.6	-14.9	100.1
1998	129.7	-37.9	62.2
1999	115.5	-2.7	60.5
2000	112.1	-4.0	58.1
2001	110.0	-9.5	52.6
2002	104.9	-21.9	41.1

Source: IPD

Over the same period timber prices, having reached a peak in 1994, had by 2001 declined to around 50% of their 1992 level. Part of this price trend is a reflection of the glut of Baltic timber referred to earlier, a factor that may now be lessening in importance.

Returns

There are no guaranteed returns from forestry, despite the hints dropped by those seeking to sell collective investments based around it.

There have also been big variations in returns between type of property. IPD, for example quotes variations in return in the three years to 2001 as ranging from -7.2% for semi mature forests to +7.6% for young plantations. The reason for this is the drag effect that falling timber prices have on the older properties that have reached maturity.

As they reach maturity the normal process is for the standing timber to be felled and replaced. The most mature properties therefore face being locked into relatively low timber prices when the time comes to fell it, whereas younger plantations have a greater chance that the price will have long since recovered by the time they reach maturity.

Returns - key points

- Returns vary considerably between properties
- Long term real returns 5-6% per annum
- Returns like this have been absent for some time
- Returns are gross of normal running costs
- Returns are tax-free

Some investment illustrations about forestry as an investment assume long-term returns in the region of 6% to 8% in real terms. Allowing for inflation at 2% a year suggests money returns in the region of 8-10%. Most forestry experts would regard returns such as this as wildly optimistic. On the plus side, returns from many forests have not been as good as this for some time, as the table shows, but it could be argued that this only increases the likelihood of better returns in the future.

Table 9.2 - Three year rolling annualised returns from forestry

Period	Weighted average	Top 5%	Bottom 5%
1992-95	4.4	17.2	-7.8
1993-96	9.9	22.5	-5.6
1994-97	7.9	19.3	-3.7
1995-98	4.5	9.9	-6.9
1996-99	-3.0	6.4	-11.3
1997-00	-5.2	3.9	-13.8
1998-01	-5.4	3.5	-15.4
1999-02	-3.2	7.8	-13.7

Source: IPD

In practice returns like this would be received partly in the form of receipts from harvested timber and partly from an increase in the capital value of the standing timber itself. Income need not be taken if not required, or only enough taken to offset management costs, leaving the rest to benefit from higher timber prices in the future, if that is what is being assumed. Either way, income is not in regular 'lumps' and with old crops, there is limited flexibility in how it is taken.

A long-term nominal return of 7%, reinvested at the same rate and compounded over 10 years, would produce something in the region of a 100% increase in value.

Returns like this are better than can realistically be achieved in many conventional investments, particularly when the tax advantages are taken into account, although it is worth bearing in mind that returns at this rate have not, on balance, been consistently seen in the last five years.

How to buy and sell

There are two options for would-be forestry investors. One is buying direct; the other is owning a stake in forestry through a collective investment scheme.

Buying direct

At bottom, forestry is no more or no less than a specialised part of the property market. The process of buying or selling a forest property is essentially no different to buying and selling a house, with similar characteristics in the sense of the liquidity of the market and the time taken to complete legal checks and transfer title.

Having said that, there are many fewer forest properties sold each year than is the case in the residential property market. In 2001, the latest period for which figures are available at the time of writing, there were 106 recorded transactions valued in aggregate at some £18.7m, according to a report from Tilhill and FPD Savills. The average size of property sold was 114 hectares and the average value per transaction was some £175,000.

Some key points when buying woodland

- Location - how far is it from your home
- Access - rights of way, gates
- Species - aim for a diverse mix
- Water - a stream or river adds value
- Tracks and roads - check for wear and tear
- Covenants - public access, shooting rights.

The bulk of sales were at prices within 10% of the guide price set by the agent. The sale time for a forest property is generally not dissimilar to a conventional residential property, around 15 weeks from initial marketing to completion. Stamp duty and agents fees are a fact of life when buying and selling a forest property, just as they are in the residential property market. Agents charge around 2%. Purchasing costs including legal fees are generally reckoned at around 4% in total depending on the level of stamp duty to be paid.

The table overleaf shows details of the specialist estate agents involved in buying and selling forest properties and those involved in collective investment schemes in forestry.

Table 9.3 – Forestry – key web addresses and contact details

Company	Web address	Email	Phone	Type
CKD Galbraith	www.forestry-scotland.co.uk	ann.hackett@ckdgalbraith.co.uk	01463 224343	Adviser
FMS Investments	www.forestryplans.co.uk	info@forestryplans.co.uk	0117 9200 070	Adviser
Forestry Commission	www.forestry.gov.uk	enquiries@forestry.gsi.gov.uk	0131 334 0503	Manager
Forestry Investment Management	www.fimltd.co.uk	fim@fimltd.co.uk	01451 844655	Adviser
Fountains	www.fountainsplc.com	info@fountainsplc.com	01539 817100	Manager
FPD Savills	www.fpdsavills.co.uk	speck@fpdsavills.co.uk	01202 856800	Agent
Investment Property Databank (IPD)	www.ipdindex.co.uk	On site	020 7643 9257	Data
Irish Forestry	www.irish-forestry.ie	info@irish-forestry.ie	3531 284 1777	Adviser
John Clegg	www.johnclegg.co.uk	thame@johnclegg.co.uk	01844 215800	Agent
Marlborough Forestry	www.marlboroughforestry.org.nz	On site	n/a	Adviser
Tilhill	www.tilhill.co.uk	tilhill.nwales-kymmene.com	01678 530206	Manager
Woodland Investment Management	www.woodlands.co.uk	angus@woodlands.co.uk	020 7737 0070	Adviser
Woodlandfinders	www.woodlandfinders.com	mailbox@tilhill.co.uk	01786 435000	Agent

Forestry Investment Schemes

Collective investment schemes that invest in forestry have been designed to permit individuals with smaller amounts of capital to invest in forestry. In total they represent about 20% of the money invested in forestry each year.

The idea is that a pool of money is raised from investors and put to work purchasing a range of forest properties. These are managed over the life of the scheme, typically ten years, after which time the scheme is wound up, and the proceeds of the sale of the assets returned to shareholders.

While schemes like this represent a more affordable alternative for many investors, they have some drawbacks not borne by those who choose the direct investment route.

The most obvious of these is that ownership is diluted, and you have little or no control over your investment. As a shareholder in a scheme like this, all you own is a share in an unlisted company. The company owns the forest properties. Another issue is that of initial charges setting up the scheme. One recent scheme had initial charges including commission to intermediaries, professional fees and marketing costs that amounted to 6% of the money raised. In effect this means that only 94% of your money is being invested.

Projected returns from schemes like this are not guaranteed and may not be based on realistic assumptions. One scheme that closed recently in the UK projected a nominal return in excess of 8.7% per annum, which seems unrealistically high. Part of the reason was that the illustration was based on assuming an average inflation rate over the period of 3.9%, appreciably higher than the current rate.

Buying and selling forestry - key points

- Buying direct is like buying property
- Transaction costs around 4-5% on a purchase, less on a sale
- Average direct purchase £100,000 to £200,000
- Estimated returns from collective schemes need careful checking
- Tax implications of collective schemes need checking.

The other difficulty with collective investment schemes is that while income can seemingly roll up inside the scheme tax free, when the scheme is wound up, the proceeds fall within the capital gains tax regime as far as the shareholder in a scheme is concerned. Gains may possibly be sheltered by the normal annual exemption and by taper relief, which would amount to 40% if the investment were to be held for the full ten years, but this tax aspect does reduce the attractiveness of schemes like this relative to direct ownership.

There are also schemes that are offered occasionally which involve investing in forestry outside the UK, notably in Ireland. These have suspiciously high projected returns and low minimum investment levels and promise a tax-free lump sum at the end of the investment period. This is despite the fact that forestland prices are much higher in Ireland; roughly five times the UK norm. It doesn't seem to add up. The reason is that Irish forestland prices have been boosted because of entitlement to EU subsidies.

Projected returns from offshore schemes can be a little fanciful. A recent scheme, for example, had a projected rate of return in excess of 9% but a minimum investment level of €750. UK residents need to beware of schemes like this, because if income or capital distributions are brought onshore they will be assessed for tax.

If you are thinking of investing in collective investment schemes related to forestry, you need to check out the tax consequences of an investment like this with a professional adviser. Remember that because schemes like this are largely unregulated (although promoters need FSA and IMRO clearance), independent financial advisers are not allowed to actively promote them.

Where to get more information

The following is a summary of the main places where you can find useful information about forestry investing on the web. The sites are grouped according to the main themes covered in previous sections.

General

Tilhill (www.tilhill.co.uk) has a wealth of information on forestry as an investment including the tax advantages, market reports and a list of forests for sale. Tilhill can supply site assessment reports, valuations, investment appraisals, surveys and negotiate the purchase, and then provide full ongoing management support.

Tilhill manage woodland

The Institute of Chartered Foresters (www.charteredforesters.org) has a list of members in consultancy practice that can offer services such as valuing forestry properties, negotiating sales and purchases, management of forests and litigation and arbitration. Chartered Foresters are the only professionally qualified foresters and arborists in the UK and must have a minimum of five years study and experience to qualify. Many have degrees in forestry.

The Smallwoods Association (www.smallwoods.org.uk) has a guide to planning legislation and small woodlands together with other articles, which may be of interest.

The Forestry Commission (www.forestry.gov.uk) is the government department responsible for the production and expansion of British forests and woodlands, and supervises grant schemes and felling licences.

CKD Galbraith Forestry Department (www.forestry-scotland.co.uk) is part of a firm of Chartered Surveyors operating throughout Scotland. It specializes in sales and valuation for forests and woodlands. The site has much information on forestry investments including taxation, timber prices and capital assets. An online form provides access to the mailing list containing forests for sale for the next twelve months.

Other sites, which may be of interest, include Forestry and British Timber Magazine (www.fbti.co.uk), Community Woods (www.community-woods.org.uk) for those involved in shared ownership or management of woods in Scotland, the

Royal Forestry Society (www.rfs.org.uk) and The Forestry and Timber Association (www.forestryandtimber.org) the woodland owners trade union, with an excellent quarterly magazine.

Buying and selling

Apart from Tilhill, mentioned previously, there are several other prominent agents working in the forestry area.

John Clegg (www.johnclegg.co.uk) is a major seller of woodlands throughout the UK. The site has a list of woodlands for sale. The company does not give financial or taxation advice but does have on its site a summary of taxation provisions as they affect forestry.

Fountains (www.fountainsplc.com) provide forestry management services throughout the UK, and also buy and sell forests, although they tend to deal in larger parcels than those likely to be of interest to private investors.

Woodlandfinders (www.woodlandfinders.com) is an electronic market place for woodland purchasers and sellers operated by Tilhill. The site has an easy to use searchable database to find woodland for sale in a specified area of the UK. Registered potential buyers can be notified by email when new woodland that meets their criteria is added to the site. Other features include a buyer and owners guide and market reports.

FPD Savills (www.fpdsavills.co.uk) has specialist consultants to advise on all commercial forestry investment and management including purchase and sale, valuation, taxation and planting and maintenance all of which can be contacted by email from the site.

Woodland Investment Management (www.woodlands.co.uk) has a guide to buying woodland complete with a step-by-step legal guide. The site also has a list of woodlands for sale throughout the UK. The emphasis of the site is enjoyment rather than purely for investment, and prices tend to be high for the acreage involved.

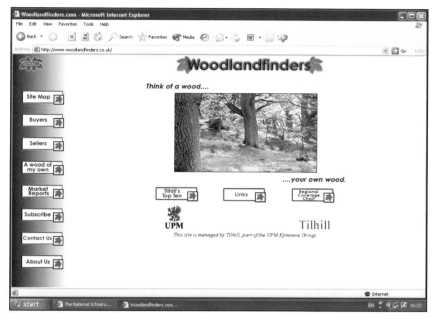

Woodlandfinders will find your woodland

Collective investment

Forestry Investment Management (www.fimltd.co.uk) has a list of woodlands available for purchase either through direct ownership or Unregulated Collective Investment Schemes (UCITS). The company offers a full investment management service, as well as maintaining lists of properties available for direct purchase.

FMS Investments (www.forestryplans.co.uk) specialises in collective, co-operative ownership of forestry mainly in Scotland. The site has a useful FAQ section covering the whys and wherefores of forestry investment and an online request form for further information.

Data

Investment Property Databank (www.ipdindex.co.uk), releases annual performance figures for UK forestry calculated from a sample of private sector coniferous plantations, and charts long term financial returns. The figures can be downloaded from the site. FPD Savills and Tilhill also issue annual reports on the forestry market and timber price trends (see www.tilhill.co.uk for more information).

Golden Prospect plc

- **Diversified natural resources investor**
- **Recognised as representing a unique opportunity in the London markets to gain diversified exposure to the gold and other junior resources sectors**
- **Listed on the London Stock Exchange AIM market since 1999**
- **Impressive core portfolio of 17 strategic equity holdings in natural resources companies listed in the UK, Australia, Canada and the USA**
- **Active trading portfolio comprising 50 equity positions in natural resources companies**
- **Strong shareholder base**

AIM: GOL

www.goldenprospectplc.com

10 | Gold

Of all tangible investments, gold is often seen as the ultimate. It has been recognised for centuries that its indestructibility and scarcity make it an ideal store of wealth. Currencies may come and go and stock markets may rise and fall. But gold is a permanent asset that will hold its value come what may.

This is not quite the whole truth. Those who bought gold at the last peak in its price in the late 1970s would have not only seen its value decline in absolute and real terms but missed out on the bull market in stocks in the 1980s and 1990s and the subsequent attractive returns seen in bonds.

In a way, though, this misses the point. Paradoxically, gold's lack of price performance versus a raging equity bull market is its attraction. It is one of the few assets that moves counter to the stock market. Nor does it depend for its value on the spending power of collectors, in the way that antique furniture, stamps or classic cars do.

It is, as one expert noted, 'the only truly divisible asset that is not someone else's liability'. It also appeals to those with a jaundiced view of the political process and the ability of governments to manage economies. As Herbert Hoover said: 'We have gold, because we cannot trust governments'.

Because of these characteristics, gold is much loved by the more apocalyptic commentators - particularly those who see geopolitical uncertainty continuing indefinitely, a wholesale loss of confidence in the dollar and a return to much higher levels of inflation. Remember that gold last hit its zenith in the late 1970s, when inflation was rising and the world had suffered two major oil price shocks.

At present, the determined attempts at reflation in the US mean, because the effects of monetary policy are hard to reverse rapidly, a risk of a sharp rise in inflation. An erosion of confidence in the dollar is already well under way. Conspiracy theorists suspect that a period of inflation may be one way - perhaps the only way - the US economy can escape from the crushing burden of household debt that has grown up in recent years.

This chapter looks at the background to investing in gold and other precious metals, and at how you can go about acquiring and holding the metal. For investors of modest means this will almost certainly be in the form of bullion coins, but there are other ways too. Note that collectable coins are a quite different market. These were covered in chapter seven.

Bullion basics

The value of gold waxes and wanes over time but ultimately it holds its value in real terms. The chart shows the real value of gold in the US since 1900. This shows it maintaining its real value over this 100-year plus period. The same is true over 200 years too.

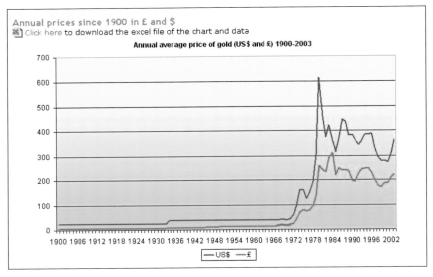

Gold price since 1900 © World Gold Council

The particularly sharp rise and subsequent fall in the price of gold between 1970 and 2002 is untypical. It has been more normal for gold to exhibit only limited amounts of volatility. Even after the rise in price seen in 2003, gold's value is currently close to the lowest point it has reached in real terms during the last century, and in terms of the price of stocks, bonds and property it is widely acknowledged to be almost as cheap as it has ever been. This argues strongly for investment in gold as a portfolio diversification right now.

The strength of gold as a store of value lies in its physical characteristics, and its scarcity, which in turn is linked to the difficulties involved in extracting it. Gold can be melted down to change its form and shape, but once extracted and refined is virtually indestructible.

Because of its density, all of the gold ever mined in the world - about 150,000 tonnes - would fit into a cube with sides of less than 20 metres, if refined to 24-carat purity. Virtually all of the gold ever mined is still in existence in some form, whether in the form of bullion bars, coins, jewellery, or as an industrial component.

Bullion basics - key points

- Relative to other assets, gold is as cheap as it has ever been
- Central bank selling and producer hedging has held back the gold price
- In any one year demand exceeds the amount mined
- Production and exploration costs put a floor of about $240 under the price
- Demand from individuals in the Middle and Far East is often underestimated

---

Mining gold is difficult. It often takes place in politically unstable countries. Even South Africa, the world's largest producer, extracts less than 400 tonnes of the metal a year. World production is currently around 2,500 tonnes a year. Even the more productive mines in South Africa produce only 8-10 grammes per tonne of ore, meaning that it takes three tonnes of ore to produce just one ounce of gold.

Production costs vary from mine to mine and from country to country, but are generally reckoned to be around $200 per ounce before taking exploration and production costs into account. For this reason mining for gold becomes uneconomic below a certain price level, generally reckoned to be in the region of $250 per ounce after exploration and development costs have been added in. This puts a floor under the spot price of gold, which is set in the free market and underpinned by an active market in gold futures.

Annual demand for gold for jewellery and industrial use is roughly 3,400 tonnes, appreciably more than is currently produced each year.

The other major influences on the market are the position of central banks' gold holdings, the degree to which gold mining companies are using the futures market to lock in prices they receive for future production, and the views of the man in the street expressed through the 'souk'.

Central banks have been large holders of gold since the 19th century and currently account for a fifth of existing stocks. Central bank independence and a more commercial approach to managing gold and convertible currency reserves has meant that some central banks have been reducing the size of their official stockholdings. This is principally because the gold they hold in reserve yields no return, although you could criticise this as being short sighted and that gold should be a strategic reserve for any central bank.

That said, the process of reserve adjustment now appears mostly complete and the banks concerned have reaffirmed that they continue to see gold as a major reserve asset for the foreseeable future. Some sales are likely in the future, but they should take place in a predictable and strictly controlled way.

The fact that central banks telegraphed their intention to sell some gold in the open market meant that the price moved against them in advance, hardly the shrewdest of moves. Central bank selling was arguably responsible for the lows in the gold price around the $250 mark seen in recent years.

Forward selling of mining output also had a significant effect on the gold price in recent years. It generally placed a ceiling on the price, above which additional supply came on to the market, driven by unwinding forward sales. The general consensus is that sales from these sources have now largely worked through the system. In turn mining companies are more optimistic about the outlook for the gold price. They therefore prefer, for the moment, to leave most of their output to be sold in the open market.

Demand from Middle Eastern and Far Eastern gold 'souks', in turn reflecting demand from the man in the street in these countries, is often underestimated as an influence on the price. Demand channelled through the 'souks' has over the last ten years taken an estimated 77% of world gold jewellery output (60% of the total physical offtake of gold).

Despite being what to Western eyes at least are simply primitive street markets, the gold dealers in the 'souks' are plugged into the international market just as closely as if they operated in London or New York.

Finally remember that by convention gold is priced in US dollars. Since gold holds it value come what may, weakness in the dollar by definition is likely to lead to an increase in the US dollar gold price. Which would you rather hold?

Is gold right for you?

Most investors with a substantial portfolio of assets invested in the stock market should view gold as a sensible diversification into an asset that should move in a way that is completely uncorrelated with movements in equity and bond prices and that will hold its value in periods of inflation and crisis. There is no getting away from the fact that gold is 'real money'.

But investing in gold requires you to answer 'yes' to a number of crucial questions.

Are you investing for the long term?

It's hard to say whether or not gold will come into its own this year, next year or the one after that. All one can say is that gold has a permanence that can be a source of considerable comfort to investors buffeted by the ups and downs of the stock market. As investment newsletter publisher Bill Bonner observes, 'while we cannot predict the future, eventually and always paper currencies disappear and gold remains'. Alan Greenspan, in testimony to the US Congress in 2001, said: 'In extremis paper money is accepted by nobody and gold is always accepted as the ultimate means of payment….'

Do you have adequate capital?

It is easy to answer yes to this question. Gold can be bought in amounts as little as $400 (about £225) for a single one ounce coin, to around £7,500 for a one kilo bar of bullion, and in larger multiples of this. Ten kilos of gold, heavy but easily portable and compact, are worth around £75,000 at current prices and exchange rates. How much you invest in gold depends on how worried you are about the current international situation and the proportion of your overall wealth you want to protect in this way.

Are you prepared for extra storage and insurance costs?

If you want to hold the gold physically on your own property, then you need to invest in both insurance and security measures, such as installing a safe in which to keep it. Alternatively you could trust it to a bank safety deposit box or buy an entitlement to gold in the form of an exchange traded fund or a certificate from a mint. These, however, are indirect means of ownership that rely on the integrity and permanence of the issuing institution, which in a cataclysm cannot be guaranteed. To be totally safe, you need to own your gold physically in a place where you can look at it. Most serious gold investors would say it is worth paying for this privilege.

Is portfolio diversification an objective?

Gold has a negative correlation with most other financial assets, and particularly with stock and bond markets. So it brings with it specific risk reduction characteristics that are independent of where its price might stand at any one time. It is an insurance policy against seemingly improbable but, if they occur, highly damaging events.

Do you have an apocalyptic view of world economics and politics?

If you do, then gold is undeniably right for you. If you think the world could collapse into chaos, that paper money will be debased and that banks will fail, then gold is for you.

If you think that there will be lawlessness, anarchy, imposition of exchange controls, and capital flight, then gold is your one sure anchor. This is always provided you are confident about being able to keep it safe and secure. It is salutary to remember that in the Middle and Far East gold has been prized as a portable liquid asset for centuries, and that the Chinese and Asian communities have been big buyers of gold in recent years.

If the answer to all these questions is yes, then gold and possibly other precious metals may well be the right way of diversifying your assets. Read on to find out how you can go about putting this strategy into effect.

Returns from holding gold

Calculating returns from investing in gold is easy. Unlike investing in art or antiques, gold is homogeneous, with a single price quoted on an international market every business day. Unlike the market in some other forms of tangible assets, the gold market has instant liquidity. If you want to buy or sell you can do so quickly and easily.

The table below shows returns from investing in gold over differing time periods in the past.

Table 10.1 - Returns from investing in gold over various time periods (Dollar terms)

Period	Average ann. rtn %	Maximum ann. rtn %	Minimum ann. rtn %	Standard deviation
1968-1996	4.21	77.6	-28.8	10.5
1896-1996	0.60	77.6	-28.7	4.5
1796-1996	0.31	77.6	-28.7	2.5
1596-1996	0.04	72.2	-29.7	1.4

The table shows that gold has always exhibited a positive return over whatever timescale you might choose, suggesting that there is a strong tendency for it to revert to the long term mean value. Its price has, however, been getting steadily more volatile over the years, as indicated by the standard deviation. Recent years have seen the sharpest extremes of year on year price movements.

Returns from gold - key points

- Gold has held its value over extremely long periods
- The gold price has a strong tendency to revert to the long term mean
- The gold price has been getting more volatile in recent years
- Gold moves counter to prices in stock and bond markets

The simplest example of the durability and power of gold as an investment comes if you calculate the return from the day in 1971 when President Nixon was forced to cut the link between gold and the dollar. This removed the shackles that had held the gold price artificially low, or the dollar artificially high. The day before Nixon's decision you could have bought an ounce of gold for $35. Today, 33 years later, you could sell it for more than eleven times that amount. That is an annual rate of return of around 8%.

The problem with this calculation is its starting point. Gold increased sharply in value during the 1970s precisely because its price had been held down artificially before then. The price of gold had not changed in relation to the dollar prior to that since FDR raised the dollar price of gold from $20.67 an ounce to $35.00 in 1934, 37 years previously.

Academic research commissioned by the World Gold Council shows a somewhat different picture when the returns from gold are compared with those of other types of asset. The results are shown in the next table. The data goes up to 1996.

Table 10.2 - Risk and return of trading gold versus other investments (in U.S dollars)

Category	Year	Average ann. rtn %	Maximum ann. rtn %	Minimum ann. rtn %	Standard deviation
Stocks	1896-1968	6.05	55.8	-37.8	4.8
	1968-1996	6.29	34.2	-34.4	7.2
LT Bonds	1896-1968	0.12	52.3	-36	3.0
	1968-1996	3.70	45.6	-16.1	8.3
T-Bills	1896-1968	0.02	42.6	-32.7	2.9
	1968-1996	2.43	9.9	-10.9	2.7
Gold	1896-1968	0.33	58.1	-27.2	3.6
	1968-1996	4.21	77.6	-28.7	10.5

The results belie gold's image as a stable store of value. In fact, though stocks and shares have better returns over most all time periods, and though gold beats holding bonds and cash, the returns seen from gold have been more volatile than most other categories.

This data excludes the later stages of the bull market and its subsequent bust, which highlights the big plus point for gold - that its returns come when stock markets are doing badly and that this is precisely when you do need something different in your portfolio.

In other words gold's returns may not be intrinsically stable in themselves, but they tend to occur in such a way that they offset the damage done to your wealth when stocks and bonds are out of favour.

How to invest in gold

There are several different ways of getting exposure to gold. We need, however, to distinguish between holding physical gold on the one hand, and a right to a specific amount of gold or an economic exposure to its price on the other.

Those with an apocalyptic view of life will insist on holding gold in physical form in a place where they can get easy access to it.

If what you want is a convenient way of holding it and the right to claim a specific physical amount of gold stored at a trusted institution, then there are other alternatives.

And if all you want is an economic exposure with no physical complications, then there are yet more alternatives you can pursue.

Physical bullion and coins

Assuming you have either a safety deposit box, or a heavy-duty safe in which to store the gold you invest in, what's the best way of buying the physical metal?

What to buy?

It depends in large measure on how much you wish to invest. Gold bulls will generally say that it is advisable to have around 10% of your assets represented by the gold 'anchor'. Bearing in mind that many investors considering a move of this sort may have substantial equity in the house they live in and other savings and investments as well, we could be talking terms of gold investment of up to, say, £50,000. This equates at current prices to about 6-7 kilos of gold.

You can perhaps reduce the amount accordingly if you are planning to invest in other tangible superhobby categories.

There is a small premium payable over the cost of the gold by weight in a bar, to cover the cost of manufacture. Larger bars carry a smaller premium than smaller ones. In no case, however, is the premium a significant amount and it will probably be recouped, less the dealer's margin, when the item is eventually sold.

Most dealers consider gold coins such as Krugerrands as equivalent to circular one-ounce bullion bars. Coins like this (and British Sovereigns, American Eagles, Canadian Maple Leafs and other variations on the theme) are sometimes available in a range of weights including one ounce, half ounce, quarter ounce and so on.

Owning physical gold - key points

- Holding 10% of your investable assets in gold provides an anchor
- Bullion coins like Krugerrands are the most practical way of owning gold
- Investment gold bears no VAT
- Hold your gold yourself, or in a segregated account at a bank
- If you have good security, holding your own gold avoids custody charges

---

Premiums on coins are generally higher than on bars but, if bought in significant quantities the premium on coins can fall to levels comparable to small bars. Coins and small bars have the advantage of divisibility.

Divisibility is important. It may be at some stage you wish to sell some of your gold to take advantage of a rise in price, or for other reasons. Holding some of your hoard in the form of coins or small 100-gram bars allows you to remove relatively small amounts and not sell more than you need at any one time.

Premiums paid do, however, depend on supply and demand at the time and can fluctuate. Large bars are usually the most efficient way to buy gold, but in certain circumstances coins can be a better investment. The Krugerrand is usually the cheapest of all the one-ounce gold coins.

Buying onshore

Gold bought for investment purposes does not attract VAT in the UK or the rest of the EU but there are a number of terms and conditions that UK bullion dealers apply, mainly related to anti-money laundering and tax aspects.

Purchasers must provide proof of identity, for example, and the first purchase of gold by any individual of more than £5,000, or an aggregate purchase of more than £10,000 of gold in one twelve month period, will be reported to Customs & Excise.

Buying offshore

Is this worth thinking about? It depends whether or not you already have an existing offshore bank account. Some investors look to Switzerland for the purchase and storage of precious metals, and specifically to private banks. The private banks are chosen because they provide safety and confidentiality. Many private banks deal in precious metals in addition to their other activities.

Types of account

It is possible you may not want to physically hold the gold you buy on your premises. It may be better kept in a bank vault. Whether you have an offshore or onshore bank account, there are three types of physical ownership (apart from holding it yourself) to bear in mind.

These are: a claims account, a custodial account or a safety deposit box arrangement. Clearly a safety deposit box needs no further explanation. They are anonymous but not 100% secure, since robberies do occasionally take place.

The claims account is basically an account where the amount you own is identified, but in physical terms may be part of a large bar stored in a bank's vaults. The only downside to this method of purchase and storage is that the bank client has a claim on the books of the bank and does not own the metal outright. Should the bank have financial problems, the bank account owner could become a creditor of the bank.

Some commercial and private banks offer a custodial account, allowing you to buy and store a 'specific and divided' amount of gold. The purchase could be of coins or bars. This arrangement is 'off the books' of the bank, and thus not subject to creditor claims. Clearly, this way of buying and storing in a segregated manner is safer but more expensive. Custody fees can be as much 3-4% of the value of the gold held.

Bullion certificates

Many investment advisers regard bullion as the hassle-free way of owning gold (and indeed other precious metals). Those of an apocalyptic view might prefer outright physical ownership, but the best certificate programme is backed by a government guarantee and therefore about as secure as you can get.

The safest precious metals investment program in the world today is the Perth Mint Certificate. The PMC is a document that gives the holder legal title to precious metals stored on either an allocated (segregated) or an unallocated (unsegregated) basis with the Perth Mint in Perth, Western Australia.

The important thing is that the PMC is safe and secure. A PMC holding is a conservative investment managed by the Perth Mint - a venerable, century-old institution. The government of Western Australia guarantees Perth Mint obligations. Western Australia is one of Australia's wealthiest states. The government of Western Australia is rated AAA. The PMC programme is the only one with a government guarantee.

There are minimum investment levels involved in owning a certificate, but they aren't that onerous. You don't have to be a millionaire to afford an initial coin investment of $10,000 (£5,500), with subsequent purchases of $5,000 (£2,750) or more. The low certificate fee (£35), coupled with no storage fee on unallocated accounts, makes this investment very attractive.

Alternatives to physical gold - key points

- Bullion certificates represent a claim on a specific amount of gold
- Perth mint bullion certificates are government guaranteed
- Gold bullion shares give you exposure to the gold price
- Spread betting on the gold price gives you geared exposure

The certificate is non-negotiable but transferable. There are approved dealers in key markets in the world. Delivery of the underlying gold or other precious metal can be made in Perth, Western Australia or in primary precious metals centres elsewhere in the world at any time. Investors have the option of holding any or all the precious metals - gold, silver, platinum and palladium - in either bullion, coin or bar form.

Gold bullion shares

These are a relatively recent introduction and amount to buying shares in a mutual fund backed by a reserve of gold, where each share represents one-tenth of an ounce of the metal held in a bank vault. The shares owned by investors are in each case traceable back to a specific numbered bar and are traded on a recognised stock exchange.

The system, initiated by the World Gold Council, is already operating successfully in Australia and London, and gold bullion shares will soon be trading in New York, on European stock markets and in South Africa.

World Gold Council home page

The management cost of the fund is 0.24% per annum and even if you add in dealing costs, the total cost of owning gold in this way compares very favourably indeed with the custody costs of holding the physical metal in a segregated account, although less well with a gold certificate programme. Since gold is priced in dollars, non-US investors also avoid the transaction fees involved in acquiring the necessary foreign exchange to buy gold, although movements in the dollar exchange will affect the value of their investment.

Gold bullion shares have been trading successfully in London for several months, with the ticker symbol GBS.

Spread betting in gold

Another way of achieving economic exposure to the gold price (and prices of other precious metals) is via spread betting.

To take advantage of this form of trading you need to open an account with a financial bookmaker like IG Index or Cantor Index. Firms like this operate by making a two-way price in a range of shares, stock market indices and commodities, usually where there is an active futures market that allows them to offset any net exposure they might incur.

In spread betting, you can bet on either a fall or rise in the price of the item in question, and dictate the size of your financial commitment by nominating the size of stake you wish to bet.

In the case of gold prices are quoted in 10-cent 'ticks'. If you place an 'up bet' (buy) gold at 4,000 ($400) at £1 a point and the price rises by $10, you make a profit of £100 or $180 at current exchange rates, roughly equivalent to holding 18 ounces of the metal. At £2 a point, the exposure is roughly equivalent to holding 36 ounces of the metal at current exchange rates.

One important plus point is that by denominating the bet in sterling you are getting exposure to the movement in the price of gold, but not to the underlying dollar exchange rate. In other words, your £1 a point bet on the gold price pays out based on the movement in the dollar price, but your winnings are in sterling. There is no translating of the dollar value into and out of sterling to do to work out your profit.

The drawback to spread betting in this way is that it is not designed to be a long-term investment medium. Most spread bets are based around futures prices. Futures have expiry dates and although bets can be rolled forward from one expiry date to the next, this does entail a cost. Spread betting on gold is best confined to situations where you believe that the price is temporarily and significantly out of line with events and may quickly correct itself.

Spread bets are based on margin requirements. Bets that lose money consistently may require you to add more funds to your account. A £1 per point bet on the price of gold would normally require you to have a minimum of £150 in your account, and in practice significantly more than this to cover day to day fluctuations in the price.

The spread in the gold price is currently around 10 points, in other words, roughly a dollar. You buy at the equivalent of $401 and sell at $400. This is small beer compared with the costs of buying and holding physical gold and compared with the price movements that can occur. Spread betting on gold also falls outside the capital gains tax regime.

Other precious metals

Gold isn't the only option when it comes to investing in precious metals. But it is the most widely known and does have a cachet that some of the others do not possess, at least in the imagination of the man in the street.

You can buy gold tax-free in the UK, in Switzerland and throughout the EU countries. However, silver, platinum and palladium (normally known as 'white' metals) are subject to VAT.

Having to pay VAT is clearly prohibitive for investment purchases. The result is that for the most part the 'white' metals are bought and stored in a VAT free zone.

In mid 2001 silver was close to an eight-year low at $4.15. It has moved up significantly recently, and the price is now 50% above that low reached more than 18 months ago.

Silver has had a chequered history. It has provided backing for currencies but also been the subject of intense speculation. The most famous recent instance was the attempt to corner the market in 1979/80 by the Texan Hunt Brothers. Now it is mainly an industrial metal and its movement is difficult to predict. Sometimes it is pulled along by the gold price: at other times its industrial demand seems to exert more influence.

Platinum is a metal even more recondite than gold. All of the platinum ever mined would only occupy a 25-foot cube rather than the 20-metre cube of gold referred to earlier in this chapter. Although demand has soared in the past decade, supplies are limited to only a few mining sources. About 75% of it is mined in South Africa.

Other precious metals - key points

- Other precious metals attract VAT, so must be stored in a tax free zone
- Silver and platinum can be bought in coins or bars
- Some precious metals can be acquired through bullion certificates
- There is spread betting in silver and platinum, though unit sizes differ

---

Platinum is an industrial metal, and a strategic one. It has many high tech applications and is also increasingly being used for jewellery. The price has already more than doubled from its low, rising from $420 an ounce to close to $860 in the past year, beating even the gold price.

Palladium is an alternative to platinum in some industrial processes, but its thinly traded price fell by more than 40% between 2002 and 2003, from about $443 an ounce to $240 and has dropped further recently. The price is currently $233 and in recent weeks it has been as low as $200.

Carmakers could substitute palladium for expensive platinum in catalytic converters and this could boost the price. Most palladium is mined in Russia and supplies tend to be held back during the first half of the year, producing strong rallies in the price.

So silver and palladium could be candidates for 'safe haven' accumulation if you are convinced of the need for having metals as your alternative investment medium. But how do you buy?

As with gold, it really depends on the size of your wallet, whether you want the satisfaction of seeing the metal you own, and whether or not you want gearing and the risk it brings with it.

Rather like gold, silver can be purchased in bars, coins, and via certificates and spread betting. White metals are available as coins, like the platinum American Eagle, Canadian Maple Leaf, and the Isle of Man Noble.

As with gold, coins like this are portable, attractive and easy to store, but need to be insured. Silver and other precious metals are also available as futures either directly or through the medium of spread betting. Or you could opt for a precious metals certificate programme such as the one run by Perth Mint.

Perth Mint - home of a good certificate programme

Outside of gold, Perth Mint offers certificates on the Australian Koala (1oz. of platinum), its palladium equivalent, and silver coins (the Australian Kookaburra and Lunar), in kilo, 10oz., 2oz. and 1oz. versions. Bars are available in a range of weights.

Spread betting basics in white metals are the same as for gold. But remember that the price quoted may not be in the form that the metal's price is quoted in the financial press. If you are spread betting on silver, for example, the price 'tick' on which your bet is based will be in US cents, not in dollars or in the 10-cent tick used in gold spread bets.

Not all spread betting firms advertise palladium as a product on which they will make a price. City Index offers gold, silver, platinum and palladium. Cantor Index only advertises gold, silver and platinum, but may make a price in palladium.

As with all spread bets, because of the leverage involved, you need to have a significant amount of cash in your account to cover margin requirements. And in markets like these, it's a good idea to place stop loss orders in case a trade goes wrong. Spread betting in precious metals, like gold, falls outside of the capital gains tax regime and deals are commission free.

Note: The author's book 'The Investor's Toolbox' (Harriman House) has more information on spread betting and how to use it for trading.

Where to get more information

The following are a number of sites where there is more information on gold and how to invest in it.

Dealers

Baird & Co (www.goldline.co.uk) is a bullion merchant based in East London. It supplies precious metal and investment products. Bullion coins and investment bars can be bought online and price information is updated twice daily on the website. Investors are offered either trading in gold or silver where the metal may be held in an unallocated account and dealt in the spot market or on the twice daily London fixing, or in an allocated account for specific numbered bars.

Chard (www.24carat.co.uk) buys and sells high quality gold jewellery, gold sovereigns, Krugerrands and other coins as well as gold bars. There are eight websites in all covering different aspects of the gold and gold coin market.

Tax Free Gold (www.taxfreegold.co.uk) offers simple investment advice, a gold price forecast and information concerning gold bars. The online catalogue is extensive and informative.

Hussar (www.hussarbullion.com) trades gold, silver and platinum group metals in all forms. The service includes financing, account management, pricing, shipping and insurance. The company originated in the Channel Islands but now has offices worldwide, and can deal with enquiries 24 hours a day. The site offers limited information, but there are contact details for further enquiries.

The Perth Mint (www.perthmint.com.au) is an informative site providing comprehensive information on gold and precious metal investment. Areas covered include purchasing gold and precious metals, live spot prices and statistical data. The certificate program and depository services are also covered in detail. The online shop is extensive, with worldwide delivery.

Spread Betting

Cantor Index (www.cantorindex.co.uk) has an online brochure covering all aspects of spread betting and live prices for gold, silver and platinum.

City Index (www.cityindex.co.uk) has an introduction to spread betting plus a downloadable brochure. Account holders have access to live prices, market reports, charting and market and investment research.

IG Index (www.igindex.co.uk) has a downloadable dealing guide. As with all spread betting firms IG is not allowed to give trading advice.

All the spread betting firms offer 24-hour online trading and will quote a price and deal immediately.

Information Sites

The Bullion Desk (www.thebulliondesk.com) was formed in 1999 by three former members of the London Bullion Market. It provides comprehensive online precious metal information. Included on the site are live prices, charts, financial data, numerous links and daily and periodic reports from sources such as HSBC, Mitsubishi, Reuters and Investec. Books on precious metal can be purchased via a direct link to Amazon.

The World Gold Council (www.gold.org) has everything you need to know about gold, silver, platinum and palladium. Among the wealth of information on offer is the daily bulletin with news, prices and numerous other items of interest.

Much of the content is free but a premium service has added benefits including real time access to prices worldwide and exclusive research from many of the leading bullion banks. The site has links to gold traders worldwide and extensive information on gold bullion securities, which the Council has played a key role in sponsoring.

STANLEY
GIBBONS
LIMITED

BY APPOINTMENT TO
HER MAJESTY THE QUEEN
STANLEY GIBBONS LIMITED
LONDON PHILATELISTS

Stanley Gibbons
Investment Department

The value of stamps as an investment has been highlighted by many investment institutions. A Salomon Brothers study of Commodities, Currencies and Bonds from 1907-1990 gave stamps the 4th highest rate of return at 10% per year; ahead of both Bonds at 9.6% and Foreign Exchange at 4.4%.

Rainbow Colour Trial Sheetlet
2001 from £9,000   2004 from £30,000
This example sold by Stanley Gibbons for £42,500 in 2004

Great Britain SG137
2001 £1,800   2004 £3,500
94.4% increase in value

Nyasaland SG69/70
Sold by Stanley Gibbons for £16,000 in 2003
A similar example recently sold in auction in excess of $38,000

Why invest with Stanley Gibbons?

- The stamp market has a huge collector base underpinning prices resulting in low market volatility.
- Stamps are traded in all major currencies and have a global market place.
- Our expert advice and guidance ensures that you only buy the best quality material.
- Buyer confidence is high knowing that we only sell material we would be pleased to repurchase.
- FREE portfolio management service.
- Secure storage and insurance facility available.
- The pleasure and enjoyment of owning a piece of history as an investment.

For further information please call the Investment Department on 020 7557 4454
or log on at **www.stanleygibbons.com/investment**

We look forward to being of service and assisting your entry into this fascinating and enjoyable area of investment
Note: Illustrations are not actual size

Chapter 11 Stamps

Weight for weight stamps are probably the most valuable tangible assets you can buy. A single stamp in mint condition weighs about a tenth of a gram but can be worth thousands of pounds. Stamp collecting is the largest hobby outside of some sports, with an estimated 30m enthusiasts worldwide.

Collectors are diverse. The Queen is an active philatelist and has one of the world's great collections. And, at odds with stamp collecting's traditional image, the Real Madrid footballer Luis Figo is also an award-winning collector. Many astute philatelists have put together a collection over their lifetime that has proved to be worth a small fortune when it comes eventually to be sold.

Superhobby investors are pursuing a somewhat different approach. They are motivated mainly by the returns that can be made over a period of years by putting together a portfolio of stamps as scarce objects in their own right. It may be that eventually they come to be interested in the history of the stamps that form part of their portfolio. But that is not a necessary part of capturing the returns that stamps can bring them.

Stamp investment is in some ways analogous to investing in the stock market. Certain stamps and genres of stamps move in and out of favour; demand for some types of stamps is broadly linked to the economy, and to the spending power of the underlying collector base.

Investors pick a portfolio of ten or twenty items to avoid undue dependence on any one particular one. They can buy additional items if they wish as they go along, adding to their portfolio over time.

The stamp dealer plays the role of an advisory broker, drawing attention to possible new portfolio additions, and perhaps highlighting the potential to take a profit in an item that has risen too far in value relative to the rest of the market.

Most stock market investors are inherently comfortable with this approach. Even the idea of dematerialised trading is relevant to stamp investment. Because condition is such an important component of an individual stamp's value, dealers often keep investors' portfolios stored under ideal conditions on their premises rather than risk storage in conditions that may detract from their value.

Stamp basics

History

Since the concept of postage stamps began life in 1840 in Britain, the idea has been imitated and developed across the world. Once stamp issuing became widespread, collectors began to take an interest.

In those countries with a monarchy, stamp issues generally change when monarchs change, providing a punctuation mark for the collector. When a monarch changes, it means that the supply of stamps issued with that monarch's image stops, and the items thus attain some kind of scarcity value. Generally speaking, the further back in time the more valuable the stamp will be.

The same was true when countries took new names as a result of political change, such as gaining independence from colonial rule. When this happened, the stamps changed, and those previously issued acquired a scarcity value. Stamps issued by Rhodesia or Nyasaland have greater cachet than those issued by their present day successor countries of Zimbabwe and Malawi.

War plays its part too. The Japanese occupation of Malaya led to special issues of stamps, as did the German occupation of the Channel Islands. Any event of this nature, particularly of relatively short duration, leads to the creation of stamps that in the future potentially have built-in scarcity value.

The ways in which stamps are printed also contribute to scarcity and create collectibility. Stamps that originate from specific printers or from numbered printer's plates can become scarce items. Those that are at the edge of a sheet and which therefore contain a blank paper margin next to the usual perforations also have scarcity value.

The way in which a used stamp has been cancelled by the application of a postmark may contribute to its value. But a smudged or poorly applied cancellation can significantly reduce a stamp's value.

> ### Stamp basics
> - High value, portable store of value
> - Condition is vital to value
> - Fragility adds to scarcity
> - Investors avoid contemporary material
> - Huge collector base provides market liquidity

Being fragile paper items, wear and tear over the years erodes the supply of older stamps. This enhances the value of those that remain, provided that their condition is maintained. Condition is vital, and a separate section is devoted to it later in this chapter.

One important reason for not collecting contemporary stamps for investment purposes has been the fact that in recent years some postal authorities have been profligate at issuing so-called 'collectors sets' of stamps with attractive pictures. Gambia and Liberia, for example, each issued more than 500 different stamps in 2001 (the UK's Royal Mail only issued 75).

This abundant supply of new material makes newly issued sets worthless for investment purposes, although it does not detract from the value of early issues. Gambia's early issues are, for example, highly sought-after. Only those taking an exceptionally long-term view or those collecting contemporary stamps for thematic reasons (say, for example, any stamps featuring birds), can expect to profit significantly from their collections.

An example of the scale of this problem is that in the Stanley Gibbons checklist 'Collect British Stamps' the period from 1840 to 1952 occupies pages 1-13, while the present Queen's reign occupies pages 14 to 163. Stamps issued in this latter era are unlikely to make good investments unless they are significant varieties or errors. Serious collectors have tended to bypass modern stamps of countries that currently operate profligate issuing policies.

One important parameter for investors is the number of collectors. Collectors provide a ready market for investment quality stamps held in portfolios, assuring investors of a fair price should they choose to sell. The number of collectors far exceeds the numbers of investors in rare stamps. Latest estimates suggest that there are around 30 million stamp collectors worldwide. The number of non-collector investors, if one can specify such a category, is probably in the low thousands in the UK, compared with collector numbers in the hundreds of thousands.

Numbers of collectors in any geographical area are less relevant than you might suppose since, for example, there are collectors of rare British stamps all over the world, and not just in the UK. Many British collectors do, however, simply collect stamps from Great Britain and present or former British colonies and Commonwealth countries.

This brings us on to the subject of collecting themes.

Collecting areas – geography

Since it is the postal authorities of particular countries that issue stamps, collecting the stamps of a particular country or group of countries is a natural collecting theme.

Those that are popular include British stamps, perhaps because Britain originated the concept of the postage stamp. Stamps from Commonwealth countries, particularly those that have historical significance in some way - Cyprus, Canada, the Falklands, and Hong Kong - are popular areas with collectors. And the USA, France, China, Russia and the Holy Land all have large collector bases.

Collecting areas - other

Collectors pursue many different themes, but popular ones include: stamps and postal material to do with transmission by air; postal material related to space travel; and items related to key events in postal history. There are many other themes. One example is pictorial postage stamps related to ornithology or animals. Some collectors collect only unused stamps: others collect only used ones. Some collectors collect stamps used for revenue and excise tax purposes, rather than for postage.

From an investment standpoint, however, investors need to stick to those areas and themes where there is a substantial body of active collectors, preferably international ones. This means that there should be liquidity in the market should the investor choose to sell, and prices will be sufficiently well bid for dealers' spreads to be narrow. For the most part this means classic British stamps from the Victorian era to the start of WW2, and those of selected foreign and commonwealth countries over a similar period.

Condition

The condition of a stamp has a dramatic effect on its price. Prices for stamps in a dealer's catalogue will typically be listed for examples in 'fine' condition, that is for a stamp without creases and tears and, if used, with a clear cancellation mark.

The issue of condition is more complex than this explanation might suggest, however. While today stamps are generally kept in albums under clear plastic strips that retain the stamp without affecting its quality in any way, earlier generations of stamp collectors used hinges or mounts to keep their stamps in their album.

Successive applications of hinges or mounts in earlier years detract from the quality of a stamp and affect its price, although more allowance is made in this respect for stamps from early years - issued, say, before 1900.

For unused stamps, of paramount importance is that the gum on the back of the stamp should be intact and original. Stamps where the gum has been disturbed by the application of mounts or hinges generally fetch lower prices, especially in the case of stamps issued during the 20th century. Discoloration or cracking of the gum on stamps also affects their price.

> ## Condition - key points
>
> - Catalogue prices are for 'fine' items
> - Mounted or unmounted
> - Used or unused
> - Perforations and margins
> - Gum
> - Quality of cancellation mark if used

Perforations and margins are another aspect of the condition of stamps. Early stamps like the penny black did not have perforations, but were cut from a sheet. It is important in examples like this that the margins should be as large and even as possible on all four sides of the stamp.

A set of intact perforations on a stamp is the ideal. More common is that one or two perforations will have been damaged but the remainder left intact. There is a whole specialised vocabulary dealing with the degree of damage to perforations, from 'nibbed' through 'short' to 'pulled' and 'missing'. More than one or two missing perforations on a classic stamp from the early 20th century is likely to reduce its value drastically.

Where used stamps are concerned these considerations also apply, but an additional variable is introduced - the quality of the cancellation mark. In the case of early stamps, symbols like a Maltese cross were often used, in a colour such as red.

Subsequently the norm became a black circular cancellation date stamp (often abbreviated to CDS). Clear and lightly applied postmarks are the things to look for, heavy smudged ones to be avoided. Some stamps were cancelled by hand in manuscript. Cancellations that are exactly centred in the stamp may also be worth a premium.

Because condition is so vital when it comes to determining the value of a stamp, this area has been fertile ground for forgers, sometimes called by the tongue-in-cheek term of 'stamp improvers'. Various tricks are used, for example to redistribute the gum on a stamp where heavy hinging has damaged it.

Another instance is with an unused stamp where the gum had been removed. This could be turned into a more attractive proposition by the addition of a forged cancellation mark, turning it from a poor quality unused example to a fine quality used one. Then again, stamps displaying forged cancellations can be collectors' items in their own right.

There is a clear trade-off between condition and price, and you need to be satisfied that the stamp meets your criteria in both respects before agreeing to buy it. This is particularly true when considering stamps as an investment.

Investment quality stamps

Investors demand stamps that hold their value. Typically these will be stamps that the dealer will guarantee to be in superior condition with, if used, a desirable single circular date stamp cancellation mark. Unused stamps will normally be in pristine unmounted condition, but this may be unrealistic for older issues. Used stamps will be classed as fine or very fine examples.

All stamps will have a minimal amount of damage to perforations, or in the case of older examples, have a full set of margins. A Certificate of Authenticity from one of the major 'expertising' bodies is desirable and may add to the resale value of the item.

The table below shows some statistics on prices of a sample portfolio of British and British Commonwealth stamps of pre WW2 and earlier, worth in the region of £10,000 in all.

Table 11.1 - Stamp investing - a typical portfolio

Country	Type/Year	Catalogue	Condition	Price (£) (late 2003)
Australia	1913 5s grey-yellow	SG13	Used VF	150
Batum Brit Occupation	1920 50r deep blue	SG27	Used Only 80-180 issued certificated	1,200
British Guiana	1888-89 $4 green	SG118	Mint Only 1133 issued	450
British Honduras	1882-87 2/6d yellow	SG21	Mint VF, only 1200 issued	75
Cape of Good Hope	1855-63 1s deep dark grn	SG8B	Mint Marginal pair	450
Cape of Good Hope	1863-64 4d deep blue	SG19	Mint Pair	225
Falkland Islands	1912-20 10s red/green	SG68	Used VF, lightly cancelled	225
Great Britain	1840 1d black plate 1a	SG2	Mint VF, certificated	4,400
Great Britain	1913 £1 green 'seahorse'	SG403	Mint VF	2,250
Iraq - Brit. Occupation	1932 1d/25r violet	SG121	Used Fine, scarce used	150
Mauritius	1863-72 1d purple-brown	SG56	Mint VF block of four	225
				10,000

Source: Stanley Gibbons

The important point is that, to perform well, stamps must combine scarcity and good condition.

Stamps in isolation are also not the only philatelic investment medium. Items of rare postal history, that is to say the use of stamps on their original envelopes and letters sent prior to the issue of stamps in 1840 have shown some of the greatest rises in value over the past few years. They are highly sought after by leading collectors.

The selection of items like this, however, needs to be made by dealers expert in this area since the value depends on a number of different factors, including the rarity of the cancellation, the number of stamps used, the scarcity and destination of the letter, or the routing of the letter.

Is it right for you?

Like gold in the preceding chapter, most investors with a substantial portfolio of assets invested in the stock market can use stamps as a sensible diversification move. Like gold, stamps can act as a hedge against inflation. Moreover they are a discreet and portable form of wealth.

Stamp prices tend to rise as the general level of prices rise. Unlike gold, however, stamps will not protect you from an apocalyptic investment background, since their value is largely determined by the spending power of the collector base.

Let's look at the questions you need to answer to determine whether stamps could form a place in your wider portfolio of investments.

Are you investing for the medium to long term?

The typical timescale for stamp investment to pay off is said by dealers to be in the region of five to ten years. Holding a portfolio of stamps for this length of time or longer should produce the optimum level of returns. While stamps are a relatively liquid market and a portfolio could be sold sooner than this, you may not get the full benefit of owning them if you sell too early.

Do you have adequate capital?

In theory there is no maximum or minimum amount to be invested, although a dealer such as Stanley Gibbons will probably stipulate that to be cost effective an investment in the region of a minimum £5,000 or £10,000 is probably the right size for a long-term portfolio. This will enable you to buy some of the scarcer items that have shown the best rises in the past. Whether or not you feel able to afford this depends on the scale of your other assets, and what other superhobby investments you are contemplating.

Are you prepared for extra storage and insurance costs?

You can hold the stamps you invest in physically on your own property. If you do this, you will ideally need to invest in both insurance and security measures, such as installing a safe in which to keep them. Security measures are arguably less necessary for stamps than for items like antiques or bullion, since they are easily concealed and their value is not readily apparent to the untutored eye.

> ### Right for you?
>
> - Time horizon 5-10 years
> - Minimum investment £2,000-£5,000
> - Storage costs 1% pa
> - Consistent gains in recent past, with low volatility
> - Interested in history and geopolitics?

Stamps are straightforward diversification rather than a store of value if times get hard. They have the advantage of portability, but against that has to be set the fact that careless handling could severely affect their resale value. Most stamp investors opt to have a dealer store and insure the stamps for them. The normal cost of this service at a well-known dealer like Stanley Gibbons is 1% of the value of the portfolio per annum.

Is portfolio diversification an objective?

Stamp prices rise in line with economic growth and inflation. They are a diversification in that sense, but unlike gold, for example, will not protect your wealth particularly well in the case of a severe economic downturn. They should therefore rise in line with the overall trend in the stock market, but not exhibit the same degree of volatility as stocks and shares.

In that sense you might consider them to be a more liquid and portable form of property. The supply of classic stamps is restricted in the same way that land is, and therefore the value of items like this tends to rise steadily in value. Unlike property and the stock market, however, the element of volatility added by purchases being made with borrowed money is by and large not present in the stamp market.

Do you have an interest in history and geography?

Philately is to some degree an interest that combines history from the mid-19th century onwards, with the endless twists and turns in geopolitics. A particularly rich vein for stamp collectors over the years has been the changes that have taken place in the Commonwealth as increasing numbers of countries have gained independence.

Countries like Hong Kong, the Falkland Islands, Cyprus and Malaysia all have a rich philatelic heritage. The stamps issued by many former British and European colonies in Africa and the Middle and Far East that have since gained independence are interesting historical curios in their own right.

To have at least a passing interest in the political and historical development of these territories is, if not a pre-requisite, then something of an asset when it comes to making a judgement about the worth of a portfolio a dealer may have put together for you, and of any acquisitions or disposals that the dealer may subsequently suggest.

Read on to find out more about stamp prices and returns.

Stamp prices

Stamps vary considerably and those items considered rare by the general public may not be the most valuable in a collection. Most people consider penny blacks to be the scarcest, but in fact a 'fine' used 1840 'penny black', for example, may be had for around £150 at the time of writing, whereas a 'tuppence blue' of the same vintage may fetch considerably more. A used £5 orange from 1883 may fetch over £3,000 in perfect condition.

A penny black - the stamp world's 'icon'

At the other end of the scale Victorian stamps issued between 1858 and 1870 had a variety of plate numbers. The rarest of these plates on a penny rose-red stamp was plate 77. Find a used example of this stamp and it is worth in the region of £120,000 - unused, considerably more. A penny black from the rarest plate, plate 11, has a catalogue value of £2,500 used but may be picked up for considerably less, perhaps around £1,800.

This brings up a major issue when it comes to buying stamps. The price in a dealer's catalogue is the price at which a dealer will sell an example in 'fine' condition. A flawless example will often command a premium over the catalogue price. It is rare for stamps to have no flaws and the price also reflects a dealers' margin. Stamps are routinely available at less than the dealer's catalogue prices at auction and elsewhere.

Commonwealth stamps can have chunky prices. A Kenya & Uganda mint black and brown £50 from the reign of George V is catalogued by Stanley Gibbons at £25,000, a pair of 6d imperforate mint British Solomon Islands Protectorate at £3,750, and a marginal £10 purple and ultramarine mint Nyasaland Protectorate Edward VII at £7,000.

Often it is the most unprepossessing items that will have the greatest value since the scarcity of an individual stamp is not readily apparent to the untutored eye. This is the attraction of the hobby to collectors - the fact that one day he or she may happen across a rare stamp and is able to acquire it for a fraction of its true value.

In reality this hope is probably a vain one. The fact remains that, more than antiques and art, stamps are arguably the best documented and most intensively researched of all collectables. There is extensive data on the price history of particular items, and a large body of collectors. London is also the recognised international centre for stamp dealing, and hence there is every chance that British investors' will get the best prices, both buying and selling, for their stamp portfolios.

Many collectables do not possess this characteristic - namely a reasonably predictable price when an item is resold.

Returns from stamp investments

Though it should in theory be possible to trace the returns from stamps from successive annual catalogues produced by dealers, little formal work has been done on this, chiefly because stamps have been largely a collectors' market rather than an investors' one ever since philately originated as a hobby in the 19th century.

It is only recently that Stanley Gibbons, the leading global stamp dealer, has compiled an index of the most actively traded stamps that allows the general level of prices to be compared from one year to the next and for returns to be worked out from it.

That said, it should be remembered that enthusiasm for stamps as a store of value has come in waves that coincide with fears of rising inflation. There was a bubble in stamp prices in the late 1970s and early 1980s, just as there was in wine and whisky for much the same reason, a bubble which, when it subsided, left some investors nursing losses. There is no evidence that such bubble conditions exist at present.

The Stanley Gibbons SG100 index is calculated less like the FTSE100 index than the RPI. In other words it is an index of the prices of a representative basket of high quality stamps from all countries, the basket being comprised of those that are the most actively traded at any one point in time. Hence its composition does change over time but the calculation should ensure that it does give a fair reflection of the general trend in the price levels for high value stamps.

The table over the page shows the course of the top ten items in the index since 1998.

Table 11.2 - SG100 Index - progress of top ten items

Country	Item	SG No.	Condition*	1998	1999	2000	2001	2002	2003	Compound gr. % pa
GB	1902 5d slate purple and ultramarine	244	M/M	20	25	30	40	40	50	20.1
GB	1873 1s green	150	F/U	35	40	45	50	65	75	16.5
GB	1911 4d bright orange	286	M/M	14	19	20	30	30	30	16.5
GB	1902 1 d slate purple and bluish green	224	M/M	19	25	30	40	40	40	16.1
GB	1911 3d purple on lemon	285	M/M	20	25	28	40	40	40	14.9
Cook Is.	1944-46 set to 3s	137/145	F/U	45	55	65	70	80	85	13.6
GB	1867 6d mauve	109	F/U	35	40	45	65	65	65	13.2
Italy	1933 Balbo triptych	379/387	U/M	84	84	84	84	140	150	12.3
GB	1924 block cipher 12 vals	418/429	M/M	65	65	75	110	110	110	11.1
GB	1867 £5 orange	137	F/U	1500	1700	1700	1800	1800	2500	10.8

* M/M = mounted mint; F/U = fine used; U/M = unmounted mint

Over the five and half years since 1997 to mid 2003, the index has appreciated 40% overall. Just like shares, well selected portfolios chosen from items from the index may outperform.

One portfolio example produced by Stanley Gibbons shows a total appreciation of 22% over the period from 2001 to 2003, comparing well with stock markets over the period in question. There are of course no guarantees that stamp values will rise at the same rate in the future: the growth may be faster or slower than this.

How to buy and sell

Unless you are already an expert philatelist, you need help selecting a portfolio of investment quality stamps to buy. Stanley Gibbons and other similar firms like Scotia Philately (set up by ex-Stanley Gibbons alumni) operate discretionary and advisory services for investment grade stamps and will usually commit to buying back stamps in a portfolio at a later date should the investor wish to sell one or all of them.

The minimum level of investment to start a portfolio of this sort is in the region of £2,000, although the optimum size is probably £5,000 or more.

It is a wise precaution to have investment grade stamps stored by a dealer, because of the potential for damaging stamps by careless handling. In this case the dealer will provide you with a detailed scanned record of the items in your portfolio and proof of ownership. You can withdraw the items from storage at 48 hours notice. As mentioned earlier, there will be modest charges for the service.

Good dealers will be aware of their clients' portfolio and from time to time be able to suggest stamps that will complement those holdings already in the portfolio. The same principles of good diversification probably apply to stamps as much as they do to stock market investing. Other than perhaps focusing a portfolio around early British stamps, it is probably not wise to have too many stamps of the same type, in case an external event affects their value.

The table overleaf shows contact details for some leading dealers.

Table 11.3 – Stamps: Dealers – key web addresses and contact details

Company	Web address	Email	Phone
Arthur Ryan	www.gbstamps.co.uk	net@gbstamps.co.uk	020 8940 7777
Bonhams Stamp Dept.	www.bonhams.com	stuart.billington@bonhams.com	020 7393 3900
Harmers	www.harmers.com	auctions@harmers.demon.co.uk	020 8747 6100
Philatelic Traders' Society	www.philatelic-traders-society.co.uk	barbara.pts@btclick.com	020 7490 1005
Scotia Philately	www.scotia-philately.co.uk	scotia01@globalnet.co.uk	020 8873 2854
Sotheby's Stamp Dept.	www.sothebys.com	On site	020 7293 5050
Spink	www.spink.com	info@spink.com	020 756 4000
Stamp Auction Network	www.stampauctionnetwork.com	n/a	919 403 9459
Stanley Gibbons	www.stanleygibbons.co.uk	aroose@stanleygibbons.co.uk	020 7557 4454

Since condition is all-important, viewing stamps is essential to appraise them correctly for investment purposes. Buying investment grade stamps over the internet is unwise, unless the dealer is prepared to guarantee that they are of a specific minimum quality. Stamp fairs are a possibility, at least for making new acquisitions.

These allow you to compare the prices offered by different dealers, and buy a particular stamp there and then, having satisfied yourself as to its quality. Large dealers with retail outlets are also likely to have better quality stock available for you to select from.

Unless it is narrowly focused on a 'hot' area, it is unlikely that a collection will be valued at more than the sum of its parts, simply because, unlike a work of art, there are usually many virtually identical stamps available of similar quality.

Canny buying and selling

- Use a reputable dealer
- Don't buy investment grade stamps 'sight unseen'
- Stamp fairs are a way of comparing prices
- Auctions establish future values

When it comes to disposing of a portfolio, a dealer may offer to buy back the stamps from you. If you are not satisfied that this offers you fair value, then it is possible to sell a significant portfolio through an auction house, where it may fetch more than the dealer's price. If you pursue this avenue it is imperative to set a reserve that allows you to be guaranteed that your portfolio will fetch more than the dealer is offering, taking into account the commission taken by the saleroom. Once the bidding surpasses this figure, you are in the money.

Recent stamp auctions have seen prices of investment quality stamps regularly fetching more than expected and significantly in excess of dealer's prices. This is part of the process of establishing new price levels for dealers to work on. This is a sure sign that the market for investment quality stamps is opening up.

Where to find more information

Stanley Gibbons has extensive philatelic literature available at its Strand showroom and publishes a monthly magazine - Gibbons Stamp Monthly - devoted to the subject. Gibbons Stamp Monthly, Stamp Magazine and Stamp and Coin Mart are all available from newsagents each month.

The British Philatelic Bulletin is published monthly by Royal Mail. An annual subscription costs £9.50. This publication is, however, mainly concerned with current British issues, which are unlikely to be of interest to would-be stamp investors.

There is however, an increasing amount of information available on the web from dealers, philatelic societies and other information providers. What follows is a small selection of those available. At the end of the chapter we look in brief at some books that would-be stamp investors and collectors will find useful.

Dealers

Stanley Gibbons (www.stanleygibbons.com) was established in 1856 and specialises in classic Great Britain and Commonwealth stamps. This site has everything you need to know about stamp collecting whether as a hobby, an investment or both. The site has a section for investors, which includes comments on the current state of the market based on the SG100 stamp index. Apart from stamps for sale the site includes a newsletter, catalogues, philatelic terms and a FAQ section.

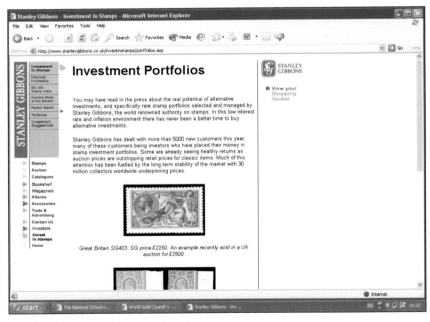

Stanley Gibbons advises on investing in stamps

As part of its plan to build the most comprehensive online philatelic resource Stanley Gibbons has four other sites on offer:

Stamp Café (www.stampcafe.com) has the latest philatelic news and information from around the world with a listing on new issues. Also featured are an advice centre and clearance items for sale from Stanley Gibbons. The site is in its early days and when it becomes fully interactive will feature email chat forums, glossaries of collecting terms and links to local philatelic societies.

AllWorldStamps (www.allworldstamps.com) is the online version of the Stanley Gibbons series of stamp catalogues.

Stamps at Auction (www.stampsatauction.com) offers a free online auction service. Registered users can track what is happening to their own lots and bids and obtain automatic notification on new lots. Also available is the 'Goldstar' service whereby a Stanley Gibbons team of experts handles the whole auction process for you.

Stamps at auction - an easy way to buy

Gibbons Stamp Monthly (www.gibbonsstampmonthly.com) is a digital copy of the magazine with the main features and articles from each month's issue plus an archive. Some articles are free to non-members.

The company also sponsors Collector Cafe (www.collectorcafe.com) an online global collecting community with a section devoted to philately, including articles and links to dealers.

Arthur Ryan (www.gbstamps.co.uk) specialises in stamps of Great Britain and is the largest mail order stamp dealer in the country. The site has a stamp price list all of which can be purchased online. A free copy of the monthly price list or the private treaty list is available by completing the online enquiry form.

The Philatelic Traders Society (www.philatelic-traders-society.co.uk) organizes the Stampex exhibitions and has links to dealers worldwide with their speciality.

Scotia Philately (www.scotia-philately.co.uk) has been trading since 1984. A selection of available stock is on the site. If an item is not illustrated and you would like to see it, email the site and the image will be left on the 'Client Room' page. A specialist register is available to enable buyers to be informed when suitable items come up. The site also has numerous links especially to sites offering postal history information. Buyers regularly travel the UK on buying trips and home visits can be arranged.

Current market values can be found at Stamp Finder (www.stampfinder.com). A searchable database provides the names of dealers with a particular stamp for sale together with the price. Other features include a 'want list' where it is possible to register for special items you may need, and a calendar of events and auctions worldwide.

The site includes an overview of stamps as an investment since 1992. It publishes individual country guides on the price histories and investment potential of individual stamps. Following from this analysis there is a list issued of 'Best Buys', which are considered likely to perform well above average. Also on offer are accessories, publications and software for sale.

Mark and David Brandon (www.stamperrors.com) deal in classic British and Commonwealth stamps and modern major errors, all of which can be bought online.

Also on the subject of errors Jack Nalbandian (www.nalbandstamp.com) a US site is a good resource centre for stamp errors. Stamps for sale are mainly US, but UK, Canadian and foreign stamps are also available.

Auctions

Sotheby's (www.sothebys.com) stamp department concentrates on selling high value single owner collections. An online catalogue will become available a month in advance of an auction. Advance notice of occasional auctions and exhibitions can be received by email.

Spink (www.spink.com) offers a wide-ranging series of auctions throughout the year with bidding either in person, by telephone or online. A catalogue is issued four weeks prior to each auction. Prices realized at auction are included on the site. There is also information on how to sell and obtain valuations.

The Stamp Auction Network (www.stampauctionnetwork.com) is an American site which includes online auction catalogues, a worldwide auction calendar, thousands of images of stamps in auction, prices realized and various auction articles and information.

Harmers (www.harmers.com), founded in London in 1884, holds up to 10 auctions a year. Unusually for an auction house they make no charge for their catalogues, which can be ordered online. The site has prices realised at auction and a catalogue archive plus books and catalogues for sale. From time to time Harmers hold open days at central locations around the country.

Information Sites

The Bath Postal Museum (www.bathpostalmuseum.org) shows how 18th century Bath influenced and developed the postal system, which was later, introduced throughout Europe and the British Commonwealth. The site has a history of the UK postal system and the key people involved.

The British Library (www.bl.uk) houses the National Philatelic Collection of the UK. The site includes numerous articles and information on its collections and various philatelic links.

The collections are estimated to comprise over eight million items from around the world including stamps, artwork, postal stationery, airmails, etc. The Library also houses a major collection of philatelic literature which is available to researchers in the Reading Room with a pass which can be applied for online.

French Stamp Directory (www.philatelie.fr) has links to dealers, auctions worldwide, magazines, organizations and accessories.

James Bendon (www.jamesbendon.com) is a philatelic publisher whose site features new books, online catalogues, special offers, an email newsletter and numerous links.

Joseph Luft's Philatelic Resources (www.execpc.com-joeluft/resource.html) had 4214 links at the time of writing covering general resources, shows and societies, postal authorities, collector's pages, downloadable images and auctions.

PhilaGuide (www.philaguide.com) is a directory of philatelic websites by a Dutch enthusiast, including dealers, stamp museums, online auctions and online publications.

Philately and Postal History (www.philatelyandpostalhistory.com) has links to clubs and societies, dealer's auction houses, philatelists and events.

Table 11.4 – Stamps – key web addresses and contact details (other than dealers)

Company	Web address	Email	Phone
American Philatelic Society	www.stamps.org	n/a	814 237 3803
Association of British Philatelic Societies	www.ukphilately.org.uk	n/a	n/a
Bath Postal Museum	www.bathpostalmuseum.org	info@bathpostalmuseum.org	01225 460333
French Stamp Directory	www.philatelie.fr	info@philatelie.fr	n/a
Great Britain Philatelic Society	www.gbps.org.uk	On site	n/a
James Bendon	www.jamesbendon.com	books@JamesBendon.com	n/a
Joseph Luft's Philatelic Resources	www.execpc.com/~joeluft/resource.html	joeluft@execpr.com	n/a
Philaguide	www.philaguide.com	On site	n/a
Philately and Postal History	www.philatelyandpostalhistory.com	helpdesk@philatelyandpostalhistory.com	n/a
Post Office Archives	www.consignia.com/Heritage	heritage@royalmail.com	020 7239 2570
Royal Philatelic Collection	www.royal.gov.uk	n/a	n/a
Royal Philatelic Society	www.rpsl.org.uk	n/a	020 7486 1044
Stamp Finder	www.stampfinder.com	n/a	n/a
Stamps.Net	www.stamps.net	mail@randyneil.com	n/a
UK250	www.stampwebsites.co.uk	info@uk25550.com	01926 863004
Wardrop & Co	www.wardrop.co.uk	stamps@wardrop.co.uk	01376 563765

The Post Office Archives and Records Office holds records of the British Post Office from the 17th Century to the present day at Mount Pleasant in Central London. (www.consignia.com/Heritage) The archives include a background on stamp production as well as proof impressions of date and cancellation stamps. Until the future of the National Postal Museum is settled limited facilities are available for researchers by prior appointment (020 7239 2570).

The Royal Philatelic Collection (www.royal.gov.uk) is housed at St James's Palace and is the most comprehensive collection in the world of UK and Commonwealth stamps. Items from the collection are occasionally on display and each season the opening display of the Royal Philatelic Society traditionally consists of items from the collection. An overview of the collection is on the site.

Stamps.Net (www.stamps.net) is a US online philately magazine with numerous articles and a basic resource centre for beginner collectors including topics such as buying stamps, philatelic terms and stamps on covers.

UK250 (www.stampwebsites.co.uk) has a list of UK sites devoted to stamps.

Societies

The American Philatelic Society (www.stamps.org) is the largest, non-profit society for stamp collectors with 50,000 members in more than 110 countries. Members can buy and sell online and receive the 100 page monthly journal. Online learning is provided by Virtual Stamp Campus (www.stampcampus.org), with a demo lesson available on the site.

The Great Britain Philatelic Society (www.gbps.org.uk) aims to 'promote, encourage, and contribute to the advancement of the philately of Great Britain'. The society meets eight times a year in central London, but also has provincial meetings. The site includes a glossary of terms, a style guide and many useful links, including dealers who are GBPS members.

The Royal Philatelic Society London (www.rpsl.org.uk) is the oldest philatelic society in the world and is strictly limited to amateur collectors. Members receive 'The London Philatelist' ten times a year. This is the society's journal, which has been published since 1892. The site includes handouts from society meetings and links to other societies worldwide. The society's London premises include a philatelic museum and library.

UK Philately (www.ukphilately.org.uk) is the home of three sites:

The Association of British Philatelic Societies (ABPS) is the national association catering for the needs of local and specialist societies, philatelic federations, individual collectors and anyone interested in philately. It organizes various events and exhibitions throughout the country, a calendar of which appears on the site.

The association publishes a journal 4 times a year and various leaflets concerning the hobby. Membership details are available on the site.

The National Philatelic Society (NPS) is one of the largest general philatelic societies in Great Britain with members worldwide. Members receive 'Stamp Lover' magazine six times a year and can buy and sell online as well as taking part in auctions. The society has an extensive library (by post if outside London) with a searchable online database. Members who live near the capital can attend monthly meetings at the headquarters in Charterhouse Street.

The British Philatelic Trust (BPT) is an educational charity established by the Post Office in 1981, from which it is independent. It's objective is the promotion of the 'study, research and dissemination of knowledge of philately'.

Miscellaneous

Wardrop & Co (www.wardrop.co.uk) are insurance intermediaries specialising in philatelic insurance. Apart from insurance information the site has numerous links including auctions, dealers and philatelic software.

Books

Stanley Gibbons publishes the world's most comprehensive range of price catalogues, whose listings and prices are the basis of the philatelic market. They include the following:

Stanley Gibbons Commonwealth and British Empire Stamps
Stanley Gibbons Great Britain Concise Stamp Catalogue
Stanley Gibbons Specialised Great Britain Stamp Catalogue (five volumes)
Stamps of the World (this includes every stamp ever issued)
Stamp Collecting - How to Start
Enjoy Stamp Collecting
Stamp Collecting - The Stanley Gibbons Guide
Stamp Collecting - Philatelic Terms Illustrated

Top Dollar Paid (The Complete Guide to Selling Your Stamps)
Stephen Datz General Philatelic Corporation Colorado 1997

The book explores the pitfalls to avoid when selling stamps including information on methods of sale, valuing stamps and stamps as investments. The main messages are reinforced by numerous anecdotal stories in an entertaining and informative style. Two other books by the same author are **Stamp Collecting** and **Stamp Investing.**

12 Whisky

It may be less well publicised than vintage wine, which we cover in detail in the next chapter, but malt whisky can prove a fascinating and potentially profitable investment medium for the discerning collector. Single malt whisky from Scotland's best distilleries carries the same cachet as first growth claret does in the wine market. It is the most highly sought-after and best, most consistent quality product available.

Basics

Like wine from the most important chateaux in Bordeaux, single malt whisky is a unique product. It has the same mystique and the same origin in a small geographical area. And it is made by a handful of small, individual producers.

How whisky is made

Single malt whisky is a whisky made from boiling to the point of evaporation, and then condensing, a fermented mixture of water and malted barley. It is called 'single' malt because it is the product of a single distillery. Peat is often present in the water used and peat fires are sometimes used to malt the barley. This is especially true of island whiskies, since Scotland's offshore islands traditionally lacked other sources of fuel. Use of peat in this way gives the whisky its distinctive peaty, smoky flavours.

The quirks of the production process, the size and shape of the stills used, and the distillery's location all influence the character of the resulting whisky. In turn this governs the degree to which it is sought-after by connoisseurs.

Much like vintage claret, which may perhaps not be ready to drink until five years after bottling, malt whisky also improves with age. In fact it has by law to be aged for at least three years before it can be described as whisky and sold to the public as such. Fine malt whisky often does not reach its best until eight, ten or even fifteen years or more after production.

The new whisky is put ('filled') into wooden casks and kept in a warehouse for this period of maturation, during which time evaporation diminishes its overall volume at a rate of around 2% a year, a phenomenon known as 'the angels' share'.

The casks in which the whisky is stored, and their previous contents, affect its subsequent flavour. Almost all casks used to store malt whisky will previously have contained sherry or bourbon. Whisky stored in this way is more distinctive and more highly prized. The best quality casks are those that have not been re-used too often. Good quality 'fresh' sherry or bourbon casks produce the best result and would-be investors need to satisfy themselves on this score before they invest.

Malt whisky is bottled for sale in its own right. It also blended with other malt whiskies and with cheaper, mass produced grain whisky to produce the blended whisky brands - Bells, Johnnie Walker, Famous Grouse and the like - with which whisky drinkers are familiar.

Although some investors have in the past sought to make money by buying grain whisky, this has generally ended in tears. There is much less investment value or collector interest in blended whisky. In reality only single malts, and then only those of certain distilleries and certain ages, have superhobby investment potential.

Rather like buying claret 'en primeur' (see next chapter for explanation), for many years the classic way of investing in malt whisky has typically been to buy in cask shortly after distillation. Investors then hold the whisky under bond for the set period of years until it can be sold as fully matured spirit of the optimum age. The evaporation that takes place in the cask during this period is, in theory, more than offset by the increase in value derived as the spirit matures.

How the whisky investment market works

The products of some distilleries are more highly prized than others. Classic whiskies like Macallan, Glenmorangie, Bowmore, Talisker and others are widely marketed in bottle and also much in demand for use in blended whisky produced for the mass market. Some malt whiskies are simply used as 'fillers' in a blended whisky and have little intrinsic merit as investments. You need to know which is which, and you may need advice on this.

Ownership of distilleries varies. Some are wholly independent, some part of small groups, others part of large multinational companies. Those with highly successful brands may not be prepared to release stock to investors over which they have no subsequent control.

It is, however, part of the way the industry works that distillers do use each other's products for blending purposes. Using whisky brokers as intermediaries, quantities of whisky are shipped from one distillery to another on a regular basis, and also out to third party blenders. Whisky is, in effect, traded in a secondary market. It is one that is nowhere near as active as wine, but it is one that enables individuals, if they wish, to acquire whisky for investment purposes.

The fundamentals of whisky investing are equally as complicated as investing in first growth clarets, but for different reasons. To understand why this is so, you need to grasp the intricacies of the whisky cycle.

Malt whisky is produced in a batch process and distilleries have limited production capacity. Some distilleries have been mothballed or closed over the years as the industry rationalised and demand for blended whiskies fell. Because malt whisky must be aged for so many years, demand has to be predicted many years ahead. Distilleries can also be victims of their own success, underestimating the popularity of a particular product and so not laying down enough stock to cover it.

Whisky investment mechanics

- There is a primary and secondary market in whisky
- Requirement for maturation creates regular supply and demand imbalances
- Prices are cyclical
- Stock is available from distilleries since closed or demolished

---

Let's take a simple example. A distillery's production in, say, 1993 is what governs the maximum available supply of its bottled 10 year-old spirit in 2003, once adjustment has been made for evaporation. If the whisky has become unexpectedly popular in the meantime, it can create a problem. There is no way in which this past production can be altered or supplemented. If more drinkers want the product, then by definition the price of the maturing whisky must rise.

In reality it is a little more complicated than that. The distillery may have originally decided to use some of 1993's production to produce 15-year old bottled whisky in 2008, or 12 year old in 2005. If it wants more of the 10-year old, it could get it by 'borrowing' from these stocks, but only by reducing the amount available for the older aged products.

It follows from this that it is possible to look back at the pattern of production a decade ago and predict with some degree of accuracy which whisky might be in short supply in particular 'age statements' (10 year-old, 12 year-old, 15 year-old, and so on) in particular years in the future. Prices should react accordingly either when the whisky is still in cask, or in auction prices after the product is bottled. Once a whisky is in bottle, it will mature no longer, but keep indefinitely.

A final very important point is that there have been many examples of distilleries that have been closed for many years or, worse still, demolished. Once a distillery is demolished, the scarcity value of its production, in cask or in bottle, increases. In many instances it becomes of greater interest from an investment standpoint. As is the case with wine, the scarcity only increases as bottles are opened by non-investors, and drunk.

The table shows which distilleries fall into this category

Table 12.1 - Distilleries currently closed or demolished

Closed	Demolished
Ardmore	Banff
Brora	Ben Wyvis
Glen Esk	Coleburn
Glen Flagler	Convalmore
Glenglassaugh	Glen Albyn
Glenugie	Glen Lochy
Hillside	Glen Mhor
Killyloch	Glenur-y-Royal
Linlithgow	Kinclaith
Rosebank	Lochside
St Magdalene	Millburn
Scapa	North Port
	Port Ellen
Reopened	
Bladnoch	
Glendronach	

This all sounds potentially interesting from an investment standpoint. You can buy in cask and in theory make money as the whisky matures, or buy scarce items in bottle as collectors' items.

Yet despite these elements of forward predictability of supply and potential scarcity, in the past whisky has proved a hard area in which to make money as an investor.

Avoiding the scams

In the past the scotch whisky industry has attracted all manner of scam artists and fraudsters.

In the 1960s, for example, many American investors were lured into schemes to buy grain whisky. Grain whisky is the cheap mass-produced main constituent of blended whiskies, to which selected malt whiskies are added to give it the resulting character. These grain whisky investors failed to understand that it was a relatively easy matter to increase production and as the investors came on board prices collapsed. Many investors kept the whisky for much longer than was originally intended. When eventually casks were opened, it was found that most of the whisky had evaporated.

Scams

- Whisky investment scams have been common
- Common ones involve paying too much for whisky
- Less common ones involve outright fraud
- Some have involved grain whisky as well as malt whisky

In the late 1980s and early 1990s a number of investment schemes were launched which involved investors paying excessive prices for malt whisky. This is similar to some scams in the wine market. In these instances, the whisky purchased is real enough, and title to it is good. It is simply that the investor has been lured into paying so far over the odds that any hope of achieving an investment return has been destroyed.

Other, more dishonest, schemes defrauded investors by simply taking their money and not giving good title to the whisky. Usually the frauds came to light when investors attempted to take physical possession of their whisky and were unable to because others had made off with it in the meantime, or because it simply did not exist in the first place.

Schemes like this, faithfully catalogued on the website www.whiskyscam.co.uk, appear to be less common now. The fact that they arose should not necessarily dissuade you from contemplating investing in whisky now, provided precautions are taken. But what they do suggest is that you need to be extremely cautious about what you buy, whom you buy it from, the proof of ownership of the whisky you get, and the price you pay.

Whiskyscam - check here first

Legitimate investment media and collecting themes

There are several ways in which whisky can be legitimately purchased for investment purposes: These are: purchase of multiple casks of whisky via a whisky broker, with or without advice being offered; buying whisky direct from a distillery; and buying collectable whisky in bottle from a specialist retailer or at auction.

So you can buy whisky in cask or hogshead (a larger version of a cask containing some 156 litres of spirit) either from a whisky broker or else through the schemes that some distilleries operate whereby whisky can be purchased at source and stored on the premises.

But remember that if you are doing this there are some provisos.

If you are buying whisky via a broker or direct from a distillery you may need to specify the type of barrel (or 'wood') in which the whisky is to be stored. Cheap wood will affect the value of the end product and the price your investment will ultimately realise. Bourbon casks are typically used and cost in the region of £30 each.

Storage and insurance charges, calculated per cask or per litre, also go on top. If you buy through a broker, there will be commission to pay.

If you buy direct, remember that distilleries normally sell maturing whisky direct to the public as a way of boosting their cash flow. They may try to create an aura of exclusivity to justify charging more than the whisky will fetch in the open market.

You need to check this at the outset. According to one expert, distilleries selling new whisky direct to the public usually do so at prices close to what 10 or 12-year whisky would fetch in the open market, thus removing much of the potential return an investor could capture.

> ## Whisky investment media
> - New from distillery in cask
> - New or aged in cask from a broker
> - Via a club membership/share issue
> - Collectable whisky in bottle

These complications do not arise in the case of the market in collectable whisky already in bottle. This is a flourishing subset of the malt whisky business with a number of different themes pursued by collectors. Some collectors simply try to collect one bottle from each malt whisky distillery. Some pursue all of the ages and bottle types of their favourite distillery. Some collectors collect as many types of malt whisky bottled in the year of their birth as they can.

One advantage to collecting whisky in bottle is that storage costs can be kept to a minimum. Once bottled, whisky will keep indefinitely without any alteration in condition and therefore there is no need for specialist storage facilities as, for example, there is with wine.

Collectable whisky can be acquired in bottle from specialist retailers such as the Whisky Exchange (www.thewhiskyexchange.com) - tel. 020 8606 9388 - or at auction. It can be sold in the same way.

McTears is a specialist auctioneer for scotch whisky in Glasgow. Major auction houses in London also hold periodic auctions of collectable bottles of whisky.

Is it right for you?

Let's look at the questions you need to answer to determine whether whisky could form a place in your wider portfolio of investments.

■ Are you investing for the medium to long term?

Like wine investment, buying whisky is not necessarily an ultra long-term business. But for the most part you need to be patient. This is because all whiskies take a number of years to reach their full potential. If you are, for example, buying in cask immediately after the whisky is produced, you are looking at an eight-year and possible a ten- or fifteen-year period before the whisky will achieve its maximum return. Collectable bottles can take eight to ten years to produce a worthwhile return, although after this time the gains for scarce items can be substantial. Bowmore Black Bottle, for example, prized Islay malt first bottled in 1964, has shown a tenfold gain in price in the past decade.

■ Do you have adequate capital?

In theory there is no minimum amount to be invested. However, whisky brokers and distillers are reluctant to deal in single casks. They prefer a buyer to contract to buy maybe five casks or a similar number of hogsheads, in which case the minimum investment is probably in the region of £1,500-2,000. In order to create a balanced long-term investment portfolio you may need to invest two or three times this amount to get an acceptable spread of whiskies. On the other hand, eminently collectable bottles of whisky can be acquired quite easily for less than £100 at the lower end of the scale. At the upper end of the market, prices of upwards of £10,000 have been regularly achieved at auction.

■ Are you prepared for extra storage and insurance costs?

It is generally not an option for investors in whisky in cask form to store the product on their own premises. The norm is for a distillery to store casks on investors' behalf in its bonded warehouse until such time as it is either sold on or bottled. Having whisky stored under bond is vital, since in the UK duty accounts for a large percentage (around 75%) of the ultimate selling price. Charges made by distillers for storing whisky in cask take the form of 'rent' for space in the bonded warehouse. Add in fire insurance, and these additional costs normally amount to about £10 per hogshead per year (perhaps £8 for a standard cask, which takes up slightly less space).

Right for you?

- Basically a longer term investment
- Minimum investment £100 to £10,000
- Significant storage and insurance costs for cask whisky
- Cask whisky prices are cyclical; not too different from the stock market
- May be CGT free but rather a moot point

Collectable bottles of whisky can, by contrast, be stored at home, subject only to arranging the normal insurance cover and making sure that labels are not exposed to extremes of damp and that bottles are stored somewhere they will not be broken accidentally.

Is portfolio diversification an objective?

There is little hard and fast information available to the general public about the performance of whisky prices over the long term. Whisky prices in cask are subject to the vagaries of the industry. Because whisky has to be matured for such a lengthy period, it is - as we have recorded earlier - quite common for there to be imbalances in stocks of certain whiskies, either shortage or surplus. When these occur, they can affect prices significantly.

For this reason expert market knowledge is needed to invest successfully. One can question whether or not this volatility really makes cask whisky a suitable diversification away from the stock market. As in the stock market, timing buys and sells correctly assumes a fair degree of importance, although whisky cycles and stock market cycles may well not coincide.

Collectable bottles of whisky, on the other hand, are a slightly different market. They are akin to rare books or stamps, where the spending power and enthusiasm of the collector base is the key factor in determining prices and increases in value.

Do you need to have knowledge of whisky and of Scotland?

It is unwise to invest in whisky without having at least some curiosity and knowledge about how and where it is produced. Visiting distilleries can be a pleasant pastime and you can be assured that the industry is a convivial one.

Are there tax considerations?

One of the big issues for investing in cask whisky is that, like wine, it could in theory be considered a wasting asset by the Inland Revenue and therefore, provided you do not buy and sell whisky often enough to be regarded as a dealer, there would be no capital gains tax levied on the proceeds of any sales.

However, this is very much a moot point. Once bottled, of course, spirits have greater durability in bottle than many wines, and therefore the Revenue may not look kindly on the idea of tax-free capital appreciation, especially if you are keeping whisky in the form of collectable bottles.

Prices and returns

There is little hard information on prices of individual malt whiskies and prices do not appear to move in a readily predictable manner.

The only given is that the price of five year old whisky will, other things being equal, be more than the price of a one year old whisky at that time, and a ten year old whisky from the same distillery may be worth more still. But it is an open question whether or not the price differences will in the normal course of events reflect any more than a charge for distillery rents and rolled up interest costs, which are expenses all investors must bear.

One example from a whisky broker serves to illustrate the point. New malt whisky spirit (known as 'new fill') could be bought through a whisky broker at the time of writing for, in round figures, £2.30 a litre, whereas spirit from the same distillery at twelve years old fetched around £4.30. A year previously the same 12 year-old whisky fetched £6 a litre. The variations in price occur because of the vagaries of production some years ago and the difference between this and the demand for the finished product now.

In short, it appears that while returns can be reasonably good if purchases and sales are timed correctly, there are lots of pitfalls. Prices can be volatile.

In the case of collectable bottled whisky slightly different considerations apply. It is best to consider collectables like this as historical curios, not dissimilar to antiques or 19th century first editions, even if not quite as old.

Price gains here can be substantial, especially in those whiskies bottled by distilleries that have since been closed or that have been demolished. Whiskies from demolished distilleries can only get scarcer.

Distilleries like Ben Wyvis, Glen Albyn, Glen Flagler, Glen Mhor, Kinclaith, and Millburn as well as Islay's Port Ellen and several others, are all highly collectable, as are very old whiskies from popular malt whisky producers like Bowmore, Macallan, Talisker, and Glenfiddich. This appears to be a much more fruitful area for investment, and a diverse collection can be assembled at relatively low cost.

The table opposite page shows examples of whiskies that can be purchased today from distilleries long since demolished, and their prices.

Table 12.2 - Price of collectable whisky from demolished distilleries

Distillery	Age (yrs)	Price (£ per bottle)
Banff	1966	100.00
Ben Wyvis	1972	699.00
Coleburn	1964	99.00
Convalmore	1978	56.50
Glen Albyn	1974	52.95
Glen Lochy	1965	95.55
Glen Mhor	1965	96.00
Glenur-y-Royal	1971	99.00
Kinclaith	1967	999.00
Lochside	1981	99.00
Millburn	1966	150.00
North Port	1964	175.00
Port Ellen	1979	120.00

Source: The Whisky Exchange

Prices of bottles from different years vary considerably. Factors affecting prices include the amounts bottled from any one year and the distinctiveness of the bottle itself or the label.

Some distilleries have played up to this by issuing a series of numbered bottles and limited editions with distinctive labels. Prices of bottlings from ongoing distilleries also fetch high prices if they are scarce in number in a particular age statement. The ultimate is perhaps the 1937 Glenfiddich, where only 61 bottles were made, and which is currently priced at around £10,000 in dealers' catalogues.

How to buy and sell

There are several methods of buying and selling. These are:

Using a broker

This is much the best way of buying cask whisky, provided you use a reputable broker. The table over the page has a list of long established whisky brokers who may be prepared to deal for individual investors.

As we note above, however, you should take advice from a broker as to which might be the best types of whisky to buy at any particular point in time and also accept their advice about selling. Brokers will charge commission but will be able to advise on storage and insurance. They will probably require you to buy several casks to make it worthwhile contacting a distillery on your behalf or to include you in part of a larger order with other customers.

There may be equally valid investment opportunities in grain whisky as in malt whisky, although this is an area with a somewhat chequered past history for investors.

The advantage of grain whisky is that you will be able to buy it in greater quantity and sell it on more quickly. As a mass produced product, grain whisky is more uniform and is not aged for as long as malt whisky prior to being used to produce the well known blended products. It therefore suffers less from the stock-induced cyclical volatility in prices that pervades malt whisky.

Whisky brokers

Company Location	Telephone	Contact	
Armstrong & Company	0131 225 7809	Ann Armstrong	Edinburgh
Macfarlane & Company	0141 303 4512	Scott McFarlane	Glasgow
Lundie & Company	0141 221 0707	Alan Lundie	Glasgow
Peter J Russell	01506 852205	Gordon Doctor	Glasgow

Buying through a reputable broker is much the best way of ensuring that you get the right cask whisky at the right price and the cheapest storage costs, and also by far the cheapest way of getting access to maturing whisky.

Dealing direct with the distillery

In recent years a number of distilleries have offered schemes whereby individuals can buy whisky in cask direct from the distillery. Typically these schemes trade on some form of exclusivity to justify charging a somewhat higher than normal price at the outset. Often the picture is further confused because distillers will frequently include several years of storage and insurance costs in the price.

The pay-off comes at the end of the maturation period when the distillery allows the buyer to sell the whisky on to a third party, to sell it back to the distillery, or to have it bottled for their own consumption or for sale as a collectable.

Distilleries that do this at present include Bruichladdich distillery on Islay, and Tullibardine. Blackwood, a proposed new distillery on Shetland, may do. The schemes all have their individual quirks, so you need to check the precise terms before signing up. Prices vary. Some whisky brokers suggest that this is an expensive way of buying whisky in cask.

> ## Canny buying and selling
> - Brokers may be reluctant to deal with 'private clients'
> - Distilleries sell direct, but prices can be high
> - Club membership complicates investment decision
> - Collectable bottles market comparable to antiques

Some other distilleries operate whisky purchase schemes linked to share ownership or club membership. Ladybank, for example, is a proposed new boutique distillery near St Andrews. It will have 45,000 litres of annual production capacity, making it approximately half the size of the current smallest distillery in the industry, Edradour.

Ladybank has been raising money by means of a members club, and may also allow members the opportunity of purchasing whisky in cask. At present members are entitled to a free case of bottled Ladybank malt whisky from each year of the first ten years of the distillery's production. Membership costs £2500 and includes a range of other benefits.

Because of the distillery's small scale of production it is highly likely that the bottles will become collectors' items, although it will take at least a decade or more to establish whether the whisky produced will rank in quality terms with the all-time greats.

In general, distillery schemes like this, while above board and perfectly viable, may not represent a particularly good deal for an individual purely looking at whisky investment in isolation. The whisky tends to sell at a 'retail' market price, but the buyback offer is at a 'wholesale' price. At any rate, the purchase price is often at a substantial premium to the price in the broking market for whisky of equivalent age and quality.

Complicating the investment decision with the paraphernalia of ownership or membership, which investors may neither want nor need, may not be attractive either unless it gives you something that will genuinely be unobtainable through any other medium. The extras make it harder to judge whether or not the investment element of the package stacks up.

Buying collectable bottles

Buying collectable bottles is a separate and distinct branch of whisky investment. It is akin to collecting antiques, with a nod in the direction of vintage claret. Collectable bottles, especially from distilleries that have been closed or demolished, are an irreplaceable part of the history of the scotch whisky industry. As the remaining bottles are consumed, as some are, their scarcity value can only increase. This is an investment for the patient, but returns over the years have been good for those who picked wisely, and probably less volatile than buying whisky in the cask market.

Buyers can purchase through the retail trade or at auction, Retailers include organisations like The Whisky Exchange. This is a London based mail order business specialising in collectable malt whisky. Collectable bottles can also be had from distillery shops (for those distilleries still open and receptive to visitors), at whisky festivals, where special bottlings destined to become collectors' items are sometimes sold, or at auction.

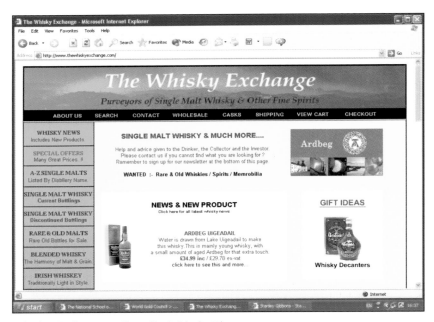

Whisky Exchange sells collectable bottles

McTears in Glasgow is a specialist auctioneer. As well as auctioning art and antiques, McTears has auctions of collectable whisky several times a year. Their website www.mctears.co.uk has details of forthcoming auctions and results of past ones, including which of the various lots sold and what prices they realised compared to their pre-auction estimates.

Where to go for more information

As outlined earlier, buying direct from a whisky broker is likely to prove a useful route for many investors. However, few brokers have web sites and must be contacted by telephone (see table on 242).

Buying direct from a distillery can work out okay, but as already mentioned prices are often at a premium and other ownership-related considerations cloud the decision.

Nonetheless, for what was once a particularly conservative industry, malt whisky distilleries have become more active at promoting their services and products on the web. Some web sites are better than others. The following distilleries (some fairly recently established) have sites that offer deals to would-be investors.

Ben Nevis Distillery (www.bennevisdistillery.com) offers little information on its site except for contact details.

Blackwood (www.shetlandwhisky.com) is a proposed new distillery in Shetland. Its site has product information and contact details for prospective investors.

Bruichladdich (www.bruichladdich.com) is a long-established Islay whisky and the distillery is now an independent Scottish company. The site contains everything you could possibly wish to know about the product's past and present from the various stages of production to tasting reviews. There are details of how to purchase two types of whisky in cask with storage charges and insurance rolled up into the price.

The Isle of Arran distillery (www.arranwhisky.com) at Lochranza is one of Scotland's newest distilleries. The site has information on the product range plus news and reviews.

Ladybank (www.whisky.co.uk) has a web site devoted to this new distillery, with its unusual 'club' ownership structure. The site contains membership details for the private club and distillery facts and figures.

Ladybank Company of Distillers - a new malt distillery

Sites that offer a more objective information-style component include the Companions of the Quaich (www.thequaich.com). This has numerous links to single malt whisky sites including brands, resources and societies. A quaich is a Gaelic bowl used for the communal drinking of whisky.

The Scottish Malt Whisky Society (www.smws.com) is for people who enjoy malt whisky. Amongst other benefits members receive a twice-yearly newsletter, with articles about whisky, the industry and personalities involved, plus a bottling list published six times a year. The society is based in Edinburgh with a branch in London. The site has much free content including a tasting notes archive and a whisky map showing the leading distilleries.

Scotchwhisky.com (www.scotchwhisky.com) aims to bring whisky enthusiasts from around the world together on the internet. It covers various topics such as the history of whisky, news, book reviews and product information. The site also has a useful section on whisky as an investment.

The Scotch Whisky Association (www.scotch-whisky.org.uk) is the trade organisation for the whisky industry. The site includes a history of whisky, a map of distilleries, a members' directory and a list of whisky brands.

Whisky Scam (www.whiskyscam.co.uk) is a helpline set up in 1998 by a Cumbrian lawyer to help those caught out by whisky scandals in the 1990's. The site has much useful information on the pleasures and perils of whisky investment.

Table 12.3 – Whisky – key web addresses and contact details

Company	Web address	Email	Phone	Category
Ben Nevis Distillery	www.bennevisdistillery.com	colin@bennevisdistillery.com	01397 702476	Distiller
Blackwood	www.shetlandwhisky.com	joanna@shetlandwhisky.com	01595 694455	Distiller
Bruichladdich	www.bruichladdich.com	On site	01496 850477	Distiller
Companions of the Quaich	www.thequaich.com	n/a	n/a	Information
Isle of Arran	www.arranwhisky.com	On site	n/a	Distiller
Ladybank Distillery	www.whisky.co.uk	enquiries@whisky.co.uk	08454 501885	Distiller
McTears	www.mctears.co.uk	whiskyvaluations@mctears.co.uk	01412 234456	Auction
Scotch Whisky	www.scotchwhisky.com	whisky@scotchwhisky.com	01506 885721	Information
Scotch Whisky Association	www.scotch-whisky.org.uk	On site	n/a	Information
Scottish Malt Whisky Society	www.smws.com	enquiries@smws.com	0131 5543451	Association
The Whisky Exchange	www.thewhiskyexchange.com	sales@thewhiskyexchange.com	020 8606 9388	Dealer
Whisky Scam	www.whiskyscam.co.uk	mwbh@gateway.net	01539 729580	Information

13 | Wine

Investing in wine has attractions for many superhobby investors. They reason that, if the worst comes to the worst, they can always enjoy their investment by drinking it.

Yet in some instances the pleasure of owning fine investment-quality wine is of necessity a remote one. Most wine merchants will advise you to store your investment at their own, or an independent, temperature-controlled bonded warehouse.

This chapter looks at investing in wine using the headings we have established for other chapters - the basics; whether or not it is right for you; the tax implications, if any; and the returns you can derive from investing in this way.

Basics

Wine is produced in many parts of the world. But from an investment standpoint investing in wine should mean investing in the 'blue chips'. This means primarily the best Bordeaux wines, including St Emilion and Pomerol, the best burgundy (such as Romanee-Conti), and a few of the best wines from Italy (say Sassicaia or Solaia) and Australia (Penfolds Grange, for example).

The history of wine making in Bordeaux dates back to Roman times. It took off when Henry II married Eleanor of Aquitaine in 1152 and received as a dowry a large part of SW France. Thereafter the English took to the wines of Bordeaux in a big way.

In 1855 Napoleon III laid the foundations for wine investment by classifying all of the vineyards in Bordeaux on a scale of 1-5. As a result we have the terms first growth (premier cru), second growth and so on. The laws enacted then have held good with almost no change to this day. They are vigorously upheld, and category changes are almost unheard of. As one wine merchant put it, 'everyone in the know, knows what should be where'.

Wines from St Emilion and Pomerol, to the east of Bordeaux (on the so-called 'right bank' of the Gironde), were not included in this original classification and have only become more appreciated from the 20th century onwards. This does not detract from their potential as investments, particularly because they tend to be produced in somewhat smaller quantities.

Because of this history and quasi-regulated structure, Bordeaux has a pre-eminent place among the world's wine regions. The geographical and climatic conditions in the area mean that it can produce more fine wine with greater regularity than any other part of France or any other country. There are many thousands of vineyards in Bordeaux but only the top-flight ones are worthy of investment money.

In virtually no other places are the greatest wines made in such limited quantity. The top 30 chateaux in Bordeaux can produce no more than 500,000 cases of wine in any one vintage, of which a third goes immediately to satisfy demand from the hotel and restaurant trade. Only the output of the best chateaux in Burgundy is smaller.

This creates conditions of scarcity that should, in theory, make wine ideal for investment purposes. This is reinforced by the fact that there is a long back history of wine prices and the quality of particular vintages. And there is an active auction market in which wine is bought and sold. There is another advantage of focusing on Bordeaux, and particularly red Bordeaux of the highest quality. It is that doing so limits to a manageable size what would otherwise be a bewildering range of investment choices.

Wine basics

- Investment grade wine means top-flight Bordeaux red
- Demand from drinkers means increasing scarcity
- Chateaux and vintages differ substantially
- Can buy 'en primeur' (futures market) or in bottle
- Advice is crucial

What should you look for in a wine for investment? The best chateaux of Bordeaux are well known to wine experts. But if you are contemplating serious investment you need guidance from reference books. Even one as simple as Hugh Johnson's Pocket Wine Book (Mitchell Beazley) is an excellent aide memoire, packed with authoritative thumbnail assessments of individual chateaux and observations on vintage quality.

The best-known names are ones like Lafite Rothschild, Latour, Haut-Brion, Mouton-Rothschild, and Margaux, but there are many others. Some of the best produce wine in very small quantities.

It is a moot point how to differentiate between first and second growth. The classification of 1855 was based on more than a century of trading practice, so second growths have been up there among the best for 250 years. Some second growth chateaux have been termed 'super-seconds'. This is because in recent years the experts feel they have produced wine of more or less the same standard as the first growths.

All can make good investments if the right vintage is bought at the right time, or bad ones if bought at the wrong time or the wrong price.

The table shows some of the best-known names in Bordeaux.

Table 13.1 - Key Bordeaux Chateaux

Name	Area	Price in £ per case (2000 vintage)
Angelus	St Emilion	n/a
Ausone	St Emilion	4,200
Cheval Blanc	St Emilion	3,850
Climens	Sauternes	408*
Clinet	Pomerol	n/a
La Conseillante	Pomerol	1,235
Cos d'Estournel	St. Estephe	575
Ducru-Beaucaillou	St Julien	642
L'Eglise-Clinet	Pomerol	n/a
L'Evangil	Pomerol	n/a
Figeac	St Emilion	514
La Fleur Petrus	Pomerol	n/a
Haut-Brion	Pessac (Graves)	2,500
Lafite Rothschild	Pauillac	2,750
Lafleur	Pomerol	5,500
Latour	Pauillac	2,950
Laville-Haut Brion	Pessac	n/a
Leoville Las Cases	St Julien	1,500
Margaux	Margaux	3,000
La Mission Haut Brion	Pessac	2,500
Mouton Rothschild	Pauillac	2,500
Palmer	Cantenac	880
Petrus	Pomerol	12,995
Pichon Longueville	Pauillac	n/a
Le Pin	Pomerol	9,900
Rauzon-Segla	Margaux	n/a
Rieussec	Sauternes	350*
Suduiraut	Sauternes	295*
Tertre-Roteboeuf	St Emilion	n/a
Trotanoy	Pomerol	n/a
De Valandraud	St Emilion	n/a
Vieux Chateau Certan	Pomerol	800
D'Yquem	Sauternes	n/a

Note: This list is based on chateaux rated **** quality by wine expert Hugh Johnson. No comment is made as to their value for money status as investments. See Hugh Johnson's Pocket Wine Book (Mitchell Beazley) for more detailed comments.

*next to price means 2001 vintage.

The 2000 vintage was generally regarded as exceptionally good, and this is reflected in prices. There are substantial differences in price between vintages. Prices of 1998 Bordeaux from the best Chateaux are between a third and a half of the prices for 2000. The 1998 is considered a reasonable vintage, though not an exceptional one.

Hugh Johnson's excellent book contains comments on which vintages are regarded as the best for each particular chateau and general comments on which vintage years are the best for laying down.

This raises the obvious point that the wine produced each year differs from chateau to chateau, and of course each vintage year is different for the Bordeaux region as a whole. Some vintages, such as 2000, have been deemed excellent across the board, and prices already reflect this. The best chateaux can produce decent wines even in a difficult vintage year. Above all, they produce wine of consistent top quality.

The quality or otherwise of a vintage is a product of the climatic conditions during the growing season and harvesting period and can therefore be determined with a broad degree of accuracy once the wine has been produced and tasted. Much depends on the quality control policies operated by the chateaux. Typically between 10% and 30% of the wine made from any one harvest may be rejected as unsuitable to be classed as vintage.

The best wine takes time to mature. It will, at some stage, reach a peak and thereafter begin to deteriorate. From an investment standpoint it follows that the best policy can be to buy wine of a quality that will last in what is known or strongly suspected to be a good vintage, and to buy it as early as possible in its life.

While some wines produced in, say, 1945 or 1961 are still superb, they are unlikely to improve further and in investment terms have little appreciation potential. Most wine experts would advise against buying anything produced before 1980 unless you can be sure it has been stored in ideal conditions.

There are several ways of buying wine. From an investment standpoint the best method to capture returns may be by buying 'en primeur'. This is buying after the wine has been produced and after an initial tasting, but prior to its being bottled for the mass market. Wine can also be bought in bottle through a wine merchant in the normal way, usually around two years later.

The timescale is roughly as follows: the grapes are harvested between the end of August and the beginning of October; the wine is then made and stored in barrels and the following April/May it is available to be tasted and rated by wine experts in this 'en primeur' form. The wine is then made available in bottled form roughly two years later. So the 'en primeur' 2003 vintage will be available in April 2004, but not available in bottle until early 2006.

Buying at the 'en primeur' stage, in effect using what is to all intents and purposes a futures market for bottled wine, allows you to get in at the earliest possible point in a wine's life cycle. But there are risks. There have been scams in the past involving 'en primeur' wine, so watertight documentation is essential. In addition with 'en primeur' there is always the chance that, despite what the experts may say, what is thought an outstanding vintage at the earliest stage may turn out to be pedestrian when it finally reaches the bottle.

Storing bottled wine is best left to the experts. Investment quality wines may take years to reach their peak and can be ruined if not stored correctly in the appropriate temperature and humidity. The ideal is for wine to be stored in a temperature that fluctuates little and which is between 10 degrees and 13 degrees Celsius with humidity of around 60% in a dark and vibration free environment.

Since few individual investors have the benefit of sufficient space of the right sort to store wine properly, it makes sense to leave the storage of your investment to an expert. The additional advantage of having your wine portfolio stored by an expert is that it can be kept under bond, in a customs-controlled warehouse. This mean it is not treated as having entered the UK market and there is therefore no duty or VAT to pay on it, as there would be if it were cleared for use in the UK.

If your sole objective is that the wine be treated as an investment, and subsequently sold, then this system is ideal. Wine is kept securely, registered in your name, and stored properly, free of tax. Clearly this is not possible if you buy 'en primeur' and in this instance you have to trust the chateau and your wine merchant to deliver the goods when the wine is eventually bottled and can then be shipped to the bonded warehouse of your choice and stored to your requirements.

For this reason it is best to use the services of an established and highly reputable wine merchant if you are planning this course of action. In any event, the best strategy is to deal with someone you know well, or someone with good credentials (a Master of Wine, for example) that can be checked out.

These quirks in the system mean that there are various styles of wine investment possible, with various risk levels attached, and various time horizons. Buying 'en primeur' is riskier, but may offer much better returns.

Is it right for you?

Let's look at the questions you need to answer to determine whether wine could form a part of your wider portfolio of investments.

Are you investing for the medium to long term?

Wine investment is not necessarily an ultra long-term business, but some of the best wines do take a number of years to reach their full potential. In some cases by buying 'en primeur', before the wine is bottled, the investor is likely to benefit from what has traditionally been the steepest increase in price, in the early years of a classic vintage wine's life. However, buying 'en primeur' is not necessary in all cases to capture the best returns from a particular vintage.

In some instances the best returns come five or more years into a wine's life, or from a sea change in the appreciation of the quality of a particular chateau. Investors need to buy wine with a five to ten-year time horizon in mind. Remember too that buying 'en primeur' does not guarantee a steady or immediate increase in value. The wine may drift for a while before increasing sharply in price two or three years into its life.

Do you have adequate capital?

In theory there is no maximum or minimum amount to be invested but wine merchants will typically recommend a minimum investment of at least £3,000 and ideally perhaps rather more than this in order to create a balanced-long term investment portfolio.

Right for you?

- Medium term investment - minimum five year view
- Minimum investment £3,000 upwards
- Advisory charges 1% a year
- Storage and insurance charges either by value or flat rate
- Prices can be volatile
- Possible CGT exemption

Many leading wine merchants, such as Berry Bros. & Rudd, operate 'cellar plans' by which an individual invests a fixed amount per month and accumulates a portfolio of wine for investment or drinking purposes over a period of years. Minimum amounts invested under plans like this are typically in the region of £150-200 per month. In fairness to those offering plans like this, it should be stressed that the firms in question are primarily orientated towards wine for future drinking rather than looking at them with a view to capital appreciation and prices reflect this. They will also charge commission if you wish subsequently to sell wine rather than drink it.

Are you prepared for extra storage and insurance costs?

It is false economy to store wine yourself in the hope of saving on storage and insurance costs. Wine merchants are able to store wine under bond in tightly controlled conditions that preserve your investment in optimum condition and save you paying VAT and duty. Charges are either a flat rate per case (typically around £5.00 to £7.50) or about 1% of the underlying value of the wine. You need to choose a wine merchant very much with an eye to the firm's expertise, but also bear in mind the cellar charges and if you feel they are excessive, negotiate an alternative arrangement. Merchants specialising in wines for investment will typically charge for their services, either an upfront figure of say 5% or perhaps an annual 1% fee.

Is portfolio diversification an objective?

Some wine investment firms would have you believe that wine prices outperform both the stock market and some other classes of alternative investment over the longer term. In selected instances this has been true, but there are many mundane wines that do not behave in this way.

Stamps, coins and art are dependent on the relative prosperity of the collector market. Wine prices reflect demand from drinkers as well as investors. This has pluses and minuses. Those who invest are doing so in conditions where not only is supply restricted, but also where supply will contract as consumers (as opposed to investors) drink it. As this happens the wine therefore become increasingly scarce.

On the other hand, investment grade wine is something of an affluent person's hobby, and wine in general is subject to extreme fashion swings. At the time of writing, some high quality French wine prices are suffering because of a de facto boycott of French products by American consumers. How long this factor remains in force is uncertain, but it could go on for some time to come and be compounded by recent weakness in the international value of the US dollar.

Do you have an interest in wine and travel?

It is perhaps unwise to invest in wine without having at least some curiosity and knowledge about how and where it is produced. Even for a teetotaller like me a visit to a vineyard is a pleasure to be savoured and one can derive almost as much pleasure from 'nosing' a fine wine as one can from drinking it. Experiencing the wines of different parts of France, and the complexity of wines from different parts of Bordeaux, is a concomitant to wine investment. You need to be prepared for it.

Are there tax considerations?

One of the big plus points for investing in wine is that the Inland Revenue sometimes consider wine to be a wasting asset. Therefore, provided you do not buy and sell wine often enough to be regarded as a dealer and therefore make yourself subject to income tax on your profits, there may well be no capital gains tax levied on the gains made on sales of any wine in which you have invested. Those banking on a tax-free return, however, should bear in mind that this is not guaranteed. Fortified wine, which has a much longer drinkable shelf life, may not be exempt from CGT when an investment is finally sold. You should check this point with an accountant before investing.

Prices and returns

This is an area that is hotly disputed. Let's begin with the basics. The starting point for a fine wine portfolio is probably a lump sum investment of, ideally, around £10,000. Investing this amount allows a wine merchant to assemble a balanced portfolio. Prices of individual wines on a per case basis vary but first growth Bordeaux from classic chateaux are typically in the region of £700-800 per case.

Data on returns is difficult to evaluate, but there is a general belief that in the long term (25 years or more) fine wine can outperform most other tangible investments. According to Decanter Fine Wine Tracker, fine wine prices have risen eight fold since 1978, a compound return of 8.7% a year.

Before we take that too literally, many performance calculations do depend on the starting point you choose and the vintage you select.

As an example of what we mean, journalist Jim Budd's 'Investdrinks' website at www.investdrinks.org produced a table that showed the prices of wine from several vintage years from some of the best leading claret chateaux over a three year period. These showed that increases in value are at best patchy. The results are summarised in the table overleaf.

Table 13.2 - Investment grade wine – sample price changes over three years 1999-2002

Chateau	Best perf vintage yr	Price ch. % over Three yrs. for best vint	Worst perf vintage yr	Price ch % over three yrs. for worst vint.	No. of vintage years1976-1998 with three year gains of:	
					>20%	>10%
Cheval Blanc	1990	51	1995	-10	7	7
Haut Brion	1990	35	1998	-3	4	7
Lafite	1982	53	1998	-5	3	8
Latour	1986	43	1995	0	5	9
Margaux	1985	47	1995	0	7	9
Mouton Rothschild	1982	28	1996	-14	2	5
Petrus	1982	65	1996	-2	7	7

Source: investdrinks.org

This shows those chateaux that show the most consistent performance and the scale of the gains in good years, and of the declines in bad years. Wines from average or poor years clearly make poor investments, but over a span of 22 vintage years only a third of vintages show gains over a three-year period in excess of 20% and then only at the top performing chateaux.

With the hurdle rate dropped to 10% over three years, the batting average improves somewhat, but in all cases fewer than half of the vintages produce gains of this magnitude.

This shows returns to be very variable and suggest that expert advice and purchasing only the best quality names will work as an investment strategy.

This conclusion is confirmed by Liv-ex (www.liv-ex.com). Liv-ex is the London International Vintners Exchange. This is an independent trading and settlement organisation serving the fine wine trade. Liv-ex produces an index of prices of the top 500 wines from what it describes as 'the most celebrated regions and vintages'. This index, with a base date of May 2001, currently stands at 110.3, with the red Bordeaux index at 109.2 and Burgundy the best performer over the period at 125.9.

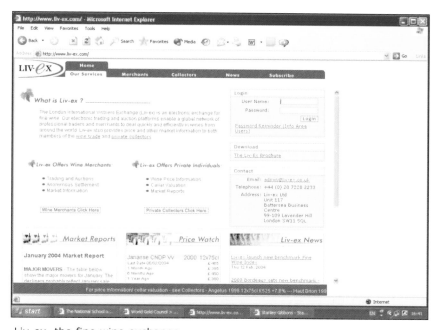

Liv-ex, the fine wine exchange

The table below shows the percentage change in price for the top ten gainers during 2003.

Table 13.3 - Big price gainers in 2003

Label/Chateau	Vintage	Price in 2002 (£)	Price in 2003 (£)	Change (%)
Lafleur	2000	2,700	5,500	103.7
Latour	2002	680	1,125	65.4
Leoville Las Cases	2000	925	1,350	45.9
Petrus	2000	9,450	12,995	37.5
Leoville Payferre	2000	335	460	37.3
Chave, Hermitage	1990	1,535	2,100	36.8
Mouton Rothschild	2000	1,850	2,500	35.1
Lafite Rothschild	2000	2,050	2,750	34.1
Antinori, Tiganello	1996	305	410	34.4
Le Pin	2000	7,950	10,500	32.1

Source: Liv-ex

Over the same period, however, there were losers too. 1982 Petrus slipped 8.6%, 1995 Latour 8.8%, 1998 Haut Brion by 12%, 1998 Leoville Las Cases by 14.3%, and 1998 Vieux Certan by 19.6%. There is no sure fire route to making money, and what is in vogue one year may not be 12 months later.

This evidence does not wholly square with the assertions made by some wine merchants that in the period from 1975 onwards a competently managed wine portfolio would have more than kept pace with the stock market during the 1990s bull market. What is true is that wine seems to have appreciated since then, albeit in a modest way, whereas the stock market has dropped back.

The wine market on average, like many other tangible asset categories, may display rather less volatility than the stock market, but does it really deliver?

There are some things to be said in its favour. While Bordeaux has occasional bad years, some winemakers can make acceptable wines even in these years, and it becomes evident from the outset whether or not the wines from any year are suitable for investment. A poor year or two only serves to enhance the scarcity value of good vintages.

In fact, one reason for the potentially useful returns from wine investment is the fact that investors can retain their wine for a reasonably long period, during which a sizeable quantity of a particular vintage will have been bought and drunk by non-investors, thereby increasing the scarcity value of the remainder.

There is also the possibility that an influential wine writer will give a particular chateau the seal of approval and revolutionise its pricing almost overnight. The well-known wine writer Robert Parker famously achieved this with Chateau Petrus, whose cause he championed. While other wine writers may or may not share his opinions, there is no doubt that he wields considerable influence, particularly among American buyers.

So good returns can happen. Many investment firms specialising in wine make eye-catching claims. As an example, Premier Cru Investments, which manages fine wine portfolios on behalf of investors, says in its promotional literature that a typical portfolio invested since 1994 has shown an average annual growth of 25.5%, while the period since 1975 has seen annual returns in the region of 19%.

Before investing, however, it would be wise to verify any claims made about performance. Ask how the portfolio would have performed measured from a different starting point, and go through the routine checks described in the next section.

Just as some investors in the stock market are highly successful and others do less well, with wine investment it is as well to remember that there are no guarantees that past performance can be repeated, no repealing of the law that states that high returns usually come with high risks attached, and that wine investment is unregulated.

How to buy and sell

It takes some educated guesswork to spot those wines that will produce the best returns from an investment standpoint. Rather like picking shares, it is a matter of spotting which ones offer the right combination of quality and value.

It is also pretty clear from what we've found out already that you need to be careful about the way you approach investment in wine.

There have been a number of scams that have trapped investors in the past, and examples of ostensibly bona fide wine investment operations where, after a company has gone into liquidation, investors find it difficult to establish title to the wine they think they own.

So there are a number of ground rules to observe to make sure your investment is safe.

Avoiding the scams - a check list

- Check the price of the wine independently
- Check the standing of the firm proposing the scheme
- Make sure the investment is right for you in terms of timescale
- Make sure you can have the wine stored independently in your name
- Only pay against invoice with confirmation of storage
- Establish what charges will be before you invest

The first is to run an independent check on the price of the wine that you are being offered by anyone suggesting it as an investment. Websites of leading wine merchants generally allow you to do this as does www.wine-searcher.com. A good source is Fine and Rare Wines (www.frw.co.uk), which has updated prices on a wide range of chateaux and vintage years. Liv-ex, referred to earlier, also gives a regular update in the public part of its web site on recent prices for the most popular chateaux for the better vintages from 1982 onwards.

Check the price at Wine-Searcher

Many scams involve buying bona fide wines, but buying them at prices in excess (sometimes well in excess) of their current market value. So check out the price before you commit to an investment.

Second, check that the firm with which you are dealing has not been involved in dodgy dealing before. The website www.investdrinks.org carries the names of companies whose dealings are suspect. If in any doubt run a Companies House (www.companieshouse.gov.uk) search on the company and its directors to see whether or not they have a bona fide business.

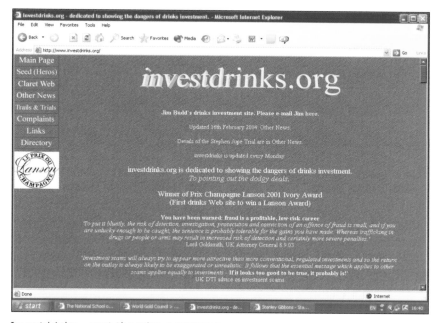

Investdrinks - spot the wine scamsters

Third, make sure the portfolio of wines you are planning to invest in is right for you in terms of its risk profile and in terms of the time the wine is likely to take to achieve its peak value. Makes sure that the wine is recognised as a high quality product and not simply an undiscovered gem that is likely to remain undiscovered for some time. As a rough rule of thumb, for example, if a particular chateau does not merit at least a three star rating in the Bordeaux section of Hugh Johnson's book, referred to earlier, then the chances are it does not merit inclusion in an investment portfolio.

Fourth and extremely importantly, establish exactly how and where the wine you buy is to be delivered and stored. Only deal with firms that will confirm that wine is specifically identified with your name on the case and stored in an independent warehouse like Octavian, which operates a large specialist facility in Wiltshire, or London City Bond (www.lcb.co.uk).

Storage in a public bond in this way means that the wines in question are specifically identified as your property and cannot be removed from the warehouse without your specific written consent. This also means that in the event of the firm through which you buy the wine going bust, creditors cannot get their hands on the wine you own.

Fifth, pay only against invoice and confirmation that the wine has been delivered either direct to you or into storage under your name at the warehouse. Do not give money to people whose bona fides you have not been able to verify.

Finally, establish what charges you will bear. Firms differ in the charges they make. Some charge an upfront fee of perhaps 5% of the total value of the wine, others an annual 1% management charge. Storage costs are levied on a per-case per year basis. Some firms pass these on straight to the client; others add a mark-up of their own on top.

It is also worth remembering that the biggest names in the wine business may not necessarily be the best when it comes to proffering advice about investment. Many operate 'cellar plans' whereby you can buy wine for laying down (and have it stored for you) by making a regular investment of £150 per month or more. But most large wine merchants have based their business on selling wine for consumption rather than investment purposes.

While they may be perfectly able to source and store cases of wine if you know what you want, they may not want to put together or monitor wine portfolios for individual investors, unless the individual in question has very large amounts of money to use in this way.

Where to go for more information

For the consumer there is generally no shortage of information about wine. Magazines like Decanter, Wine & Spirit International, and all the national daily and especially Sunday newspapers have regular columns about wine written by acknowledged experts.

For investors, a little further digging is required. Prominent wine merchants are a good starting point and many have sophisticated web sites aimed primarily at selling wine to would-be drinkers. Nonetheless these can prove useful sources of information for investors and an all-important check on prices quoted by those promoting investment schemes.

The following are a few examples:

Berry Bros. & Rudd (www.bbr.com) has an entertaining, informative site, but with the accent on drinking the wine rather than buying it as a long-term investment. The site has details of the company's 'cellar plan' with information on buying, selling and storage plus the objectives and benefits of the plan. The 'wine knowledge' section has news, newsletter, wine FAQs and details of tastings and wine courses. Wine can be purchased online and there are numerous guides and charts.

Christie's (www.christies.com) has been auctioning wine since 1776. Christie's wine newsletter can be subscribed to online. The site has information regarding forthcoming auctions worldwide, plus information on wine tasting and courses. Catalogues can be ordered online with digital versions also available. Those buying wine through auction should remember that the buyer's premium can add significantly to the price you pay.

Corney and Barrow (www.corneyandbarrow.com) established its fine wine broking in 1992. The current wine list can be downloaded from the site and wine can be bought online. The company does not limit itself to France and deals in fine wine from around the world.

Magnum Fine Wines (www.magnum.co.uk) specialises in wine investment and the web site has a comprehensive section devoted to the process including sections on storage, how to buy and sell, and investment news together with a sample portfolio. A performance graph compares wine prices since 1975 with other forms of investment over the same period. Wine can also be bought online and tasting notes are included.

Premier Cru (www.premiercru.com) has detailed information on wine investment with a downloadable brochure. Topics covered on the site include market history, tax-free investment and investment charges. Wine can also be bought online across the price range varying from £120 to £5,500 per case. Relevant details are included such as year and chateau region.

Sotheby's (www.sothebys.com) holds approximately eleven wine sales in London annually and six in New York. A list of forthcoming auctions is available on the site together with downloadable catalogues.

Based in Cheshire, Vineyards of Bordeaux (www.vineyardsofbordeaux.com), as the name suggests, has much information on wines of the Bordeaux region. Wine can be purchased online once registered and the company has a significant number of clients it advises on wine investment.

Among sites more geared to the pure provision of information on wine, Investdrinks (www.investdrinks.org) is a site dedicated to the dangers of drinks investment. Jim Budd, who set up and runs the site, specialises in tracking down the perpetrators of drinks frauds. He lists the companies to avoid as well as those he considers reputable and who have committed not knowingly to supply firms offering dubious investment schemes or perpetrating scams.

The directory of fraudulent companies makes interesting reading. It is accompanied by information taken from their Companies House returns. The site is full of advice and help for would-be investors, together with advice for investors who have been the victims of fraud.

Fine and Rare Wines (www.frw.co.uk) is an online wine broker. The site is useful for up to date prices on a wide range of wines from round the world with prices updated daily. An extensive list of Bordeaux vintages allows would-be investors to check accurately the current price of wines being suggested for investment purposes.

Jancis Robinson (www.jancisrobinson.com) is a Master of Wine (the most prestigious and sparingly awarded qualification in the industry) and well known broadcaster and writer. She has an informative site with wine news, a list of books on wine, an exhaustive archive of her articles for the Financial Times, and a directory of merchants, auction houses, publications and trade associations. Further information is available to subscribers.

Wine-Searcher (www.wine-searcher.com) provides an impartial service for wine availability and pricing. The free part of the site is useful for locating hard-to-find wine and is searchable by country. The subscription service locates the best prices and stockists of your chosen wine, with worldwide price comparisons.

Wine Spectator (www.winespectator.com) has a roster of more than 10,000 wines reviewed in the last year. Account holders have access to a database of 110,000 wine reviews. Other information includes wine news, the basics of wine, vintage charts and advice on collecting.

Table 13.4 – Wine – key web addresses and contact details

Company	Web address	Email	Phone	Category
Berry Brothers and Rudd	www.bbr.com	On site	0870 900 4300	Dealer
Christies	www.christies.com	info@christies.com	020 7839 9060	Auction
Corney and Barrow	www.corneyandbarrow.com	wine@corbar.co.uk	020 7265 2400	Dealer
Fine and Rare Wines	www.frw.co.uk	On site	020 8960 1995	Dealer
Jancis Robinson	www.jancisrobinson.com	n/a	n/a	Information
Liv-ex	www.liv-ex.com	info@liv-ex.com	020 7228 2233	Exchange
London City Bond	www.lcb.co.uk	cs@lcb.co.uk	01375 487110	Warehouse
Magnum Fine Wines	www.magnum.co.uk	wine@magnum.co.uk	020 7930 6925	Dealer
Premier Cru	www.premiercru.com	inquiry@premiercru.com	020 8905 4495	Dealer
Sothebys	www.sothebys.com	serena.sutcliffe@sothebys.com	020 7293 5050	Auction
Vineyards of Bordeaux	www.vineyardsofbordeaux.com	james@vineyardsofbordeaux.com	01204 535302	Dealer
Wineprice	www.wineprice.com	info@wineprice.com	n/a	Data
Wines of Bordeaux	www.winesofbordeaux.com	ukinfo@winesofbordeaux.com	0870 111 8990	Dealer

Chapter

14 | **Auctions and Dealers**

In the course of reading this book I hope you have found one or more areas that interest you and fit your pocket. If so and before you invest, make sure you read up further on your chosen area. It goes without saying that what you've read here on each topic can only scratch the surface of the subject.

In a favourite area of mine like Victorian watercolours, there are, for example, several large books detailing the work of various artists, painting techniques, collecting themes and other topics. You need to study these and talk to dealers in these items and to auction house specialists and maybe attend a couple of auctions to get a feel for the market before you even think about buying.

One of the great debates in many collectable areas is whether it is best to buy through a dealer or through an auction house. There is no one correct answer to this question. In some areas we have covered in this book - film and forestry, for example - auction markets do not exist. But in most others, you have a choice of buying and selling either at auction or through a dealer. The next section looks at how to choose.

Auction versus dealer?

The conventional answer to this question is that you buy through a dealer and sell at auction. This is a sweeping generalisation, but two main reasons are usually given for this advice.

One is that by selling at auction, you may benefit from aggressive competition between buyers, which can drive the price to unexpectedly high levels.

The second is that many individuals avoid buying at auction because of the hefty charges that auction houses impose, in the form of the so-called buyer's premium. This is generally a percentage added to the 'hammer price' (the price at which the bidding stops and the lot is sold to the highest bidder). On lower priced items at large salerooms it may be as much as 20% plus VAT of the hammer price. Even on high priced items it may be as much as 12% plus VAT.

In reality there is a trade-off between the two. While you may incur hefty charges buying at auction, you do avoid paying the dealers' markup, which can be a hefty amount. With auctions, your charges are a known quantity at the outset.

The table opposite shows contact details for major auction houses in different superhobby categories.

Why dealers use auctions

However, it isn't as straightforward as that, as the presence of many dealers at auctions will testify. Some dealers who attend auctions are bidding on behalf of clients, but many are buying for their own stock. They will bid for lots up to a level at which they calculate that, even including the buyers' premium they can add their own margin to a particular lot and still find ready buyers.

There are other reasons too why dealers frequent salerooms.

Salerooms may be the only source of scarce items that they know they will have buyers for. Some collectors know they have items that the market wants, and will calculate that a sufficiently scarce item will attract a lot of interest. It is not necessarily in their interest to sell it to a dealer, because a dealer's bid is likely to be on the low side.

A rational dealer's motivation on the other hand is to make as much profit from a scarce item as possible, perhaps exploiting the seller's ignorance about how much the piece might really be worth. The auction is the only true arbiter of value for that item on that day. Even then, it is an imperfect one.

Dealers also bid at auctions, and collectors and superhobby investors should consider doing so too, because there are often opportunities to snap up worthwhile items at advantageous prices.

The essence of auctions

Auctions rely on assembling a crowd of interested buyers and on occasion for reasons beyond their control, only a few turn up. The buyers that do turn up may not be interested in all the lots, and in this eventuality, low bids on particular lots may be successful.

If so, this means that even allowing for the buyers' premium, buying at auction will almost certainly be cheaper than buying from a dealer. By the same token, it means that a collector can also outbid a dealer and still get the item cheaper than he might pay at the dealer's outlet.

There is a proviso attached to this. You need to be confident enough about your superhobby investing to know the true value of the item in question and that it is the genuine article. You can only do this by attending the auction in person and viewing the item before the sale.

Table 14.1 – Auction Houses – key web addresses and contact details

Company	Web address	Email	Phone	Category
Baldwins Auctions	www.baldwin.sh	auctions@baldwin.sh	020 7930 9808	Banknotes
Bloomsbury Book Auctions	www.bloomsbury-book-auct.com	info@bloomsbury-book-auct.com	020 7883 2636/7	Books, prints
Bonhams	www.bonhams.com	info@bonhams.com	020 7393 3900	Various
Christies	www.christies.com	info@christies.com	020 7839 9060	Various
Dix Noonan Webb	www.dnw.co.uk	chris@dnw.co.uk	020 7499 5022	Coins, banknotes
Glendinings	www.bonhams.com	Andrew.Litherland@bonhams.com	020 7393 3900	Coins
Harmers	www.harmers.com	auctions@harmers.demon.co.uk	020 8747 6100	Stamps
McTears	www.mctears.co.uk	whiskyvaluations@mctears.co.uk	0141 221 4456	Whisky
Sotheby's	www.sothebys.com	On site	020 7293 5050	Various
Spink	www.spink.com	info@spink.com	020 7563 4000	Coins, stamps, medals, banknotes
Stamp Auction Network	www.stampauctionnetwork.com	n/a	919 403 9459	Stamp
Tennants	www.tennants.co.uk	enquiries@tennants.co.uk	01969 623780	Various, regional

---

Auction essentials

- Dealers use auctions as a source of stock
- All auctions have a similar format and cast of characters
- You may be able to buy cheaply at auction
- You need to be selective
- You need to work out charges in advance

In most instances however, you will not succeed in getting an item substantially below its estimate in the auction catalogue. Many (though by no means all) sellers set a reserve price on an item they sell through auction, below which the auctioneer will not sell. But there are exceptions.

This reserve price will not be more that the low end of the auctioneer's catalogue estimate, but could be significantly below it. Not all items have reserves on them. By bidding up to just below the bottom end of the estimated price you stand a chance of getting an item at a good price, and below what you might pay for it at a dealer. The auctioneer's language will normally give a clue as to whether the reserve has been met, a topic we'll go into in the next section.

Let's also remember that bidders make decisions for reasons other than price. I could have bought an attractive 46-volume first edition set of the works of Sir Walter Scott for £45 at a book auction but did not, simply because a] I don't like Sir Walter Scott, b] I don't have the room to keep it and c] it would have been inconvenient to transport. I did pay considerably more than this for a small Victorian watercolour that fitted in my briefcase. Large unwieldy items may sell for less than small compact ones.

How auctions work

You can buy most types of superhobby investment categories at auction. The list of items auctioned includes stamps, books, coins, art, antiques, cars, wine, whisky and so on. Most auctions have a number of characteristics in common.

Before the sale

The auction will be advertised well in advance so that would-be buyers will have plenty of time to make arrangements to be there in person. Except for particularly homogeneous items with precise grading like stamps, wine, or whisky, it makes sense to attend an auction in person and in particular to view the items you intend to bid for prior to the auction to satisfy yourself as to their condition and genuineness.

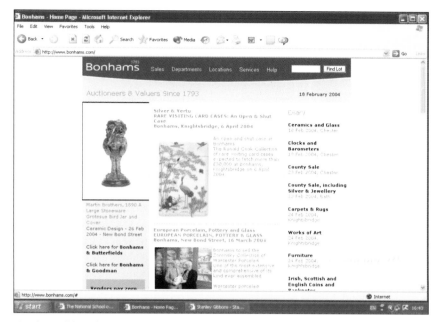

Bonhams' helpful home page

Even in situations where this is not strictly necessary, it makes sense to attend in person if humanly possible to take advantage of opportunities that may occur where bidding in the room is slack, or to gauge the momentum of bidding for a particular item.

If you are selling items at auction, it is worth attending in person, although auctions are recorded and are open and transparent. If you do attend, you can verify for yourself the progress of the bidding and the eventual price.

A catalogue will normally be published some time before the auction. This may range from a photocopied sheet, in the case of an auction at a small provincial saleroom, to a lavishly produced perfect bound book in the case of a high value auction at a leading London auction house. In the case of the latter, the items will be illustrated in colour.

Auction mechanics

- Sale advertised
- Catalogue published, with estimated values
- Viewing of items
- Sale day - dealers, private, telephone, and absentee bidders
- 100 lots an hour

Some auction catalogues, particularly those from large salerooms, sometimes include a guide as to the source of the item, and for important lots, its provenance. In many cases this can, however, be fairly sketchy and may not be a foolproof guarantee of authenticity. Provenance may not be available for all items, although if an item is from a noted collection this is itself a reasonable guarantee.

Large auction houses employ experts on particular areas and the presence of these experts is in itself a reasonable assurance that items offered for sale will be the genuine article, although attention needs to be paid to the precise description in the catalogue. Large auction houses offer what might best be described as conditional and time-limited guarantees that items sold are not counterfeit.

Conditions include the buyer producing independent experts acceptable to both sides to check disputed authenticity. Buyers must also return the goods in the same condition as when they were sold. Subject to this, the auction house may return the full amount paid.

This does not apply if the description of the item in the original catalogue accorded with the opinion of experts at the time and all reasonable steps available to verify authenticity at the time had been taken. Guarantees last for several years, but in view of the conditions set, it is best to assume that you make a purchase on the basis of the old maxim of 'caveat emptor' (buyer beware).

There are unlikely to be such formal guarantees at small local salerooms.

On the day

What happens on the day of the sale? Auction rooms generally have a fixed cast of characters. There are bidders in the room, who may be dealers or private buyers. There are clerks manning telephones, each in contact with a telephone bidder (who normally remains anonymous), and the auctioneer, whose job it is to auction the lots and to bid on behalf of absentee or 'commission' bidders, who have set a maximum price beyond which they will not go.

Lots are auctioned in the order they appear in the catalogue. An auctioneer will typically sell 50-100 lots an hour. Bidding starts at some way below the minimum estimate value and progresses by predetermined amounts (normally around 10% of the previous bid). Auctioneers may start and continue the bidding themselves if the price is below the reserve. If bidding on behalf of an absentee bidder the auctioneer will normally indicate this by pointing to himself (or herself).

Auctioneers will normally indicate when commission bids have been exceeded and bidding then continues in the room until all but one bidder drops out. The auctioneer will give fair warning that the lot it is to be sold to that particular bidder and then signal the end of the auction for that lot by a rap of the gavel. If the reserve has not been met, this is sometimes indicated by a simple and rather terse 'unsold'. If the auctioneer fails to note a successful bidder's number, this can also be an indication that the reserve price has not been met.

Astute observers of auctions can sometimes spot subtle changes in the auctioneer's language that indicate if a reserve has been met despite a lot being below the minimum estimate. If the auctioneer uses the phrase 'selling then at .....', this could be the time to jump in with a bid.

The table below shows some of the phraseology used by auctioneers and what it means.

Auctioneer-speak

Says	Means
Against you at (price)	Another bidder is bidding more, do you want to bid
On the telephone at (price)	Telephone bidder has bid (price)
Against the room at (price)	Telephone bidder is bidding (price)
Bid is with me at (price)	Auctioneer is bidding (price) for a commission bidder
That clears me	Commission bids have been exceeded
Commission bids all out	Commission bids have been exceeded
Against you all	Commission bid exceeds all other bids
All done	Hammer about to go down
Fair warning	Hammer about to go down
Selling then at (price)	Price is above reserve and hammer about to go down
Unsold (after hammer)	Reserve price has not been met

If you wish to bid in an auction you need to register prior to the sale and, at large auctions, will be given a 'paddle' or a sheet of paper will a number on it, to indicate your identity to the auctioneer and that you are a bona fide registered bidder. After a sale, provided you have paid in full in cleared funds, you can take your purchase away with you. Some auction houses will allow you to store your purchase for five days free of charge at the buyers risk. Shipping can also be arranged at the buyers' risk and expense.

If it turns out you can't pay, normally within five days, the auction house has the opportunity either to cancel the sale, or to re-auction the lot or sell it privately, with the defaulting buyer being responsible for any shortfall. An alternative may be for the auction house or the seller to pursue the defaulting buyer through the courts. The moral is: if you can't afford it, don't bid. Defaulting buyers will normally find it hard to show their face at another auction.

If you wish to bid in absentia, you can fill in a form and send it by post or email, or take it to the auction house. In the event of two or more identical absentee bids being the highest, the one received earliest carries the day.

Christie's web site has auction details

Telephone bidding works the same way as if you were in the room, with competing bids being relayed to you by an auctioneer's representative in the room by an open telephone line. Telephone bidding is not normally offered for lots estimated at below £1,000. You can normally bid by telephone by simply registering with the bidding department at least 24 hours prior to the auction.

Charges

The charges levied by auction houses are a bone of contention with many dealers and collectors alike but they are known in advance and bids can be tailored accordingly.

The charges take two basic forms, with one or two extras on top. These charges are the buyer's premium, a levy added to the 'hammer' price and payable by the successful bidder. Seller's commission is deducted from the hammer price and paid to the buyer. The difference between these two prices represents the amount that the auction house takes for its services.

Buyer's premium varies from auction house to auction house. London salerooms take 20% plus VAT on the first £70,000. Sellers commission is typically 15% for the £1,000-3,000, and 10% thereafter.

Let's look at how this works out in practice.

Let's look at an object that goes under the hammer at £10,000. The charges work out as shown below:

Charges on an item with £10,000 'hammer' price.	
Buyers premium (20% plus VAT)	£2,350
Buyer pays	£12,350
Sellers commission (10% plus VAT)	£1,175
Seller receives	£8,825
HM Customs & Excise receives VAT of	£525
Saleroom receives	£3,000

The bottom line here is that there is a 40% difference between what the seller receives and what the buyer pays. The saleroom receives three-quarters of this difference and VAT accounts for the remainder.

While this seems a little unfair, let's not forget the dealers are in business to make money too and there are differences between what dealers pay for items they want to sell, and the price they put on them when they sell them to customers. It seems fair to assume that there is a sizeable markup applied by dealers, who have overheads to recoup just as auction houses do.

The point with dealers, however, is that while you might not know what the markup is, there is some wiggle room. Most dealers will negotiate on price, especially if you are a regular customer.

Auction house charges do not end with the buyer's premium and seller's commission. There are occasionally charges for placing a reserve on the item. It is also normal practice for sellers to pay a fixed amount for items illustrated in the catalogue. Buyers may also bear charges for credit card payment for lots acquired, and may also have to pay charges for shipping, packing and storage, if appropriate. Charges are made for insuring items while in the care of the auction, although sellers can opt out of this, or arrange their own.

When buying or selling through auction, or at least through large salerooms in major cities, you need to take these charges into account. Successful bidders basically need to add 25% to the price of the lot they are bidding for to work out what they will eventually pay.

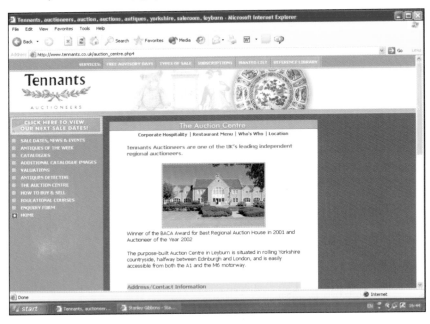

Tennants - the largest regional auctioneer

The table opposite shows a summary of the main charges at various auction houses.

Table 14.2 - Auction house charges

Company	Web address	Buyers Premium	VAT incl.	Sellers Commission	Reserve charge	Estimate charge
Baldwins	www.baldwin.sh	n/a	n/a	n/a	n/a	n/a
Bloomsbury Book Auctions	www.bloomsbury-book-auct.com	17.5% of first £10,000 10% thereafter	n/a	12% in excess of £3000 15% below that amount	n/a	n/a
Bonhams	www.bonhams.com	19.5% on first £70,000 10% on excess over £70,000 Less outside London	No	15% up to £1000 10% upto £70,000 0% thereafter	Minimum £5	Free
Christie's	www.christies.com	Variable depending on location eg 19.5% up to £70,000 12% thereafter	Nog	scale varying from 10% up to £59,999 to 2% on £2,999,999 Case by case thereafter		Free
Harmers	www.harmers.com	15%	No	10% over £2000 12.5% £1-2000 15% up to £999		
Sothebys	www.sothebys.com	20% 0n first £70,000 12% thereafter	No	Contact dept concerned	Yes	Free
Spink	www.spink.com	15%	No	Agreement between seller and auctioneer	5% on final bid if fail to reach reserve	n/a
Tennants	www.tennants.co.uk	10%	No	15% on first £500 falling to 10% over £1000	£8.50 per lot if unsold	Free

Online auctions

Online auctions like QXL and eBay have increased in importance in recent years. But are they the right place for a superhobby investor to go prospecting for material?

Before we look at the mechanics let's just consider a couple of obvious pluses and minuses.

The big plus about online auctions is that they are continuous and they attract a very large number of buyers and sellers. You need to devote time and money going to physical auctions and you also have to wait until one of the auction houses, either a local or nationally known one, puts one on in your chosen area of interest. These may only happen a few times a year. On sites like eBay items are being auctioned every day.

Online auction essentials

- Mainly eBay
- Register to bid
- Continuous searchable flow of auctions
- Pay through Paypal and other mediums
- Description usually accurate; policing via feedback
- Quality of items collectable but often sub-investment grade

---

The large number of potential sellers means that there is a wide choice of items if you are a would-be buyer. In some ways this is an advantage to the buyer, because the buying interest is diffuse. If you happen to find an item you are interested in, there may only be a couple of other bidders, and you may end up buying the lot cheaper than you would have done in a large well publicised auction in a noted saleroom.

The obvious minus from the standpoint of an online auction is that goods must be bought sight unseen. All you will have to go on is a digital photograph of the item, which may not show the detail you need and is, in any case, no substitute for seeing and handling the item in real life.

Online auctions attempt to keep sellers from misdescribing and overgrading items whose condition is vital to their value by operating a feedback system. This allows buyers who have had good service to register positive votes and those who feel they have been let down to file negative feedback. Accumulated feedback ratings are displayed on the site, the aim being to drive traffic away from those with poor feedback and towards those with excellent customer ratings.

The usual auction rules apply, the only difference from a live auction being that the auctioneer's gavel is replaced by a strict time limit. The highest bid standing when the clock ticks down to zero wins the item, subject to a reserve. This has given rise to a certain amount of gamesmanship, with bids being submitted at the very last minute to beat the clock and yet not allow other bidders time to respond.

eBay also operates other varieties of auction. Some items are offered as auction items but with a fixed 'buy it now' price that secures the item and stops the auction. Items are offered with or without reserves.

Those wishing to buy in this way have to register to be able to bid. If they do bid successfully, the seller and buyer then continue the discussion regarding delivery options and payment via email. A note below the item generally contains details of acceptable forms of payment (some sellers will not accept credit card payment), delivery options, policy on returns and so on.

A useful adjunct to regular bidding on eBay is a Paypal account. This is a secure money transfer system operated by eBay and linked to your email address that allows you to send cash to another Paypal account holder. Users can transfer money into and out of their Paypal account from their bank. Most sellers on eBay will accept payment via Paypal.

Experienced superhobby investors will probably use eBay only sparingly, when particularly interesting items come up. Some professional dealers operate on eBay, and there are dealers on eBay who, though starting out as amateurs, have built a reasonable business buying and selling.

As regards the honesty of the items on offer, I have checked this for two areas that interest me in particular (books and watercolours) and sellers generally do appear to describe the items warts and all. Many items are of a condition that would be unsuitable for superhobby investing, but there are some that are not and experienced collectors could probably pick up the occasional bargain in this way.

Dealing with the dealers

One of the plus points of dealing with large salerooms is of course that they have a high public profile and they are sensitive to adverse publicity. This is particularly so among the top rank of auction houses. Local salerooms can, in my experience be rather more variable in their standards and it is vital here to attend the auction in person simply as a check that your instructions are being followed to the letter.

One problem auction rooms face is collusion among dealers before an auction whereby groups of dealers will agree among themselves which lots are attractive and who wants what, and then agree not to bid against each other, and share out the ownership of the items after the event. 'Rings' like this are illegal and distort the market. But you as a private individual can outbid the dealers because you do not have to factor in their markup.

When it comes to buying through dealers and building relationships with them, there are a couple of golden rules. One is to make sure that the dealer understands your objectives as a superhobby investor and only shows you top quality items. You need to choose your dealer with this in mind - specifically to choose a specialist in the area you have chosen, and one that deals in investment quality material. You may pay slightly more, but you know in the end that the dealer has a reputation to maintain, and wants to keep you as a customer because you could become a reliable source of income for him.

It is usually the quality of dealer's stock that will mark him or her out as the sort of person you will want to deal with, something that you will instinctively be aware of the minute you enter his shop or gallery.

The importance of building relationships with dealers varies from category to category. Some observers, for example, suggest that classic cars, should probably be bought at auction or privately, rather than through dealers. There is such stiff competition in the book trade that means that most second hand book dealers will keep their prices competitive. Even so book auctions are often cheaper than dealers, although quality can be more variable. For art and antiques, building a relationship with a dealer is vital, even though you may also from time to time buy at auction or elsewhere. For stamps, coins and banknotes, specialist dealers like Stanley Gibbons are an essential source of investment grade material in prime condition.

There are, however, a number of other supplementary reasons why buying through a dealer may be worthwhile.

In the first place you will get the benefit of specialist knowledge and experience (although this can also be obtained from auction house specialists). While a dealer is trying to sell you something and therefore to present it to you in the best possible light, with your bullshit detector turned on, you should be able to see through this and appreciate the merits of the item being discussed.

Auctions are places for snap decisions. A dealer's premises, by contrast are unhurried. You can view an item, talk about it, think about it, discuss it with your spouse, go away, come back, ask to take it home on approval, get first refusal on it and a whole range of other options that are not available in the case of auctions which by their nature are 'sudden death' affairs.

Thirdly, dealers travel widely and generally buy stock shrewdly. While some try to pass off inferior items at excessive prices, well-informed buyers will be able to spot this. I once saw a book dealer, for example, sell a third-rate copy of JRR Tolkien's The Hobbitt to an uninformed buyer at the height of the excitement about the 'Lord of The Rings' films for probably three times what the book was worth. If you know your market, and the dealer knows you know, you will only get shown items that fit your criteria and the temptation to pull the wool over your eyes will be that much less.

Good dealers label items well so that you should know pretty accurately what you are buying. In the event that an item has been misrepresented, the best dealers are generally part of trade associations that will have arbitration procedures for settling disputes of this nature. When you are buying through an auction the guiding rule remains 'caveat emptor', but in both cases you ultimately have recourse to law if you feel an item was misrepresented.

Dealers like to both buy and sell. When you build up a relationship with a dealer he may be prepared to buy back items from you for resale, in part exchange for other items or sell it on your behalf on commission. Provided you are satisfied that his bid is as good as the item would fetch at auction after allowing for charges, it can make sense to pursue this as an avenue for buying and selling.

Finally in the event that a piece you buy from a dealer is forged, stolen, or otherwise tampered with and not as represented to you at the time you bought it, you have some comeback legally. The dealer is normally acting as a principal. He owns the goods he is selling to you. This contrasts with the position of an auctioneer, who is normally simply acting as an agent for the seller.

Other sources of investment grade material

Fairs

Fairs, which gather together dealers in one discipline in one place, are often good places to buy and sell, if you know your market and have a good appreciation of the price and value of particular items. Competition between dealers, particularly at larger fairs, tends to keep prices keen.

One slight caveat here is that it makes some sort of sense to attend fairs that are not held in particularly ostentatiously affluent areas, since dealers will automatically mark up prices to reflect the likely affluence of the clientele. The more mundane the surroundings, the more likely you are to discover a bargain.

Another issue is condition. You need to be able to satisfy yourself by inspecting an item that it is in sufficiently good condition to be of investment grade.

Fairs are, however, good places to meet and talk to dealers and other collectors and superhobby investors, and to gauge the strength of the market and the relative price of particular items. There are major fairs held annually, or with greater frequency, for books, coins and banknotes, stamps, art and antiques.

Charity Shops

Charity shops acquire items typically from individuals decluttering, perhaps prior to a house move, or disposing of the effects of a deceased relative. In some cases they may acquire antiques, paintings, old books and the like, which have a value to collectors. It is rare, though not unknown, for investment grade material to crop up in outlets like this, although those running shops like this have an increasingly astute eye for the value of the items that pass through their hands.

It is, however, undeniable that they have become a significant factor in the market. Oxfam, for instance, is now the largest UK retailer of second hand books, much to the chagrin of small professional book dealers. There are occasional bargains to be had, in the form of first editions that have gone unnoticed, or else in older leather bound volumes priced at less than they would fetch at auction. The same is probably true of other disciplines, but you need patience and a keen eye to sift though the dross.

Postscript

With that last chapter on auctions and dealers we've reached the end of the book. If you are still reading at this stage, I hope you have enjoyed this journey through what I believe are some of the more interesting and unusual investment opportunities around.

Of course, there are no guaranteed sure things. But one of the great attributes of investments like this is that they add another dimension to investing. It becomes more than just the simple matter of working out your profits and losses. If you buy, for example, as I have done, some nice pictures, a few first editions, and some investment-grade stamps, you have the beginnings of absorbing interests that can last a lifetime, as well as attractive objects to look at and enjoy in your own home.

In the course of researching this book I have also found that, for example, visiting dealers and attending auctions and fairs - as all superhobby investors must inevitably do - takes you to new and different parts of the country and allows you to meet and talk to, and to buy from and sell to, fellow enthusiasts. At the very least, it is a good way of passing damp winter weekends.

What I think we have also found is that the returns from many of the superhobby categories we have looked at bear favourable comparison with the long term returns from bonds and equities, with perhaps less of the volatility traditionally associated with the securities markets.

Finally, there are many areas we could have looked at in the book: ceramics, posters, sporting memorabilia, watches and clocks, scientific instruments, jewellery and so on. If enough people buy this book, it is possible that we may be able to remedy these omissions in a new edition or a follow up book. That, of course, is for the future, but in the meantime enjoy your superhobby investing!

Appendix

- **Classified contact details for organisations mentioned**

   These tables are intended to mention all of the companies referred to in the books, whether alluded to briefly or discussed in detail.

Antiques

Company	Web address	Email	Phone	Category
Antique Collectors Club	www.antique-acc.com	sales@antique-acc.com	01394 389950	Data
Antiques Atlas	www.antiques-atlas.com	Iain@Antiques-atlas.com	0161 613 5714	Links
Antiques Magazine	www.antiquesmagazine.com	subscriptions@antiquesmagazine.com	0121 427 8731	Publication
Antiques Trade Gazette	www.atg-online.com	info@antiquestradegazette.com	020 7420 6600	Publication
Antiques World	www.antiquesworld.co.uk	contact@antiquesworld.co.uk	n/a	Links
BADA	www.bada.org	info@bada.org	020 7589 4128	Association
BBC Antiques	www.bbc.co.uk/antiques	antiques.roadshow@bbc.co.uk	n/a	Information
Bonhams	www.bonhams.com	info@bonhams.com	020 7393 3900	Auction
British Antique Furniture Restorers	www.bafra.org.uk	headoffice@bafra.org.uk	01305 854822	Association
Brit. Ass'n of Paintings Conservators-Restorers	www.bapcr.org.uk	secretary@bapcr.org.uk	0239 246 5115	Association
Christies	www.christies.com	info@christies.com	020 7839 9060	Auction
Fiske & Freeman	www.fiskeandfreeman.com	info@fiskeandfreeman.com	n/a	Dealer
Invaluable	www.invaluable.com	customer.services@invaluable.com	020 7487 3401	Links
LAPADA	www.lapada.co.uk	lapada@lapada.co.uk	020 7823 3511	Association
Olympia Antiques Fairs	www.olympia-antiques.co.uk	info@olympia-antiques.com	0870 126 1725	Dealer
Phillips	www.phillips-dpl.com	inquiry.desk@phillips-dpl.com	020 7318 4010	Dealer
Sotheby's	www.sothebys.com	On site	020 7293 5050	Auction
Tennants	www.tennants.co.uk	enquiry@tennants.co.uk	01969 623780	Auction
Trace	www.trace.co.uk	enquiries@trace.co.uk	0800 018 0208	Information
UK Institute for Conservators	www.ukic.org.uk	ukic@ukic.org.uk	020 7721 8721	Association

Art

Company	Web address	Email	Phone	Category
24 Hour Museum	www.24hourmuseum.org.uk	info@24hourmuseum.org.uk	n/a	Other
Agnews	www.agnewsgallery.co.uk	agnews@agnewsgallery.co.uk	020 7290 9250	Dealer
Art Loss Register (The)	www.artloss.com	artloss@artloss.com	020 7928 0100	Data
Art Review	www.art-review.com	info@artreview.co.uk	020 7236 4880	Publication
Art Sales Index	www.art-sales-index.com	info@art-sales-index.com	01784 451145	Data
Artprice	www.artprice.com	info@artprice.com	n/a	Data
Bonhams	www.bonhams.com	info@bonhams.com	020 7393 3900	Auction
British Arts	www.britisharts.co.uk	n/a	n/a	Information
Christie's	www.christies.com	info@christies.com	020 7839 9060	Auction
Contemporary Art Society	www.contempart.org.uk	gill@contempart.org.uk	020 7612 0730	Information
European Fine Art Fair	www.tefaf.com	info@tefaf.com	31 411 64 50 90	Information
Galleries	www.artefact.co.uk	n/a	n/a	Publication
Kara Art	www.karaart.com	On site	n/a	Information
Londonart	www.londonart.co.uk	info@londonart.co.uk	020 7738 3867	Dealer
Mei & Moses	www.meimosesfineartindex.org	n/a	n/a	Data
NuMasters	www.NuMasters.com	enquiries@NuMasters.com	020 7592 0880	Dealer
Phillips	www.phillips-dpl.com	inquiry.desk@phillips-dpl.com	020 7318 4010	Dealer
Photographers Gallery(The)	www.photonet.org.uk	On site	020 7831 1772	Dealer
Poster Classics	www.posterclassics.com	bruce@posterclasics.com	011 33 450 772052	Dealer
Sotheby's	www.sothebys.com	On site	020 7293 5000	Auction
The Art Newspaper	www.theartnewspaper.com	feedback@theartnewspaper.com	n/a	Publisher

Banknotes

Company	Web address	Email	Phone	Category
Baldwins Auctions	www.baldwin.sh	auctions@baldwin.sh	020 7930 9808	Auction
Banknotes	www.banknotes.com	audrius@equay.com	828 651 0030	Dealer
Barry Boswell World Banknotes	www.collectpapermoney.co.uk	barry.boswell@btinternet.com	01327 261877	Dealer
Bonhams (Glendinings)	www.bonhams.com	info@bonhams.com	020 7393 3900	Dealer
Dix Noonan Webb	www.dnw.co.uk	chris@dnw.co.uk	020 7499 5022	Auction
Ian Gradon	www.worldnotes.co.uk	ian@worldnotes.co.uk	0191 3719700	Dealer
International Bank Note Society	www.ibns.it	On Site	n/a	Association
Maastricht Paper Money Show	www.papermoney-maastricht.org	On site	31 77 477 4047	Information
Society of Paper Money	www.spmc.org	On site	n/a	Association
Spink Banknote Dept.	www.spink.com	info@spink.com	020 7563 4000	Auction

Books

Company	Web address	Email	Phone	Category
Abebooks	www.abebooks.co.uk	info@abebooks.co.uk	n/a	Dealer
Addall	www.addall.com	n/a	n/a	Dealer
Alibris	www.alibris.com	On site	n/a	Dealer
Antiquarian Book Review	www.antiquarianbookreview.com	On site	01494 562266	Publication
Antiquarian Booksellers Association	www.abainternational.com	admin@aba.org.uk	n/a	Association
Any Amount of Books	www.anyamountofbooks.com	charingx@anyamountofbooks.com	020 7836 3697	Dealer
Bibliofind	www.amazon.com	n/a	n/a	Dealer
Bibliology	www.bibliology.com	n/a	n/a	Links
Biblion	www.biblion.com	onsite	020 7629 1374	Dealer
Blackwells Rare Books	www.rarebooks.blackwell.co.uk	rarebooks@blackwells.co.uk	01864 333555	Dealer
Bloomsbury Auctions	www.bloomsburyauctions.com	info@bloomsburyauctions.com	020 7883 2636/7	Auction
Bonhams Book Dept.	www.bonhams.com	books@bonhams.com	020 7393 3900	Auction
Book and Magazine Collector	n/a	janice.mayne@dpgsubs.co.uk	0870 732 7070	Publication
Book Guide (The)	www.thebookguide.co.uk	n/a	n/a	Links
Bookaway	www.bookaway.com	n/a	n/a	Information
Bookcovers	www.bookcovers.co.uk	daniel@care4books.com	01924 495 768	Dealer
Bookfinder	www.bookfinder.com	On site	n/a	Dealer
Christies	www.christies.com	On site	020 7839 9060	Auction
Exedra Booksearch	www.exedra.co.uk	info@exedra.co.uk	020 7731 8500	Dealer
Firsts in Print	www.firsts-in-print.co.uk	peter@firsts-in-print.co.uk	0198 352 1748	Dealer
Firsts in Prints	www.firsts-in-print.co.uk	peter@firsts-in-prints.co.uk	01983 521748	Dealer
Francis Edwards	www.francisedwards.co.uk	sales@francisedwards.co.uk	020 7430 2535	Dealer
HD Bookfairs	www.hdbookfairs.co.uk	exhibitionteam@aol.com	020 8224 3609	Dealer
Int'l League of Antiquarian Booksellers	www.ilab-lila.com	onfo@ilab-lila.com	n/a	Association
Maggs Bros.	www.maggs.com	enquiries@maggs.com	020 7493 7160	Dealer
Provincial Bookfairs Association	www.pbfa.org	info@pbfa.org	01763 248400	Links
Robert Frew Books	www.robertfrew.com	shop@robertfrew.com	020 7580 2311	Dealer
Scottish Book Collector	www.essbc.demon.co.uk	jennie@essbc.demon.co.uk	0131 228 4837	Publication
Sotheby's Book Dept.	www.sothebys.com	On site	020 7293 5050	Auction
Spink	www.spink.com	info@spink.com	020 7563 4000	Auction

Cars

Company	Web address	Email	Phone	Category
Bonhams	www.bonhams.com	cars@bonhams.com	020 7393 3900	Auction
Car Collector	www.carcollector.com	editorial@carcollector.com	n/a	Information
Classic Car	www.classiccar.com	news@classiccar.com	n/a	Links
Classic Cars	www.classiccars.co.uk	On site	n/a	Links
Classics and Customs	www.classicsandcustoms.com	On site	n/a	Links
Complete Automobilist	www.completeautomobilist.co.uk	orders@completeautomobilist.co.uk	01778 426 222	Dealer
Footman James	www.footmanjames.co.uk	On site	0845 458 6782	Insurance
Gregor Fisken	www.gregorfisken.com	cars@gregorfisken.com	020 7584 3503	Dealer
JD Classics	www.jdclassics.co.uk	On site	01245 400060	Dealer
OldClassicCars	www.oldclassiccar.co.uk	dodgenut@44onthefloor.co.uk	n/a	Information
Paradise Garage	www.paradisegarage.co.uk	sales@paradisegarage.co.uk	020 7584 0660	Dealer
Ugly Cars	www.uglycars.co.uk	On site	n/a	Information
Vintage Supplies	www.vintagecarparts.co.uk	info@vintagecarpparts.co.uk	01692 650455	Dealer

Coins

Company	Web address	Email	Phone	Category
American Numismatic Society	www.money.org	ana@money.org	800 367 9723	Association
Baldwins	www.baldwins.sh	coins@baldwin.sh	020 7930 6879	Dealer
Bonhams Coins (Glendinings)	www.bonhams.com	Andrew.Litherland@bonhams.com	020 7393 3900	Auction
British Association of Numismatic Societies	www.coinclubs.freeserve.co.uk	bans@mernick.com	020 8980 5672	Association
British Coin Collector	www.britishcoincollector.co.uk	mail@bitishcoincollector.co.uk	n/a	Association
British Museum	www.thebritishmuseum.ac.uk	coins@thebritishmuseum.ac.uk	020 7323 8607	Information
British Numismatic Society	www.cm.fitzmuseum.ac.uk/coins/britnumsoc	No email	n/a	Information
British Numismatic Trade Association	www.numis.co.uk	bnta@lineone.net	01797 229988	Association
British Royal Mint	www.royalmint.com	information@royalmint.gov.uk	n/a	Information
Chard Coins	www.24carat.co.uk	enquiries@24carat.co.uk	01253 343081	Dealer
Coincraft	www.coincraft.com	info@coincraft.com	020 7636 1188	Dealer
Coin Dealers Directory	www.numis.co.uk	conatact@numis.co.uk	01253 343081	Information
Coin News	www.tokenpublishing.com	info@tokenpublishing.com	01414 46972	Publication
Coin Resource	www.coinresource.com	info@coinresource.com	n/a	Information
Coincraft	www.coincraft.com	info@coincraft.com	020 7636 1188	Dealer
Cornucopia	www.cornucopia.org.uk	nick.poole@resource.gov.uk	020 7273 1410	Data
Dix Noonan Webb	www.dnw.co.uk	chris@dnw.co.uk	020 7499 5022	Auction
Fitzwilliam Museum	www-cm.fitzmuseum.cam.ac.uk/coins	fitzmuseum-coins@lists.cam.ac.uk	01223 332915	Information
Morton and Eden	www.mortonandeden.com	info@mortonandeden.com	020 7493 5344	Dealer
Noble Investments (UK)	n/a	igoldbart@aol.com	020 7581 0240	Dealer
Oriental Numismatic Society	www.onsnumis.org	secgen@onsnumis.org	n/a	Association
Royal Numismatic Society	www.rns.dircon.co.uk	RNS@dircon.co.uk	n/a	Association
Royal Mint, The	www.royalmint.com	information.office@royalmint.gov.uk	0845 60 88 300	Dealer
Simmons Gallery	www.simmonsgallery.co.uk	simmons@simmonsgallery.co.uk	020 8989 8097	Dealer
Spink	www.spink.com	info@spink.com	020 7563 4000	Auction

Films

Company	Web address	Email	Phone	Category
Allenbridge Group	www.taxshelterreport.co.uk	On site	0800 3399 99	Adviser
Astute Money (Chambers IFA)	www.astute-investor.co.uk	info@astute-investor.co.uk	01225 428444	Adviser
Baker Street Finance	www.bakerstreetfinance.tv	enquiries@bakerstreetfinance.tv	020 7487 3677	Other
British Film Institute	www.bfi.org.uk	On site	020 7255 1444	Statistics
Civilian Capital	www.civilian.com	info@civilian.com	323 938 3220	Dealer
Close Investments	www.closeinvestments.com	info@cbil.com	020 7426 4000	Dealer
Future Film Group	www.futurefilmgroup.com	stephenn@futurefilmgroup.com	020 7434 6600	Dealer
Horwath, Clark, Whitehill	www.horwathcw.com	wolfj@horwath.co.uk (Man)	0161 214 7500	Adviser
Irish Revenue	www.revenue.ie	bbrien@revenue.ie	0167 48988	Information
James Baxter	www.jamesbaxter.co.uk	enquiries@jamesbaxter.co.uk	020 7939 9600	Adviser
Kreis Consulting	www.kreisconsulting.com	On site	0141 564 1523	Dealer
Matrix Group	www.matrixgroup.co.uk	films@matrix-securities.co.uk	020 7292 0899	Dealer
McCann Fitzgerald	www.mccann-fitzgerald.ie	n/a	353 1 8290000	Adviser
MPAA	www.mpaa.org	n/a	n/a	Data
Neilsen EDI	www.entdata.com	On site	020 7170 5200	Statistics
Offshore-Onshore	www.lowtax.net	marketing@lowtax.net	01494 474480	Adviser
Oz Cinema	www.ozcinema.com	On site	n/a	Information
Pact (Media Industry Alliance)	www.pact.co.uk	john@pact.co.uk	020 7331 6000, 0141 222 4800	Association
Revenue Ireland	www.revenue.ie	jbarry@revenue.ie	n/a	Adviser
Screen Daily	www.screendaily.com	On site	020 7505 8080	Data
Screen Digest	www.screendigest.com	On site	020 7424 2820	Statistics
Screen Finance	www.informamedia.com	On site	020 7017 5533	Information
Screen International	www.screendaily.com	On site	020 7505 8097	Statistics
Tax Efficient Review	www.taxefficientreview.com	On site	020 8458 9003	Publication
Teather & Greenwood	www.teathers.com	tom.hulme@teathers.com	020 7426 9583	Dealer
UK Film Council	www.ukfilmcouncil.org.uk	info@ukfilmcouncil.org.uk	020 7861 7884	Statistics

Forestry

Company	Web address	Email	Phone	Category
CKD Galbraith	www.forestry-scotland.co.uk	ann.hackett@ckdgalbraith.co.uk	01463 224343	Adviser
Community Woodlands Association	www.community-woods.org.uk	On site	n/a	Association
FMS Investments	www.forestryplans.co.uk	info@forestryplans.co.uk	0117 9200 070	Dealer
Forestry and British Timber Magazine	www.fbti.co.uk	On site	01732 377660	Publication
Forestry and Timber Association	www.forestryandtimber.org	info@forestryandtimber.org	0131 538 7111	Association
Forestry Commission	www.forestry.gov.uk	enquiries@forestry.gsi.gov.uk	0131 334 0503	Information
Forestry Investment Management	www.fimltd.co.uk	fim@fimltd.co.uk	01451 844655	Adviser
Fountains	www.fountainsplc.com	info@fountainsplc.com	01539 817100	Adviser
FPD Savills	www.fpdsavills.co.uk	speck@fpdsavills.co.uk	01202 856800	Adviser
Institute of Chartered Foresters	www.charteredforesters.org	icf@charteredforesters.org	0131 225 2705	Association
Investment Property Databank (IPD)	www.ipdindex.co.uk	On site	020 7643 9257	Data
Irish Forestry	www.irish-forestry.ie	info@irish-forestry.ie	3531 284 1777	Adviser
John Clegg	www.johnclegg.co.uk	thame@johnclegg.co.uk	01844 215800	Dealer
Marlborough Forestry	www.marlboroughforestry.org.nz	On site	n/a	Adviser
Royal Forestry Society	www.rfs.org.uk	rfshq@rfs.org.uk	01442 822028	Association
Smallwoods	www.smallwoods.org.uk	enquiries@smallwoods.org.uk	01743 792644	Information
Tilhill	www.tilhill.co.uk	tilhill.nwales-kymmene.com	01678 530206, 01524 272249	Adviser
Woodland Investment Management	www.woodlands.co.uk	angus@woodlands.co.uk	020 7737 0070	Adviser
Woodlandfinders	www.woodlandfinders.com	mailbox@tilhill.co.uk	01786 435000	Dealer

Gold

Company	Web address	Email	Phone	Category
24 Carat	www.24carat.co.uk	enquiries@24carat.co.uk	01253 343081	Dealer
Baird & Co	www.goldline.co.uk	sales@goldline.co.uk	020 7831 2838	Dealer
Bullion Desk (The)	www.thebulliondesk.com	On site	01799 516 956	Information
Cantor Index	www.cantorindex.co.uk	cs@cantorindex.co.uk	020 7894 8800	Dealer
City Index	www.cityindex.co.uk	enquiries@cityindex.co.uk	020 7550 8500	Dealer
Hussar	www.hussarbullion.com	darren.hacquardAhussarbullion.com	n/a	Dealer
IG Index	www.igindex.co.uk	helpdesk@igindex.co.uk	020 7896 0011	Dealer
Perth Mint	www.perthmint.com.au	info@perthmint.com.au	61 8 9421 7218	Dealer
Tax Free Gold	www.taxfreegold.co.uk	chard@24carat.co.uk	01253 343081	Dealer
World Gold Council	www.gold.org	On site	020 7826 4700	Information

Scripophily

Company	Web address	Email	Phone	Category
Adam Historical Shares	www.adamshares.de	AdamShares@aol.com	n/a	Dealer
Galerie Numistoria	www.numistoria.com	gcifre@numistoria.com	33 1 4927 9271	Dealer
GKR Bonds	www.gkrbonds.com	gkr4@hotmail.com	01376 571711	Dealer
International Bond & Share Society	www.scripophily.org	chairman@scripophily.org	01225 873271	Association
Numistoria	www.numistoria.com	contact@numistoria.com	33 1 49 27 92 71	Dealer
Old Securities	www.husi.ch	On site	0271 455 36 23	Dealer
Scott Winslow	www.scottwinslow.com	onlinesales@scottwinslow.com	n/a	Dealer
Scripophily.com	www.scripophily.com	service@scripophily.com	1 888 786 2576	Dealer
Scripophily.nl	www.scripophily.nl	molen@worldonline.nl	31 50 534 8795	Dealer
Special Stocks	www.specialstocks.com	On site	n/a	Dealer

Stamps

Company	Web address	Email	Phone	Category
AllWorldStamps	www.allworldstamps.com	info@allworldstamps.co.uk	n/a	Information
American Philatelic Society	www.stamps.org	On site	814 237 3803	Association
Arthur Ryan	www.gbstamps.co.uk	net@gbstamps.co.uk	020 8940 7777	Dealer
Association of British Philatelic Societies	www.ukphilately.org.uk	On various sites	On sites	Association
Bath Postal Museum	www.bathpostalmuseum.org	info@bathpostalmuseum.org	01225 460333	Information
Bonhams	www.bonhams.com	stuart.billington@bonhams.com	020 7393 3900	Auction
Brandon Galleries	www.stamperrors.com	mark@stamperrors.com	01483 503335	Dealer
British Library	www.bl.uk	philatelic@bl.uk	020 7412 7635/6	Information
Collectors Cafe	www.collectorcafe.com	editor@collectorcafe.com	n/a	Information
French Stamp Directory	www.philatelie.fr	info@philateli.fr	n/a	Links
Great Britain Philatelic Society	www.gbps.org.uk	On site	n/a	Association
Harmers	www.harmers.com	auctions@harmers.demon.co.uk	0208 747 6100	Auction
Jack Nalbandian	www.nalbandstamp.com	nalbandianj@earthlink.net	401 885-5020	Dealer
James Bendon	www.jamesbendon.com	books@JamesBendon.com	n/a	Publisher
Joseph Luft's Philatelic Resources	www.execpc.com/~joeluft/resource.html	joeluft@execpr.com	1 262 242 512	Links
Mark and David Brandon	www.stamperrors.com	mark@stamperrors.com	01483 503335	Dealer
Philaguide	www.philaguide.com	On site	n/a	Links
Philatelic Traders' Society	www.philatelic-traders-society.co.uk	barbara.pts@btclick.com	020 7490 1005	Association
Philately and Postal History	www.philatelyandpostalhistory.com	helpdesk@philatelyandpostalhistory.com	n/a	Information
Post Office Archives	www.consignia.com/Heritage	heritage@royalmail.com	020 7239 2570	Information
Royal Philatelic Collection	www.royal.gov.uk	n/a	n/a	Information
Royal Philatelic Society	www.rpsl.org.uk	secretary@rpsl.org.uk	020 7486 1044	Association
Scotia Philately	www.scotia-philately.co.uk	scotia01@globalnet.co.uk	020 8873 2854	Dealer
Sotheby's	www.sothebys.com	On site	020 7293 5050	Auction
Spink	www.spink.com	info@spink.com	020 756 4000	Auction
Stamp Auction Network	www.stampauctionnetwork.com	n/a	919 403 9459	Auction
Stamp Café	www.stampcafe.com	On site	n/a	Information
Stamp Finder	www.stampfinder.com	On site	n/a	Links
Stamps at Auction	www.stampsatauction.com	help@stampsatauction.co.uk	n/a	Information
Stamps.Net	www.stamps.net	mail@randyneil.com	n/a	Publication online
Stanley Gibbons	www.stanleygibbons.co.uk	aroose@stanleygibbons.co.uk	020 7557 4454	Dealer
UK250	www.stampwebsites.co.uk	info@uk250.co.uk	01926 863004	Links
UK Philately	www.ukphilately.org.uk	On site	On site	Association
Wardrop & Co	www.wardrop.co.uk	stamps@wardrop.co.uk	01376 563764	Insurance

Theatre

Company	Web address	Email	Phone	Category
Box Office Data Report	www.officiallondontheatre.co.uk	n/a	020 7557 6700	Data
Denton Wilde Sapte	www.dentonwildesapte.com	info@dentonwildesapte.com	020 7242 1212	Adviser
Harbottle & Lewis	www.harbottle.co.uk	neil.adelman@harbottlecom	020 7667 5000	Lawyer
KD Management	www.kdmanagement.co.uk	mandy@kdmanagement.co.uk	020 7357 6633	Producer
Marc Sinden Productions	www.sindenproductions.com	mail@sindenproductions.com	020 8455 3278	Producer
Park Caledonian	www.parkcaledonian.biz	dgoldberg@parkcaledonian.biz	020 8 543 8882	Adviser
Society of London Theatres	www.solt.org.uk	susanne@solttma.co.uk	020 7836 0971	Association
The Stage	www.thestage.co.uk	editor@thestage.co.uk	020 7403 1818	Publication
Theatrical Managers Association	www.tmauk.org	enquiries@solttma.co.uk	020 7557 6700	Association

Whisky

Company	Web address	Email	Phone	Category
Ben Nevis Distillery	www.bennevisdistillery.com	colin@bennevisdistillery.com	01397 702476	Distiller
Blackwood	www.shetlandwhisky.com	joanna@shetlandwhisky.com	01595 694455	Distiller
Bruichladdich	www.bruichladdich.com	On site	01496 850477	Distiller
Companions of the Quaich	www.thequaich.com	n/a	n/a	Information
Isle of Arran	www.arranwhisky.com	On site	n/a	Distiller
Ladybank Distillery	www.whisky.co.uk	enquiries@whisky.co.uk	08454 501885	Distiller
McTears	www.mctears.co.uk	whiskyvaluations@mctears.co.uk	01412 234456	Auction
Scotch Whisky	www.scotchwhisky.com	whisky@scotchwhisky.com	01506 885721	Information
Scotch Whisky Association	www.scotch-whisky.org.uk	On site	n/a	Information
Scottish Malt Whisky Society	www.smws.com	enquiries@smws.com	0131 5543451	Association
The Whisky Exchange	www.thewhiskyexchange.com	sales@thewhiskyexchange.com	0208 6069388	Dealer
Whisky Scam	www.whiskyscam.co.uk	mwbh@gateway.net	01539 729580	Information

Wine

Company	Web address	Email	Phone	Category
Berry Bros & Rudd	www.bbr.com	On site	0870 900 4300	Dealer
Christies	www.christies.com	info@christies.com	020 7839 9060	Auction
Companies House	www.companieshouse.gov.uk	enquiries@companies-house.gov.uk	0870 33 33 636	Information
Corney and Barrow	www.corneyandbarrow.com	wine@corbar.co.uk	020 7265 2400	Dealer
Fine and Rare Wines	www.frw.co.uk	On site	020 8960 1995	Dealer
Investdrinks	www.investdrinks.org	jim@investdrinks.org	n/a	Information
Jancis Robinson	www.jancisrobinson.com	n/a	n/a	Information
Liv-ex	www.liv-ex.com	info@liv-ex.com	020 7228 2233	Exchange
London City Bond	www.lcb.co.uk	cs@lcb.co.uk	01375 487110	Warehouse
Magnum Fine Wines	www.magnum.co.uk	wine@magnum.co.uk	020 7930 6925	Dealer
Premier Cru	www.premiercru.com	inquiry@premiercru.com	020 8905 4495	Dealer
Sotheby's	www.sothebys.com	serena.sutcliffe@sothebys.com	020 7293 5050	Auction
Vineyards of Bordeaux	www.vineyardsofbordeaux.com	james@vineyardsofbordeaux.com	01204 535302	Dealer
Wineprice	www.wineprice.com	info@wineprice.com	n/a	Data
Wine-Searcher	www.wine-searcher.com	anne.welch@wine-searcher.com	n/a	Information
Wine Spectator	www.winespectator.com	On site	n/a	Information
Wines of Bordeaux	www.winesofbordeaux.com	ukinfo@winesofbordeaux.com	0870 111 8990	Dealer

Index

the alternative investment show

Advice: **For investments to appreciate, You'd be well advised to visit this show!**

- **All readers may claim a complimentary pair of tickets for both the 2004 and the 2005 shows, saving £30**

- Visit the website and register for your COMPLIMENTARY show tickets today!

The Alternative Investment Show (AIS) is the UK's only exhibition for those interested in making money and improving their lifestyle through alternative investment. In association with the author and publishers of 'Superhobby Investing', you are cordially invited to enjoy the manifestation of the book that is The Alternative Investment Show.

To register for your complimentary tickets visit the website at www.harriman-house.com/ais

For more information on the show visit the website at www.alternativeinvestmentshow.com

---

The Alternative Concept:

The show features over 100 exhibiting companies offering investment opportunities which can provide considerable financial and tangible returns, where the appreciation is as much in the pleasure of ownership as in the potential future value.

Antiques

Expert Speakers & Exhibitors:

In addition to the many and varied exhibitors, the show provides a unique opportunity to talk with, listen to, and learn from a stellar cast of speakers including the author - Peter Temple. Visit the website for more information on speakers and exhibitors.

Classic Cars

Unique Opportunities:

Nowhere else will you find such an eclectic gathering of potentially lucrative and certainly enjoyable investment options. The show provides an ideal environment for private, professional and institutional investors to find fortune and fulfilment through alternative investment.

Overseas property

A Multifaceted Event:

Whether you wish to use the show as a research centre, lecture theatre, trading floor or networking forum, the opportunities are numerous and the decisions yours to make.

Investments from every chapter of this book will be at the Alternative Investment Show!

To register for complimentary tickets visit
www.harriman-house.com/ais

For more information on the show visit
www.alternativeinvestmentshow.com

Or call the events team on:
+44 (0)20 8971 8281